C000060569

AUSTRALIA TOMORROW

Edited by Jake Thrupp

Connor Court Publishing

This book is dedicated to the patriots of Australia who strive to make this country better for all.

Published in 2021 by Connor Court Publishing Pty Ltd

Copyright © 2021, Jake Trupp (as editor)

All rights reserved. No part of this book may be reproduced or transmitted in any form or by any means, electronic or mechanical, including photo copying, recording or by any information storage and retrieval system, without prior permission in writing from the publisher.

Connor Court Publishing Pty Ltd
PO Box 7257
Redland Bay QLD 4165
sales@connorcourt.com
www.connorcourt.com

Phone 0497-900-685

Printed in Australia

ISBN: 9781922449795

Front cover design: Van Le, (www.vanle.info).

The views expressed in this anthology are the personal views of the contributors and should not be attributed to any other individual or organisation.

"A majority that stays silent does not remain a majority"

– Tony Abbott

Contents

FOREWORD

The Hon. John Howard OM AC
Prime Minister of Australia 1996-2007

I have always argued that politics at its essence is a battle of ideas, not a public relations contest. Campaign skills and a strong party organisation are essential, but nothing beats the relevance of ideas and the passion with which they are advocated.

This collection of essays speaks to the future of liberalism in Australia.

The ideas canvassed are all relevant to the kind of Australia we wish our children to have. Not only do they deal with the cultural challenges of contemporary society but also they directly confront the threat to free speech which so frequently masquerades as providing protection against discrimination. The central role of high-quality education is highlighted in the excellent piece from Dallas McInerney.

The breadth of the contributions is exceeded only by the quality of the contributors. They are a diverse group of men and women, all motivated to write in a positive way about our nation's future. There is both a streak of robust liberalism as well as a proper regard for valued institutions permeating so many of the contributions. I commend Jake Thrupp for assembling and editing such a free-flowing prospectus about Australia's future.

The Honourable John Howard OM AC served as Australia's 25th Prime Minister between March 1996 and November 2007. He is the nation's second longest serving Prime Minister, was a Member of Parliament for 33 years, and was Treasurer in the Fraser Government.

PREFACE
Peta Credlin AO

Even though the Liberal Party is in office nationally and in three states, it's still at a very low ebb.

Some of this is third term blues. Some is ongoing dismay at the removal of a widely admired first term Prime Minister and at the waste of the Turnbull years. But most is members' demoralisation at these seemingly endless lockdowns and bewilderment that Liberal governments are often their authors.

The whole point of politics is not just to be in government; it is to make a difference and live out, in policy terms, what you believe in. As so many Liberal supporters say to me, in many respects, it is hard to see, right now, the difference between the Liberal governments and the Labor ones.

People don't join the Liberal Party just for the thrill of their "side" winning on election night. They join because they believe Liberal victories will make our country better and safer for small business, for families and for institutions that have stood the test of time. We are supposed to be the party of greater freedom and lower spending; and even though we all know that extraordinary times sometimes demand extraordinary measures, it is simply breath-taking that Liberal governments have walked away from these ideals, seemingly, without a single regret.

When it comes to restrictions on freedom and ever-bigger government, there's no doubt that Labor would be even worse;

but the Liberal Party, in Canberra and in the States, has run up the biggest burden of debt and deficit in our peacetime history; and, either implemented or connived, at restrictions on human freedom that are absolutely unprecedented even in wartime – all to combat a virus which, even before vaccinations became widespread, had an infection fatality rate of about 0.3 per cent.

So, this is an important volume of essays if we, as Liberals, are to recover our drive to make a difference; and if our country is to be put back on the road to national renewal, because, for all our faults, I am sure that task will fall to us.

Just as Cory Bernardi broke away prior to the 2019 election, with quite a few decent party members following, the fate of breakaways to the Right is invariably to leave the Liberal Party both less conservative and more vulnerable to defeat at the hands of an ever-more-green-left Labor Party. And, even as I write this, it is rumoured that senior figures within the Liberal Party and others who are understandably disillusioned, are contemplating leaving the party which, in effect, means fighting an election against their former political home which effectively may offer momentary satisfaction but strengthens the claims of a Labor/Greens government. Inevitably, their voices will be crying in the wilderness, their good advice unnecessarily discredited.

All of the contributors to this volume are determined to build a better Australia: with energy security based on reliable 24/7 power so that we can be a country that makes things; with better managed water resources so that we really can be the good food source for our region; with much stronger armed forces so that our country cannot be bullied and our friends won't be invaded; and with politically correct brainwashing banished from our schools so that the scale of our achievement in producing a country that is as free, as fair and as prosperous as any, is better appreciated.

The best way to do this, of course, is to "stay in and fight" within a party of government.

The Morrison Government will not be able to limp towards the next election and demand a reward for its management of the pandemic. It will need to offer voters a positive programme to justify a fourth term and, in any event, elections are a contest and you don't win them by being a paler version of your opponent. To that end, there are plenty of ideas here that could be adopted and refined and plenty of contributors to this volume still willing it to succeed.

If our country does happen, post-election, to be saddled with what I fear would be the worst Labor government in our history, there is much here that could be drawn on by everyone who thinks that the Liberal Party remains our best hope for a brighter future.

Peta Credlin AO is a weekly columnist with *The Australian, Sunday Telegraph, Sunday Mail and Sunday Herald Sun*. Since 2017, she has hosted her successful primetime program Credlin on *Sky News Australia* each weeknight at 6pm. For 16 years, Peta was a policy adviser to Howard government ministers in the portfolios of defence, communications, immigration and foreign affairs. Between 2009 and 2015, she was Chief of Staff to Tony Abbott as Leader of the Opposition and later as Prime Minister. Peta is admitted as a barrister and solicitor in Victoria, with legal qualifications from the University of Melbourne and the Australian National University. In 2015, she received the Australian Women's Leadership Award for the ACT and in 2016, was named a joint winner of Harper's Bazaar magazine's "Woman of the Year". She is a Board Director at The Robert Menzies Institute at the University of Melbourne.

INTRODUCTION
Jake Thrupp

Australia is a great country but it could be greater.

The centre-right side of politics, for too long, has been timid when it comes to reasserting its values, beliefs and ideas, all of which are designed to strengthen Australia, not weaken it.

This self-doubt of centre-right values, spurred by constant attacks from sections of the media and the corporate world, has now crept into our national psyche, breeding a cultural self-doubt amongst the public. It is as if we must apologise over long held Australian values based on egalitarianism and never question the elitist opinion birthed from this country's bloated bureaucracy.

It is a slippery slope.

Further, there is increasingly less tolerance for inevitable human mistakes, just that you are banished for good if you dare misspeak or mouth uncomfortable truths.

If we want Australia to progress, we must snap out of this immaturity surrounding debate where we are shielded from honest, strong opinions. "Pussyfooting" (to use Gina Rinehart's expression in her essay) around big issues and big ideas is doing us a massive disservice. We are global laggards because of it.

More than ever, Australians must start pushing back against the nihilism of contemporary life. Since when is the meaning of life about making a placard and marching for the latest fashionable, feel-good cause, especially if those fashionable causes, when you dig more deeply, are littered with inaccuracies and often are no more than a shopfront for Marxism. It is gesturing at its finest, not producing a single practical outcome for ambitious, dispirited Australians. Is the ennui towards modern life now this great?

Life is lived in order to be lived! The social and technological advancement we enjoy today is like never before in human history. The mobility, social care, personal wealth and opportunities offered to all citizens, today, should be celebrated. Some are awarded an easier path but, certainly, with hard work and when granted appropriate opportunity, all Australians can be equipped with the tools to live their best lives. How could anyone object to the centre-right principle of reward for effort? Well, some do!

Throughout history, people have taken to the streets to protest certain government policies. That is sometimes the only avenue afforded to a group where tin-ear politicians refuse to take notice. But never before have we seen Australians take to the streets to show their hatred towards their own country. These protestors also tell us there is absolutely nothing to celebrate or be proud of when it comes to the story of Australia.

Perhaps the former Prime Minister, Tony Abbott, summed this up when he said, "Part of the human stain is our tendency to look for the minor flaws in people rather than try to discern their fundamental strengths."

That sentiment is applicable to those who endlessly dissect our nation.

In recent times, the Australian public has become more divided than ever and it seems that many are unaware of the responsibilities they should shoulder as part of our nation.

Why is it that Australians now find it totally acceptable to shame, bully, harass and cancel their fellow countrymen, through social media, purely because of a difference of opinion? The mental and economic harm that can be caused from such tactics calls for government regulation. How can Australian political discourse ever improve if defamatory and ad hominem attacks are acceptable in the unregulated Wild West of social media?

An even more frightening development in this country is that if a person wishes to share a viewpoint or piece of information which does not mirror the official governmental position, that person is labelled as unworthy and uninformed.

In this politically correct world we talk endlessly, do we not, about "diversity", yet we seem incapable of tolerating a diversity of opinions. Instead, as Tom Switzer writes about in his essay, the Left's obsession with "cancelling" people and initiating boycotts is now the level to which we have stooped. In other words, the Left are incapable of engaging with uncomfortable ideas.

One of the worst developments, as James McGrath's essay highlights, is that Australia's public broadcaster, the ABC, is anything but a bastion of diversity when it comes to opinions. Our taxes are paying for a $1 billion-plus public broadcaster which is hostile towards centre-right viewpoints where Liberal Party politicians are treated as persona non grata. Supercilious inner-city ideologues are more than welcome to opine in a way which attracts applause from their Twitter fanbase, but should they be entitled to do so on taxpayers' dollars?

David Maddox, political editor of London's Sunday Express and lead writer for their Daily Express, in his guest essay, describes the same deterioration of Britain's BBC and its inability to represent the views of mainstream Britain. It is another example of the institutional push by the politically-correct talking class to oust Western values.

At a time when Australians now have over 21 million smartphones, almost as many smartphones as the country has adults, with most connected to the internet, when will a Liberal government promote the principles of choice and turn the ABC into a subscription service.

If you want it, you pay for it.

This raises an important point. The Liberal Party, in partnership with the National Party, have won 7 out of the last 9 federal elections. This proves that the Australian public have rejected, regularly, what the modern Labor Party represents – a political brand viewed as being weak on illegal immigration, hostile towards Christian religion, admiring international bodies like the United Nations and, quite literally, obsessed with climate change.

The Australian public, time and time again, have entrusted the centre-right to govern at a federal level. The majority of Australians cannot stomach the lecturing from regressive elites about how they should live their lives. What they inherently wish for is freedom, the adherence to human rights, reward for effort, equal opportunity, self-responsibility and economic settings which encourage business to prosper, not flounder.

However, those of us on the centre-right must acknowledge that there is a difference between being active in power and purely holding office. Winning elections, virtually by default, because the opposition is so unelectable is hardly a ringing endorsement.

We are entitled to ask what all these victories, 7 from the last 9, have achieved in terms of cementing centre-right values in Australia. What has been done to strengthen Australia during this period of governance?

As Jason Falinski's essay observes, we have allowed Australia to be overrun by the "talking class" who largely inhabit the governmental space. The talking class are largely an unproductive class, paid for by the unrepresented working class. Over-regulation is their weapon of choice, attempting to force mainstream Australians to live by their distorted values. This is the same talking class who traffic in alarmist hysteria and show little resilience towards the simple values of life.

Now is the time for the Australian centre-right movement to remind voters what makes this country so special, what obstacles can be overcome and what greatness can be achieved if we band together.

The Rita Panahi essay is a compelling statement of the dispiriting, dare I suggest, dishonest motives of the Left, at a time when we all want the Australia of tomorrow to be better than it is today. That is what politics is about, shaping the opinion of the majority and convincing them your worldview is the way forward.

Politicians should only be entering parliament with one goal – to leave their community and, more broadly, their nation, in a better place than they, themselves, inherited.

Unfortunately, as Professor David Flint reminds us in his essay, Australia has long suffered from analysis paralysis. Politicians have failed to build the visionary infrastructure our country so desperately requires. Perhaps it is time to reform democracy to have greater public involvement in decision-making?

When will those who hold political office actually do something? On things like critical infrastructure, the pesky political class never miss an opportunity to miss an opportunity. Politicians, too often, blink and baulk over big ideas which will boost the prosperity of individuals.

Why is it so hard to build dams in order to harvest water? Without water, our land cannot be productive; regions cannot survive and a growing population cannot be sustained.

Growth is good but must be sustainable. Those who advocate for a "big Australia", as Professor Judith Sloan's essay reinforces, will only further decrease our living standards because government fails to draw up a population policy to accommodate such growth. The political class are asking Australians to work harder but live off less, without ever actually seeking a mandate for this from the people. No one is opposed to immigration, but the rate of it is inconsistent with what ought to be the central objective of making all Australians better off.

Australia's population reached 25 million people in 2018, more than two decades faster than predicted. How do we provide water and energy for these people with the current policies in place? What about the congestion on our roads and the ability for young Australians to buy a home? A quarter of Sydney apartments are now occupied by families. They cannot afford a house. Our cities are seeing entire suburbs being rezoned for apartments. And with automation and robotics, fewer jobs will be available in the future. Pre-coronavirus, we had over 12 per cent youth unemployment and 18 per cent underemployment.

We are asleep at the wheel.

Even then, Australia's migration program must be in the national interest. Julian Leeser writes about the principles which ought to govern any discussion on migration policy in Australia. Those who contribute to their communities will always be greatly admired. The episode involving a refugee family living and working in the tiny Queensland town of Biloela proves that those who come here and roll up their sleeves win applause from the Australian public. We are a fair and compassionate people.

On this theme of analysis paralysis, why are the Luddites in government so slow to give the green light to nuclear energy?

Australia has 40 per cent of the world's uranium reserves yet we ship it offshore but deny ourselves the benefit of its use. This is a reliable, virtually carbon-free, low-cost baseload power, which generates commerce for the regions where small modular reactors are built.

Matt Canavan deals with this splendidly in his essay. Yet nuclear power has been banned in Australia since 1986.

The Minerals Council of Australia argues that if Australia were to increase its uranium production by just 20 per cent, there would be an economic benefit of $10 billion a year and 20,000 new jobs by 2040.

But time is not on our side. These highly advanced small modular reactors which, unlike old reactors, do not need to be placed near large water catchments, take 10 years to get up and running.

These are simple policy initiatives that will bring down the cost of living for Australian households and provide decent-paying jobs.

Along with others, in this anthology, addressing this failure, Michaelia Cash's essay reasserts the importance of creating new jobs and the dignity that accompanies work. Investing in the skills sector is so important to keep our country ticking. The fixation on having every Australian student go to university to attain a degree has created a massive distortion in the labour market. How can we build a better Australia if the construction industry is anaemic? Frankly, we can do with fewer human resources middle-management types and more of those in the trades – plumbers, electricians, carpenters and plasterers.

Middle Australia must unequivocally believe that the centre-right is their political sanctuary.

Caroline Di Russo, in her essay, describes Middle Australia as those people who are living busy lives with the least amount of fuss; those who are raising children, paying off the mortgage and saving for an annual holiday. These Australians are not overly engaged in politics but are well-versed in fairness.

This cohort, Middle Australia, are the majority of Australians. They are centre-right in the sense that they are uneasy with government interfering with their freedom. They want to be free to flourish.

They understand that in a country, change occurs. They understand that when progress is achieved, it must not be at the expense of replacing entire institutions which have stood the test of time. Modern conservatism is about preserving that which is good and changing, incrementally, that which needs to be changed.

The British Prime Minister Benjamin Disraeli harnessed similar sentiments, describing change as a constant feature in a progressive society. But it is the timing and incremental nature of that change which is critical to a conservative's thinking.

Disraeli asks whether change ought to be "carried out in deference to the manners, the customs, the laws and the traditions of a people or whether it should be carried out in deference to abstract principles and arbitrary and general doctrines."

Only those who encompass a hatred of who we are, our achievements and our institutions, would be willing to live by the latter and, like their statue-toppling cousins, burn the whole joint down.

Proud Australians are not about toppling inherited institutions and values, things like the legal system, the rule of law, the presumption of innocence, the Westminster system of government, together with all the democratic privileges we enjoy. The bulk of Australians want to build new statues to celebrate modern successes and contemporary values; they want to build hope in the next generation; they want to honour the monuments to our history, good or bad. That is how we learn.

This is why the centre-right in Australia must become more committed and more dominant. We are the political side which grants the best conditions for human beings to realise their true self.

Unlike the Left, we do not want to equalise outcomes and take from those who have been rewarded for their effort only to redistribute to others. We do not want to produce an entire group of people who are solely dependent on welfare. We do not want to encourage victimhood and box people into categories. We do not want to suffocate your earning potential. We do not want government to grow so big that every aspect of your life is met with a bureaucrat, a piece of legislation or a tax. We also do not believe that government should be brought into the private home. If this entire socialist overhaul of our way of life was allowed, may we ask, '*cui bono*'?

The centralisation of power only benefits those at the top, not the worker. Your freedom and your very ability to control your own destiny would be severely compromised. That is the threat.

Those who expect to reap the blessings of freedom must undergo the fatigue of supporting it.

These threats should be enough to mobilise any hardworking Australian who adheres to centre-right values. They are modern-day conservative values which, contrary to the fake news narrative, should embrace compassion.

After all, the tenets of conservatism, liberalism, democracy and capitalism, have freed masses of people and lifted them out of poverty; they have given people a voice for the first time ever, an opportunity to create wealth and live their own lives without being dictated to by government. Compassionate conservatives must fight for and defend civil liberties and must be prepared for sometimes uncomfortable political action against those countries denying such liberties to their own people.

Over time, cracks have appeared in the conservative edifice and its thinking. But there has always been a willingness from the centre-right side to reform and refine. Remember, in life you buy the package, not the bits you like the most.

It is time to stop apologising for our beliefs. It is time to stop walking away from the necessary defence of those values which are central to the Liberal philosophy. After all, what is there to lose? Just the nation we love.

In this pursuit, we can learn from great Liberal Party leaders of the past.

Robert Menzies taught us to be the voice of middle Australia.

Harold Holt taught us to have faith in our future.

John Gorton taught us to be courageous and take political risks.

Malcolm Fraser taught us about moral obligation.

Andrew Peacock taught us to be authentic.

John Howard taught us to be confident in our convictions.

Brendan Nelson taught us the importance of sacrifice.

Tony Abbott taught us how to draw battle lines.

This anthology of essays by prominent centre-right thinkers, politicians and business leaders, highlights the reality that there is no shortage of remarkable ideas from our side. As Prime Minister Howard has noted in his generous and outstanding foreword, what is missing is the will to implement them.

The purpose of this publication is not to oppose but to propose.

Nonetheless, we cannot afford to be blind to ideological forces, within other political parties and, sadly, sometimes within our own who, by their utterances and their efforts, show a disturbing disdain towards our country and its often voiceless people. What is worse, they often seem unapologetic about the harm their behaviour is causing to the nation's fabric. And we must accept, rather than blindly ignore, that much of this ideologically dangerous direction is authored by, and promoted by, a bloated bureaucracy.

We must understand these forces seek to regulate us, not to lead us.

This anthology offers the ideas and the direction for Australia tomorrow.

I firmly believe that the Liberal Party is the party of the strugglers and strivers. But we must wake from our slumber, mobilise our supporters by giving them something to believe in and to fight for and prove to Australians that we have the ideas and policy gumption to govern them for the next decade and beyond.

We must ask ourselves what sort of Australia do we want?

It is no longer good enough to win elections by default.

From this day forth, action will be what defines us.

This anthology, I hope, helps to show the way.

Jake Thrupp is a graduate of the University of Sydney with a Bachelor Degree in Politics and Political Economy. Since his teenage years, he has been involved in campaigns for the Liberal Party on the NSW Far North Coast and the Gold Coast. Jake is currently Senior Producer for Alan Jones, working on his primetime television program on *Sky News Australia*. He also writes regularly for Brisbane's *Courier Mail* newspaper, *The Spectator Australia* and London's *Daily Express*.

1

WHEN THE WAR IS OVER: REVIVING LIBERALISM FOR POST-PANDEMIC AUSTRALIA

Nick Cater

On a late autumn evening during the darkest days of World War 2, Robert Menzies delivered a radio talk describing the pathway Australia should follow, once victory had been won.

Australians and the freedoms they enjoyed had never been in such peril. Three weeks earlier, 152 Japanese bombers escorted by 36 Mitsubishi fighters had unleashed a deluge of munitions upon Darwin. Tunnels in Sydney's Town Hall station were being converted into air raid shelters and, within a fortnight, Japanese submarines would enter Sydney Harbour and fire missiles at naval vessels at anchor. Yet Menzies, confident that Australia and its allies had the courage to win the military conflict, turned his attention to the culture war and the creeping threat of socialism.

It would be laughable to compare the coronavirus with our wartime enemies, despite the virus's suspicious origins in China, a country ruled by Communists who wish to overturn the peaceful rules-based order that has been our protection for the last 70 years or so. Yet, in some ways, the public health campaign that consumes us now is not dissimilar to the total wars we fought last century. The emergency powers evoked by our governments, resemble those imposed in wartime. Much of the machinery of state has been directed towards the campaign and priority has been given to warfare over the needs of non-combatants; and, once again, our liberties are at stake, this time, not from the intentions of a hostile enemy, but from what we are doing to ourselves.

Four years ago, 75 years to the minute after Menzies' Forgotten People address, his words were heard again on the Macquarie Radio network in a moving recitation by actor Peter Cousens. Among the three hundred people who witnessed the speech, as it was delivered live in Old Parliament House were three former Liberal leaders, two of whom had lost their jobs to the same party room challenger. Their common nemesis, the serving Prime Minister, was diplomatically seated on a separate table. Agreeing on the order of proceedings had taken some negotiating, since the protocols guiding precedence are somewhat fluid in such circumstances. As the event's organiser, I kept the proposed finale for the event to myself, to avoid complicating matters still further.

The Forgotten People broadcast is not short. Menzies was allotted 45 minutes in the schedule by 2UE and its affiliates, beginning at 9.15pm on May 22, 1942. I was concerned that such a lengthy performance and the complexity of the language might test the attention span of an audience in the age of Twitter. In commercial radio, ears are money. Would Macquarie Radio's management blame me for selling them a pup?

I left my seat and moved to the back of the room where I could watch the audience react. From the opening words to the powerful conclusion, Cousens had their undivided attention. No one glanced at their phone or was struggling with the weight of their eyelids. The audience responded to Menzies' ironic dry humour with wry laughter and were transfixed by the melody of the crafted oration. This was much more than a journey back in time, however. The message of Forgotten People is enduring and speaks directly to our contemporary challenges:

> "The great vice of democracy – a vice which is exacting a bitter retribution from it at this moment – is that for a generation we have been busy getting ourselves on to the list of beneficiaries and removing ourselves from the list of contributors, as if somewhere there was somebody else's wealth and somebody else's effort on which we could thrive.
>
> To discourage ambition, to envy success, to have achieved superiority, to distrust independent thought, to sneer at and impute false motives to public service – these are the maladies of modern democracy, and of Australian democracy in particular."

The 35 radio talks in the Forgotten People series, broadcast weekly in 1942, were a feat of intellectual leadership without parallel in Australian public life. Published as a book, the following year, they framed the philosophy that united a fractured centre-right under the banner of the Liberal Party of Australia in 1944 and remain a source of inspiration and instruction to this day. Menzies' thoughts gave the party the intellectual clarity and moral purpose that enabled it to win 19 of the 29 federal elections it has fought. The secret of the party's electoral success, despite the human frailties of its members, is not difficult to fathom. When the party remains true to the principles Menzies articulated; when it empowers the unorganised and un-self-conscious middle-class, it does well. When it becomes distracted by the interests of the rich and powerful, special interest groups or rent-seekers, it fares badly. It is as simple as that.

No centre-right party in the English-speaking world has been blessed with such a firm foundation. Other conservative leaders have inspired us over the years – Margaret Thatcher and Ronald Reagan, for example, but none of them had the opportunity to shape their parties at conception nor is it certain that they had the fortitude and intellect to have done so. The Liberal Party, and its permanent Coalition partners, has been in office in Canberra for 50 of the 75 years since it fought its first election, a record better than Republican presidents or centre-right parties in Britain, New Zealand and Canada.

Yet socialism, like coronavirus, will probably never be eradicated and will always remain in our system. The utopian instinct it satisfies is alive in every generation and the expansion of higher education that begun under Menzies provided a fertile environment for it to spread. Communism, as Marx and Engels conceived it, has thankfully had its day. Its essential thinking however, that the state is better able to manage human affairs than an independent people, is as strong as ever. The instinct to order society from the top, with coercion if necessary, rather than trust citizens to establish social order by consent, grows stronger. If we have learned nothing else from this pandemic, we have surely learned that.

The presence of our 25th, 28th and 29th Prime Ministers for the anniversary recital of Forgotten People, together with our 12th Prime Minister's daughter, Heather Henderson, was a testimony to the enduring strength of the Liberal tradition which Menzies founded. The man who was to become Australia's 30th prime minister was also present. The then Treasurer was occupied with the task of restoring the budget to balance, fired by the Liberal conviction that the money we carelessly refer to as government money has been taken from citizens, or borrowed on their behalf. Dealing with the legacy of Labor's spending sprees is an obligation that can absorb Liberal governments, but it is not their only purpose. There is a moral as well as an economic imperative: the restoration and protection of dignity and justice that are almost always eroded by Labor's levelling schemes. Addressing them requires a degree of emotional intelligence that economically focussed governments sometimes find hard to muster; but as Menzies was fond of reminding Liberals, the most important things in a civilised democracy cannot be measured in pounds, shillings and pence.

> "If the motto is to be 'Eat, drink and be merry, for tomorrow
> you will die; and if it chances you don't die, the State will look
> after you; but if you don't eat, drink and be merry and save, we
> shall take your savings from you' ... then the whole business of
> life would become foundation-less. Are you looking forward to
> a breed of men after the war who will have become boneless
> wonders? Leaners grow flabby; lifters grow muscles. Men
> without ambition readily become slaves."

There have been many backseat drivers as our governments have tried
to steer an uncharted course through this pandemic. I have been one
of them, believing that there is a different road that could have been
taken, one that would have jarred less with our liberal principles.
This is not to diminish the achievements of our governments, who
have demonstrably saved lives that would otherwise have been lost.
The challenge of dealing with a novel virus, as infectious as this one,
that preys particularly upon the elderly and sick, the people towards
whom we have a duty of care, is considerable. Our leaders have been
called upon to make weighty decisions with limited information
or time. Australia is blessed with a world-class health service and
lockable borders, both of which have served us well. The cause of much
of what has gone wrong has its origins in our unusual Constitution
with its divided responsibilities and the age-old problem that the
governments who spend most of the money don't have to raise it.

Nevertheless, there were other strategies we might have adopted
that would not have carried such an immense human cost. There
were plausible solutions that would not have required the state to
trespass so far, or so insensitively, into our personal lives, that would
not have required draconian policing or the deployment of the army
on our streets. The control of social behaviour by the enforcement of
arbitrary state regulation is part of daily life in some countries, but it
is not the way we do things here.

Social order in Australia is maintained with a force more powerful than coercion. In a tolerant liberal democracy like ours, the rules are willingly obeyed by people who have regard for the welfare of the community of others to which they belong. Consent is the binding force of Australia's social fabric and the rule under which our police should operate. They are not members of a disciplined hierarchy, operating at the government's command, but citizens in uniform who secure the willing co-operation of the public to ensure obedience to the law. They must refrain from usurping the powers of the judiciary, recognising that it is not their job to judge guilt or punish the guilty. These conventions are part of our precious inheritance of liberalism. We should not lightly disregard them, especially under the pretext of protecting the public. Ultimately, the rule of law, common law and the separation of powers provide the best protection any people, anywhere could desire.

Liberals, in contrast to libertarians, understand that there are circumstances when our liberties must be curtailed, since our rights are attached to a duty to safeguard the rights of others. Our concern to protect everyone's health, as best as we can, and prevent avoidable deaths in a pandemic will, of course, require the temporary curtailment of some freedoms. Liberalism, however, is a philosophy, not a rule book, where duties and rights are balanced by common sense. One person's right to a healthy retirement, for example, untroubled by a novel virus that can be particularly cruel to a people of a certain age, should be respected as far as we can. Yet that right is not absolute. It must be balanced against the freedom to worship, the freedom to earn a living or operate a business or the freedom of teenagers to mingle with their peers to alleviate adolescent distress.

In everyday life, these are matters that free people, who respect the rules, can generally work out for themselves. When that decision is made by a chief health officer we are in trouble; for, while we expect public health experts to be better versed in virology than the rest of us, none of them possesses the wisdom of Solomon.

As liberals, we don't seek perfection from our bureaucracies, we just pray that the exceptional powers they have been granted will not last. We long for the day when QR codes, permits for interstate travel and two-metre rules are just a bad memory. We look forward to partying like it's 1945 when the tape is removed from park benches and we can stand upright in a pub with a beer in our hands. Those of us who put on a paper mask rather than one made of cloth, as a gesture of hope that all things must pass, trust we will one day be vindicated.

Menzies was studying law at the University of Melbourne when emergency measures were enacted in World War One. His prize-winning essay, 'The Rule of Law During the War,' written in his teens, demonstrates a clearer appreciation of the delicacy of freedom than many of our adult leaders have shown today:

> "Some infringements of the 'Liberty of the subject' are inevitable in any war. Such infringements have been considerable during the past two years; the power of the Executive has been much increased and the full authority of the common law Courts greatly hindered.

> "All these things may be justified by the gravity of the national emergency; by virtue of this alone do we acquiesce in such an extensive abrogation of the Rule of Law.

> "Should the almost arbitrary power of the Executive prove to be anything else but temporary, a very great disaster would have befallen the English Constitution."

As I write this essay in August 2021, I am confident the war we have been called upon to fight will be over by Christmas. Which Christmas, I cannot say, nor does it seem clear what victory will look like, since the coronavirus shows no willingness to surrender. Whenever we reach this uneasy truce, the immediate task for liberals is reconstruction, to repair the damage to the liberal democracy we once imaged was the birth right of every Australian.

We cannot be sure of that now.

We must begin by taking stock of the transfer of power from individuals to the State and begin returning them one by one. We must emancipate our fellow citizens from the tangle of emergency rules that has enslaved them. There should, of course, be several thorough independent inquiries into what has occurred; but their aim will not be to punish or to shame, but to learn how to do better, since mistakes provide the knowledge for innovation.

Inevitably, it will require a little more humility from our governments which must reconsider what is properly their business and the risks which they should shoulder. When victory was declared against Japan, on August 15, 1945, Menzies was quick to recognise that Australia's future lay in the hands of its people:

> "The first task of government, therefore, is to restore what we call 'private business activity' instead of treating it, as Labour politicians frequently do, as Public Enemy Number One.

> "I also ask you to remember that employment in public works is in its nature very spasmodic; that it provides temporary jobs, and that it very seldom offers a real prospect of continuous employment, with progress and promotion."

Government cannot create jobs or prosperity except by sleight of hand. The wealth we will need to unburden future generations from the debt we have accumulated in the last 18 months will be earned by industrious and enterprising citizens. The role of government should be limited to the creation of the conditions in which competitive enterprise thrives. It is to encourage people to take risks with the hope of reward without the need to seek permission, knowing that the rules are fair. This is the kind of permissive society for which

Liberals should crave.

Whatever it is that divides good people on the centre-right, we can be confident we have a unity ticket on this one. The economic arguments that split Liberals in the 1980s have been settled. Anyone who is still not convinced of the primacy of competitive markets, in most sectors most of the time, is in the wrong party.

As Cousens reached the powerful climax of Menzies' Forgotten People address in Old Parliament House, the post-traumatic shock of the events in the Party Room eight months earlier momentarily lessened. Three quarters of a century after its delivery, Menzies' rhetoric had an audience transfixed:

> "I do not believe that we shall come out into the overlordship of an all-powerful State on whose benevolence we shall live, spineless and effortless – a State which will dole out bread and ideas with neatly regulated accuracy; where we shall all have our dividend without subscribing our capital; where the Government, that almost deity, will nurse us and rear us and maintain us and pension us and bury us; where we shall all be civil servants, and all presumably, since we are equal, heads of departments.

> "If the new world is to be a world of men, we must be not pallid and bloodless ghosts, but a community of people whose motto shall be, 'To strive, to seek, to find, and not to yield.'

> "Individual enterprise must drive us forward. That does not mean we are to return to the old and selfish notions of laissez-faire. The functions of the State will be much more than merely keeping the ring within which the competitors will fight. Our social and industrial laws will be increased. There will be more law, not less; more control, not less.

"But what really happens to us will depend on how many people we have who are of the great and sober and dynamic middle-class – the strivers, the planners, the ambitious ones. We shall destroy them at our peril."

Once the applause had subsided, and the passion of Cousens's performance recognised by our gracious MC, Alan Jones, it fell to me to close the evening with a final unscripted performance. I began by asking Heather Henderson to join me on the platform as we acknowledged her father's great legacy. I then acknowledged his successors one by one who led the federal parliamentary party in government or opposition, beginning with Harold Holt.

When I reached the name of John Howard and invited him onto the stage, some in the room could tell where this was going. Brendan Nelson duly stepped up, followed by Malcolm Turnbull and finally Tony Abbott. With press photographers present, armed with rapid-repeat shutters, inviting Turnbull and Abbott to share the same stage for the first time since the Prime Ministership had changed hands was not without risk. One frame capturing either or both looking anything but rapturous could land up on the front page, drawing attention away from a great performance and the enduring power of Menzies' words. No such image appeared, nor do I believe one could have been taken.

We had been reminded that night why the Liberal Party of Australia had been put on this Earth and why its philosophy of freedom is favoured by most Australians in most federal elections. We had been reminded of the power of ideas to unite and inspire a party and a nation. And we had been reminded that the political centre of gravity in Australia is neither Vaucluse in the seat of Wentworth nor in the towns along the Warrego Highway in the seat of Wright. The heart of our nation is in the indefinable place Menzies identified where the Forgotten People reside:

"I do not believe that the real life of this nation is to be found either in great luxury hotels and the petty gossip of so-called fashionable suburbs, or in the officialdom of the organised masses. It is to be found in the homes of people who are nameless and unadvertised, and who, whatever their individual religious conviction or dogma, see in their children their greatest contribution to the immortality of their race."

Nick Cater is Executive Director of the Menzies Research Centre and a columnist at *The Australian*. He is a former editor of *The Weekend Australian* and a former deputy editor of *The Sunday Telegraph*. He is author of *The Lucky Culture*.

2

THE LIBERAL PARTY: WHERE TO NOW?

Senator the Hon. Concetta Fierravanti-Wells

Over the past decade, whilst thousands of Australians have joined the Liberal Party, it is clear thousands have also left. Why? What drives members to make such decisions, and why are some still disillusioned with the Party?

In a world dominated by a 24-hour media cycle and social media, we experience much more pressure from an activist culture turbocharged by these new and evolving technologies. The toxic by-product of social media was never intended by those creative minds who developed the tools to improve our social engagement.

To an extent, social media has been a force multiplier utilised by the unhinged. It has also been used by vocal fringe groups to give the impression that they are more powerful and influential to shape public opinion and government policy, "Sleeping Giants" is a case in point.

Against this background of activism and toxic culture, political parties of all persuasions are influenced by 'wokeness', 'cancel-culture', and, to an extent, climate activism, all of which, have tended to disregard the rule of law and hide the facts.

The Liberal Party Federal Constitution ('the constitution')

To analyse the question of why members have left the Liberal Party, the best place to start is with the philosophy in the constitution and where the Liberal Party has strayed off course.

The constitution sets out a series of objectives that remain a clear statement of aims that the Party has for Australians. People joined the Liberal Party based on these articulated values and beliefs. It is not as if they were written yesterday – the policy themes were developed over time and incrementally adjusted through consultation. Recent decisions have now been made against a background of activism and toxic social media culture where consultation and promises were the casualties.

I would like to examine some of the relevant tenets in the constitution where perceived failures of various Liberal governments have occurred by not following its mission statement.

The Liberal Party has moved too far to the Left

The constitution speaks of *dedication to political liberty and the freedom and dignity of man*. It also refers to *freedom of speech, religion, and association*. From the eyes of the majority of our support base, the Liberal Party has moved too far to the Left.

The failure to find the appropriate balance between freedom of speech under s.18 of the *Racial Discrimination Act* and outcomes of the same-sex marriage 'voluntary postal vote' remains a festering sore that will damage those who promised religious freedom would be preserved in accordance with, not only international law, but also the constitution.

Australians are a 'live and let live' society. The same-sex marriage debate and its result, determined by a 'voluntary postal vote' rather than a referendum of the people, is now history; but people of faith remain disillusioned. They believe the result would have been different if the Federal Government had fulfilled its promise to hold a referendum of the people at election time.

Australians of faith still face the potential of a legal battle before courts or tribunals for simply quoting their bibles. Despite believing the 'sacrament of marriage' is solely set aside for the joining of a man and woman in matrimony, many acquiesced on the basis that they believed the government would fulfil its promise to protect their religious freedoms. That has not happened.

Despite theological differences, religious leaders remain unified in their commitment to protect freedom of speech, thought, conscience and religion. They have expressed serious concerns about the religious discrimination draft bills. Given the existing disparate Commonwealth/state and territory discrimination framework, a better and more long-term solution would be to consolidate discrimination law into federal legislation to ensure national consistency and applicability. This would afford proper equality of rights and conformity to international obligations, including the protection of religious freedom. In the absence of a proper bill to protect religious freedom, I have supported the stance by religious leaders that no bill is better than this flawed bill.

Most of us would recall the term "Howard battlers" when referring to Australians who were drawn away from the Labor Party to support the Howard Government because they believed the Coalition parties were more relevant to their needs and aspirations. Those who forget this part of our history will do so at their peril!

Failure to articulate the objectives of 'the constitution'

We have witnessed an erosion of trust in the political class. Public life is about public service to the Australian people. There is an expectation that those in public office abide by a proper code of conduct and integrity – the higher the office, the greater the responsibility.

Regrettably, negative perception of politicians has not changed; indeed, it has deepened. Recent events at Parliament House, including the Higgins matter, only reinforced the stereotyping that politicians generally are not held in high regard.

We have seen the conflating of bad behaviour by politicians with a proposed change to preselection processes to introduce quotas. Firstly, individuals should be responsible for their own actions and dealt with accordingly. Secondly, the quota push was an illogical and fallacious argument at the time and was quickly dismissed.

Preselections must be based on merit. This view is reinforced by the fact that *individual initiative and enterprise as a dynamic force of progress* is an important cornerstone of the constitution. For over 20 years, conservatives fought hard to achieve plebiscites in the NSW Division of the Liberal Party so that members can have a direct say on who they want as their representative in parliaments.

Of significance, it has been the introduction of plebiscites that has encouraged a growing membership in the NSW Division of the Party. I have no doubts that from a growing and diverse base, potential candidates will emerge who will now feel more comfortable nominating for preselection in a more transparent and equitable process.

Once elected to Parliament, it can be difficult for a politician to articulate his/her intent to affect policy change. It was the late Jim Carlton who once said to me that politics is always about compromise, you never get 100 per cent of what you want; but don't compromise on your value set and what you stand for as an individual.

In a recent Senate speech, I quoted Marcus Aurelius, Roman Emperor and philosopher: *"If it is not right, do not do it; if it is not true, do not say it".*

Family life is fundamental to the well-being of society

Another key objective of the constitution is that *family life is seen as fundamental to the well-being of society*. The passage of same-sex marriage legislation by a Liberal government was a blow to many of our supporters who saw this as a breach of faith. The toxic media campaign accompanying the 'voluntary postal vote' attacked traditional family values and religion.

This has been compounded by the promotion of the so-called 'safe-schools program' by both federal and state administrations. Parents feel helpless at the onslaught of woke culture in schools which is doing everything possible to erode their influence with their children.

The constitution expresses the objective that there be *a comprehensive system of child and adult education designed to develop the spirit of true citizenship* - noting that *wealth or privilege are not determining factors.*

The Safe-Schools program is activism at its worst. It targets children who are not mature enough to make informed judgements and decisions, effectively brainwashing young minds. The same toxic intent has extended to transgender 'brainwashing' of children, whilst again usurping the rights of parents to safeguard their own children.

Democratic principles

The constitution refers to *an intelligent, free and Liberal Australian democracy maintained by a Parliament controlling the Executive and Law controlling all.*

As Chair of the Senate Standing Committee for the Scrutiny of Delegated Legislation, I have witnessed first-hand the erosion of democratic principles, especially under COVID-19. Each year approximately 2,000 pieces of legislation are enacted. About half of this is delegated legislation – legislation enacted by the Executive.

There are over 31,000 legislative instruments currently in force, making up the law on minor and substantial matters in every field. Delegated legislation does not only deal with matters that are technical and administrative but also, it is increasingly used to legislate matters of policy significance.

Whilst there may be good reasons to delegate legislative power to the Executive, there are also few good reasons to exempt such legislation from disallowance. Disallowance is not just a technical process. It is how Parliament retains oversight of delegated legislative power, thus fulfilling its role under our Australian Constitution. Approximately 20 per cent of delegated legislation is currently exempt from disallowance. Recent changes to Senate processes limit the circumstances where instruments can be exempt and hence, afford greater scrutiny by Parliament – more democratic!

Debt, economics and sovereign risk

The most successful democracies aim for a stable and trustworthy financial system.

The Global Financial Crisis (GFC) challenged our economic stability. Labor crowed from the roof tops about its sound economic stewardship, but Australians knew better. The true heroes were Howard and Costello. Their sound economic management left Labor zero debt, budget surpluses and large sums of monies in consolidated revenue - the best insurance policy for future economic shocks.

During the GFC, banks were the beneficiaries of government intervention at the expense of the taxpayer. The abolition of Statutory Reserve Deposits by the Hawke/Keating Governments was a step too far with deregulation placing the taxpayer in the default position if banks mismanaged risk. Today, the Reserve Bank manages an insurance scheme to cover the banks' government/taxpayer indemnity rather than limit such indemnity to shareholders.

Further, the Rudd Labor Government announced on 12 October 2008, it would guarantee bank deposits up to $1 million. The Coalition managed to reduce the figure to $250,000 taking effect 1 February 2012. Post-GFC, Australia was not in a good place financially which made us very vulnerable to future shocks and it has been hard work to achieve a balanced budget.

Since the GFC, we are now experiencing COVID-19 and its accompanying economic stress, exacerbated by lockdowns. Many argue that, as a traditional, fiscally conservative government, we have been too generous with borrowed money that will burden future generations of Australians.

The constitution makes clear for us that *social provision is made for the aged, the invalid, the widowed, the sick, the unemployed and their children.*

Whilst the Liberal maxim has always been "the best form of welfare is a job", just under half of Australians are employed. The social welfare bill is growing but the dependency ratio is shrinking. According to the 2021 Intergenerational Report (June 2021), in 1981-82, there were 6.6 people of working age (15-64 years) for every person aged 65 years or over. In 2019-20 it was 4.0 people and by 2060-61, it drops to only 2.7 people.

The constitution further notes that there should be *no nationalisation of any Australian industry without the approval of the people.*

We have navigated down a risky path of de facto 'nationalisation' with respect to key strategic assets including our ports, energy, and critical infrastructure. These have not been passed to the Australian government, but to the Chinese Communist Party and their entities – a shameful policy blunder at all levels noting the sacrifices Australian forces have made in past conflicts fighting for democracy against the evils of communism. We have entered the realm of sovereign risk.

The path back

When you have lost your way, you need to retrace your steps and go back to the start. In short, go back to the basic tenets of what a Liberal government should be and reassert those articulated objectives, values and beliefs developed over decades.

Therefore, it is incumbent on those who criticise the Liberal Party for having lost its way, to do something about it. Do not walk away. Have faith and contribute from within to affect change that is needed – become more engaged!

In the first instance, preselect those who are up to the task of defending 'the constitution' and its values. Ignore the toxic social media bile and seek solace in the knowledge that history will judge you kindly.

Senator the Honourable Concetta Fierravanti-Wells was elected to the Senate in 2005 and has served as the Assistant Minister for Multicultural Affairs with portfolio responsibilities in the Attorney-General, Immigration and Border Protection and Social Services, as well as serving as the Parliamentary Secretary to the Minister for Social Services, with special responsibility for multicultural affairs and settlement service. She served as Minister for International Development and the Pacific from 2016 to 2018. Before entering politics, she worked as a lawyer with the Australian Government Solicitor and as a private secretary to the former Premier of NSW, John Fahey. For 25 years before entering the Senate, Senator Fierravanti-Wells was involved in many different community organisations and activities, including strong and extensive engagement in culturally and linguistically diverse communities. Senator Fierravanti-Wells graduated from the Australian National University with a Bachelor of Arts in Political Science and European Languages (1980), and a Bachelor of Laws (1982). She was born in Wollongong, NSW, and is the daughter of Italian migrants. She is married to Commander John Wells (RAN Ret'd).

3

COUNTERING CANCEL CULTURE

Tom Switzer

Today, a growing, malignant disease undermines liberal democracy. It has permeated every crevice of our society and is destroying free speech – all roots of classical liberalism. This phenomenon is called cancel culture.

It is a deeply illiberal mindset where you can be vilified, shamed and denied a public platform if your actions or opinions are deemed by others to be morally or politically incorrect. Livelihoods are lost, reputations ruined. Although cancel culture is more prevalent in the United States and the United Kingdom, it is still evident in Australian public life. And liberals – as in both the Liberal Party and classical liberal sense – must stand firm and push back against this dangerous illiberalism.

From public intellectuals to public figures, the "cancellation" entails not just the denial of public platforms to those who refuse to conform to stifling orthodoxies, but also attempts to use social media to seek to remove such people from civilised society and the public consciousness. The movement has led to attempts to erase our history, culture and even elements of language and comedic rhetoric.

Tolerant, civil discourse should be the fruits of a free society and be fiercely defended by genuine liberals.

Truly open exchange of ideas and arguments is fundamental to a healthy, flourishing society. Maintaining a public culture in which freedom and civility can co-exist are principles that must be upheld. A society which shames people into self-censorship, forces mindless groupthink and conformity is not only reminiscent of a totalitarian dystopia but stultifies societal progress and leads to a decadence in our culture.

Disturbingly, the cancel culture campaign is justified in the name of "tolerance" and "diversity". The activists are supposed to oppose bigotry, yet they impose a new stifling orthodoxy of their own. Cancellers believe they are righting wrongs, stamping out perceived oppression against vulnerable groups and effecting meaningful social change and retribution.

However, as we have seen with social movements, such as Black Lives Matter and the same-sex marriage campaign, intolerance is the key weapon in the armoury of the mob. It is chipping away at the defining elements of our democracy and dismantling free speech and common decency.

During the same-sex marriage debate in Australia, anyone who defended traditional marriage was treated with shock and distaste. Company board members who supported traditional marriage endured a hysterical witch-hunt while a Catholic archbishop in Hobart was accused of hate speech for voicing the church's scepticism about same-sex marriage. The contorted logic was that if you opposed gay marriage, you must be a homophobe.

In a similar vein, the Black Lives Matter movement in 2020 inflamed the practice of cancellation across the western world. BLM began with laudable intentions of protesting the injustice of black people, such as the murder of Minneapolis man George Floyd. Yet the movement has morphed into a collective effort to defeat all forms of perceived oppression and privilege through ideological conformity and mindless group think.

John Stuart Mill, the great 19th Century British liberal, warned in his famous 1859 essay *On Liberty*: "Unmeasured vituperation, employed on the side of the prevailing opinion really does deter people from expressing contrary opinion, and from listening to those who express them."

Mill's quote exemplifies the mob of cancellers. They strangle debate, kill the ethos of the liberal society, suppress ideas and seek to standardise opinion. Their actions have resulted in the censorship and erasure of our language, history, culture and our sense of national identity.

And indeed, we do not need to look far to perceive the damage that cancel culture has already inflicted on our key institutions. Universities, especially in many parts of Britain and America, have been at the top of the cancel mob's hit list.

For generations, the university has been a place designed as a crucible of debate and discussion. That meant allowing free-flowing debate and the exchange of ideas in order to acquire knowledge and intellectual substance. Yet many universities across the western world are now at the forefront of restricting freedom of speech. Across America and Europe, for example, anyone with counter-orthodox views about transgender issues, or same-sex marriage, or even aspects of capitalism, is liable to suffer the indignity of "de-platforming."

The courageous Somalia-born human rights activist, Ayaan Hirsi Ali, was silenced on American campuses for questioning the Islamic treatment of women while social commentator Bettina Arndt was blocked from accessing an Australian campus because she challenged the prevalence of rape and sexual assault incidents against university students. Dissenters to the cancel-culture mob, who are predominantly conservative or classical liberal students, were shouted down or even physically assaulted if they failed to bend to ideological conformity.

Radical leftist orthodoxy has encouraged disgust and frenzy at the thought of western civilisation being taught on campuses. For example, the controversy over the failure of the Ramsay Centre for Western Civilisation to find residency at the University of Sydney showed that some of our higher education institutions are increasingly in the grip of toxic cancel culture.

According to protesting academics at the University of Sydney, teaching students about the rich history of western arts and letters will somehow offend the principles of diversity and inclusion on campus. Student activists argued it sheltered toxic and paranoid prejudices and cast all students of a non-western background as culturally backwards.

On this premise, many of the world's leading academics, who have taught aspects of this discipline for centuries – theologians, philosophers, classicists, linguists, historians, art historians, musicians and so on – must now be re-labelled as toxic and paranoid, not to mention racist. Cancellers ignore that part of the teaching of western civilisations has been to encourage inquiry into other civilisations. Indeed, anyone who has looked at Persian, Indian, Chinese or Aztec cultures (to name but a few) will have grasped at once their sophistication and complexity.

The woke-style cancel culture attack has also penetrated younger students in primary and secondary schools. The launch of the newly revised national education curriculum demonstrates that factual accuracy has been relegated in the pursuit and vision of a radical social justice.

The draft history curriculum presents the arrival of the First Fleet as an "invasion", European settlement as "genocide" and substitutes references to "Aboriginal" and "Indigenous" with "First Nations Australians". It echoes the rhetoric of activists who have attempted to cancel Australia Day as a national public holiday and rename it as "invasion day".

These proposals are deconstructing and revising our history to teach our young that the British brought violence, racism and slavery to Australia while ignoring its formative role in establishing liberty, democracy and equality as key pillars of our nation. The end game of this will be to breed a generation of Australian students who view their society through a flawed, divisive and socially destructive lens.

In the wake of the Black Lives Matter resurgence in 2020, protestors in Australia took to the streets over Aboriginal Australian deaths in police custody. They sought to remove all symbols and legacies of our past, which they considered to be blemished by colonialism. They defaced and toppled statues of public figures like Captain Cook and Lachlan Macquarie who they considered represented racism and colonialism. Like Pol Pot, with his Year Zero, or Mao Zedong and his Cultural Revolution, they wished to change the past.

Commercial brands, such as Coon cheese and Colonial beer, were also cancelled – the cheese because it unwittingly shared an epithet with a coarse term of racial abuse, the beer because any link between enjoyment and colonialism was deemed inevitably to be wicked and mocking those who suffered from colonialism.

For too many of the present protesters, opposition is not an end in itself, but rather the means to a greater end – the reordering of a political and social settlement accepted by the vast majority of people in Western nations.

Context is irrelevant to these people. Historical figures who had attitudes or performed deeds of which today's society rightly disapprove are to be vilified and despised, with no quarter given. That is why statues and monuments are being ripped down or defaced around the world. For these people, the purpose of history is not to seek the truth, but to deploy it as a weapon, however crude and distorted, to manipulate the present.

It doesn't matter how you dress this act up, it is the imposition of the views of a minority of agitators on the rest of society without any attempt at consultation or respect for democracy. Then again, the whole point of being an anarchist is to reject democracy and to seize any excuse to attack manifestations of the establishment – whether they are statues, other monuments or police officers.

Australia's continent has certainly had distasteful episodes in its treatment of our Indigenous people, especially before our independence in 1901. But name a country whose history has not been plagued by some form of cruelty, abuse of power or ignorance? The fact is that our nation, admirable by almost every international standard, only exists because of James Cook, one of the figures protestors defaced and toppled.

Colonisation of Australia's land mass was inevitable; and, as John Howard has all too often argued, British settlement was a far better outcome than other possibilities. Think of the English language, rule of law, representative democracy, a free press and a market economy. Context is everything.

History cannot be undone; its legacies are in every society, everywhere. Censoring the past by removing statues, re-naming products or decolonising our curriculum only allows an ignorance of our history, a rejection of critical, reasoned thinking and a sharply polarised society to be propagated. Liberals need to defend civil discourse and free expression if we hope to protect our history and culture.

The cancel culture movement has veered to such extremities that even left-wing radicals like Noam Chomsky and Bernie Sanders are defending classical liberal values of free speech. They have come together with esteemed artists, authors and public intellectuals to sign a letter condemning cancel culture for stifling freedom of expression in journalism, higher education, philanthropy and the arts.

Writing in *Harper's* magazine in 2020, the ideologically diverse group said: "The free exchange of information and ideas, the lifeblood of a liberal society, is daily becoming more constricted." They went on to bemoan "an intolerance of opposing views, a vogue for public shaming and ostracism, and the tendency to dissolve complex policy issues in a blinding moral certainty." The letter followed former president Barack Obama's denunciations of "woke" culture and "purity tests".

The exclusion of views that challenge the consensus can only hurt the activists for the reason John Stuart Mill elaborated: "He who knows only his own side of the case, knows little of that." Why not, as the *Harper's* letter writers put it, try to "defeat bad ideas... by exposure, argument and persuasion, not [by] trying to silence or wish them away."

Cancel culture is a relentless campaign of ideological conformity. This, more than anything, is why responsible politicians should act to stop this manipulation of our values and the vilification of those whose only offence is not to agree with the stifling orthodoxy. If genuine Liberals, conservatives and classical liberals fail to defend civil discourse and stand up and confront cancel culture when it rears its ugly head, the foundations of democracy risk becoming permanently disfigured. Civil discourse and free speech will become luxuries of the past.

Tom Switzer is Executive Director of the Centre for Independent Studies and a presenter at the ABC's *Radio National*. He has previously worked at *The Spectator Australia*, *The Australian*, *Australian Financial Review* and the American Enterprise Institute in Washington. He was a senior adviser to the former federal Liberal leader, Brendan Nelson.

4

THE ABC: WHO DOES IT SERVE?

Senator the Hon. James McGrath

The Australian Broadcasting Corporation is somewhat like a lost teenager aimlessly floating through time trying to find himself/ herself, unperturbed by authority, yet infatuated with its own self-importance.

The ABC's lack of direction stems from the wide and unfettered nature of the Charter, which exists purely to govern the public broadcaster's operations. The outdated ABC Charter fails to define the purpose of a public broadcaster within Australia or limit what the ABC's operations should consist of in a diverse media market.

This has allowed the ABC to encroach well beyond what was ever expected by a public broadcaster, giving birth to an uncontrollable leftist mediocracy forever dependent on taxpayer expenditure.

The ABC's reluctance to accept that it has a serious problem with centre and centre-right Australians has effectively terminated its social licence. Additionally, the violent evolution of the media landscape means a radical solution is required.

The Board is a toothless tiger inhabited by members who are, at best, powerless, or, at worst, captured by the ideology of the staff collective who are the true decision-makers.

It is no better at Government level; successive Coalition Ministers have willfully failed to meaningfully attempt any reform of the ABC. At least one Minister saw himself as its 'Defender in Chief'.

Therefore, there needs urgently to be a Commission of Inquiry into the future of taxpayer-funded broadcasting with a view to shifting the ABC to a subscriber model similar to *Sky News* or *Netflix*.

Simply put, if you want the ABC, then you can pay for it.

Previously, I have argued that the ABC needs to be reformed to save itself via a staged reform agenda consisting of three broad headings:

1. Sell-off inner-city offices and shift operations regionally or to the outer suburbs;

2. A review of the Charter with a view to accepting commercial advertising; and

3. Open up all staff recruitment.

However, the time for incremental reform has passed.

The ABC costs Australian taxpayers over $1.1 billion each year, and many within the ABC and, more broadly, on the Left, advocate for more while simultaneously rejecting any notion of criticism.

Not only is this completely irrational, but it arguably demonstrates what many ordinary viewers fear – that the ABC has grown into a big self-serving bureaucracy that is out of touch with their obligation to the Australian people.

What makes matters worse is that the ABC is now displaying blatant trends of bias across varying platforms which are not consistent with mainstream Australia.

When it comes to fulfilling its obligation to the Australian people, the ABC is stuck in knowing that its own Charter fails to define its scope.

The broad nature has allowed the ABC to evolve into a media conglomerate with little to no restraint or review. Its wide ambit even arguably allows for bias, opinion and partisan irreverence, all things that most Australians would agree do not belong on the ABC.

While the ABC is enshrined in the Australian media market, this does not mean that it is not broken or free from reform. You just have to tune into 'The Drum', 'Q&A' or 'Insiders' to observe open bias in the coverage.

Just ask the ABC's own secret review into their 'biased' coverage of the 2019 election, a review only made public after a resolution moved by the author was passed by the Senate. After all, since the 1930s, the ABC has never been beyond reproach of Government review or reform, so why should it be now?

Ever since the then named Australian Broadcasting Commission opened on 1 July 1932, its operation as a government-controlled entity and, subsequently, an incorporated statutory body, has always been subject to Government policy, criticism and review.

In its infancy, the functionality of how the ABC could best broadcast wireless services to the public was contested between proponents for the American commercial model and the British publicly owned monopoly model.

The disputed development in Australia resulted in the mixed model that was funded through broadcasting licence fees. However, this inefficient blancmange did not exempt the ABC from evolving or being reviewed and reformed.

Governments of both political persuasions have amended the ABC over time. Labor's Chifley government amended the ABC Act in 1946 which required the ABC to source and report its own domestic news, rather than previously relying on rebroadcasting national tabloids.

Chifley's further amendments in 1948 attached the broadcaster's funding directly to federal government expenditure which reduced the broadcaster's reliance on private radio licence fees. This part license fee and part federal funding model continued until Whitlam abolished the licence fees in 1973, resulting in a fully funded public broadcaster.

The most comprehensive changes to the public broadcaster occurred in the 1980s which saw the ABC evolve from a Commission to a Corporation model. This substantial restructure of the organisation included segmenting the radio and television division which led to rapid growth of the production output.

This overhaul of the broadcaster arose from a growing public distaste with the Commission as identified in the 1976 review by Alex Dix of the ABC. Commissioned by the Fraser government, the Dix Review was the first serious consideration of the purpose of the public broadcaster in Australia.

The Dix Review identified that the public broadcaster should not necessarily be a niche complementary provider for where the private media market fails to reach. Rather it should accommodate the cross section of the community. This ultimately led to the introduction of the ABC Charter to give the ABC a sense of purpose and direction.

Although an admirable pursuit, the current construction of the Charter does not live up to this expectation.

The reform of the 1980s clearly demonstrates that the public broadcaster has evolved over time and its evolution has been fraught with competing views, in ideology and purpose. Not only does this demonstrate that the ABC is not beyond reproach, but its evolution in its first 50 years has caused it to lack purpose or lose its integrity within the national environment. The same, too, can be argued about its second 50 years.

Since consecutive federal governments have reviewed elements of the ABC and implemented changes (often in the form of funding), however, no recent government has comprehensively reviewed the ABC, its purpose within Australia, how it conforms with its Charter and whether it is fit for purpose. Nor has any government been able to overcome the blatant bias.

The fact of the matter is that it took a better part of half a century for the ABC Charter to be enacted in 1983; however, the Charter in its existing form fails to define the ABC's purpose, in particular, the ABC's applicability in the 21st Century with reference to how large the national broadcaster should be and to what extent they should compete in the modern media market.

In 1996, the Howard government commissioned the Mansfield Review of the role of the ABC in an attempt to strengthen its effectiveness in its delivery of services. The review concluded that "the principal function of the ABC should be defined as broadcasting for general reception within Australia".

The review made recommendations relating to the sale of the ABC's property, the possibilities of outsourcing programming and questioned the equal programming of domestic and international broadcasting. Despite this, the Howard government, mostly due to political pressures, did not successfully implement the change the ABC desperately needs, nor has any other government since.

The Rudd government's only contribution was to amend the ABC Charter to include the provision of digital media services in 2011 – something that the ABC had been doing for the better part of two decades.

This inapplicability of the Charter to the provision of digital services is a poor reflection on the Charter itself, which highlights how it remains an unenforceable quasi-obligatory mission statement that is enshrined in law. This demonstrates a crucial issue with the Charter that has allowed the ABC to expand well beyond what it was ever intended to – this is clear in the extensive and arguably excessive services the ABC provides.

Although the early debate related to the ABC's structure, over time, the conglomerate has grown and expanded into the various arms it operates today – from its four television channels, its four national radio channels, its seven digital radio stations and the 53 local radio stations that operate across the eight capital cities and 48 regional locations.

All of these are 'acceptable' within the scope of the ABC Charter. However, to continue operating an expanding conglomerate, with no ceiling on that expansion, is an unnecessary burden on the taxpayer. Therefore, the question must be asked, does all of the ABC's substantial operations pursue the purpose of a public broadcaster?

Determining that purpose is a $1.1 billion question and one that requires us to define, in today's terms, whether there is a need for a public broadcaster and, if so, what is its specific purpose and scope of its operation?

To do this, the federal government must urgently commence a Commission of Inquiry into the ABC's operation and identify what the specific parameters of its operation should include and, therefore, aim to make the ABC's Charter fit for purpose.

The review should not only define the ABC's priorities and their appropriate position within the media market, but also should serve as a mechanism to cut through the bureaucracy and minimise any waste of taxpayer money.

Refining the scope of the ABC's operations will promote strict purpose metrics that will demand compliance and mitigate any existing lack of priority for the everyday Australian.

A prime example of the ABC's lack of priority for the Australian public is the ABC's refusal to broadcast the Tokyo Olympic Games on radio, the first time since 1952. Filling the market, where commercial providers do not supply, is a crucial function of the ABC, especially when Australians are on display, whether its athletes, musicians or artists.

Essentially, the challenge before the "review" is to sieve through the ABC bureaucracy to ascertain where the true value of the ABC lies, in order to benefit the entire Australian public. The review must refine what is and is not acceptable by a public broadcaster which effectively upholds the Australian taxpayer as beneficiary of the ABC.

The review should extensively consider any aspect of the ABC's operation that falls outside of the defined parameters and those operations should be consolidated, privatised or cease operating. Defining the "purpose" of the ABC will undoubtedly be a robust conversation, but it is a necessary one.

The review of the ABC Charter is one of the three crucial steps that I have previously proposed. In my view, the ABC needs to be there to ultimately uphold the values of the Australian people, and definitely not be catering to a niche demographic or ideology.

The primary function of the ABC (or its successor in title) should be the unbiased presentation of news and current affairs to the Australian public, and should always be there in times of crisis or emergency. This is particularly critical in regional areas and the use of regional radio. Therefore, the ABC must uphold its most critical operations which arguably should remain on public funding.

In recognising what is "critical", the review should also identify what television and, more likely, radio stations that are not central to the provision of news and determine whether they could compete commercially.

If so, the ABC must either consolidate them within the commercial arm of the ABC and, therefore, allow advertising or be privatised completely. The prime example of this is Triple J, as it is a popular station with a specific target audience making it prime for commercialisation. This will either make certain aspects of the ABC self-sufficient or cease operating. Both outcomes would lower the burden on the taxpayer.

Alternatively, if the privatisation of such aspects is not within the national taste, then the review should recommend that this commercial arm operate as an opt-in subscription model, meaning that the niche and non-purpose-meeting-services are not propped up by taxpayers who never engage with them.

If anything, this semi-privatisation of the ABC's more niche services will enhance its competitiveness within the media market, all the while allowing truly public funds to be spent on truly public services.

In addition to reviewing the ABC's purpose and commercial viability, the ABC should also be forced to divest from its $426 million inner-city property portfolio and relocate to locations that reflect middle-class, mainstream Australia. This will not only expose the taxpayer employed journalists to mainstream Australia but, by selling off properties, the proceeds can be used for budget repair.

The ABC can quite easily relocate from inner-city hubs in Brisbane, Sydney and Melbourne to locations outside of the inner-city and adopt a model of satellite studios to conduct interviews located in the city. This is a model that is adopted by many competitive providers thus saving the taxpayer money. By way of example, the BBC have shifted many operations from London to Salford.

Finally, the ABC must always be transparent to the Australian public, especially in regard to appointments to broaden the diversity of views within the organisation. The review must consider provisions for bias review and internally examine how the ABC can enhance a diversity of views and representation. By opening up the appointment process and increasing the diversity of the employees, the ABC will therefore enhance its impartiality which should always be the main function of the ABC.

In any event, to even consider a possible role of the ABC in today's Australia arguably requires a broader review of its current position, purpose and functionality.

The last review of the ABC and its Charter was over 40 years ago. It is definitely time for another. This time we need to define the role of a public broadcaster from the outset and mould the ABC to fit that purpose. Only then will we possibly be able to ground this rogue teenager.

Senator the Honourable James McGrath is a Liberal National Party Senator for Queensland. He currently serves as Deputy Government Whip in the Senate and as Chairman of the Joint Standing Committee on Electoral Matters. Prior to entering the Senate, James McGrath worked in Australia and overseas, in particular the United Kingdom, in various roles including law, political campaigning and public policy.

5

VISION AND VALUES
FOR A BETTER AUSTRALIA
The Hon. Gary Hardgrave

Be they the forgotten, the battlers, or the quiet, Australians have come to rely on the traditional principles of Liberal-led governments.

These core, traditional liberal principles are compelling. Especially as we now face a real and present threat to the rights, freedoms and aspirations of the individual.

While Labor is more comfortable in the big government, big unions and big business approach to control our society and economy, the Liberal Party traditionally recognises the importance of measuring decisions in terms of how they impact the individual.

There is a need to revisit, reinforce and revitalise these traditional values to define the vision modern day 'forgotten people' seek.

In too many ways, even many Liberals, currently in Parliament, have become lazy acolytes of the big government and big business mantra of Labor.

Trust of the people is a restorative, fundamental approach. As most people in our society are law-abiding and worthy of trust, the Liberal Party should reject existing structures of rules and regulations, higher taxes and more government codification of the lives of individuals.

In many ways so much of what Sir Robert Menzies observed in the dark days of the Second World War with regard to the non-Labor parties, fractured and aimless as they were, is sadly true today.

Menzies in "The Forgotten People" speech of the 1940s spoke to the same types of aspirational individuals as did John Howard half a century later. His 'Howard battlers' in the 'For all of us' campaign of 1996 and Scott Morrison's 'Quiet Australians' of 2019 were individuals wanting less government and more common sense, guided by core principles which encourage and nurture private ambition to provide a better future for individuals, families and our nation.

These aspirational Australians cannot be classed by ethnic or social background but rather by their personal and unbridled ambition to be rewarded for effort.

If governments trust private citizens, they would tax less, legislate less and regulate less. Encouraging individuals to succeed means less government, less tax, less legislation, not more. Encouraging individuals means trusting in individuals to grow a stronger, more cohesive, more inclusive society providing, at the same time, equality of opportunity.

However, the Liberal Party can be an awkward beast. It's an organisation built on trust and the rights of the individual allowing each to bring their own ambition, their own observation, their own experience and their own personal values to debate within party fora.

For those attempting to lead the party, to organise campaigns and Parliamentary teams, the rights and freedoms of individual members, with views which may vary from others, can be problematic and frustrating but the freedom of the individual remains paramount.

It's evident the broad church of the Liberal Party can often be too broad for some of its members. The party has tended to group within broad philosophical or personality-based groupings or streams.

Sometimes the personality-based grouping leads to a Messiah complex. A 'top-down', 'whatever the leader says goes' approach often has transitional or temporary appeal but the greatest strength of stable leadership comes when a strong leader emerges from assembled like-minded colleagues to implement a 'bottom up' broad based agenda.

Throughout its long and politically successful history there have been a number of Messiah periods where all hope was placed in the character and charisma of one person to lead the party to success. However, messiahs have come and messiahs have gone, often leaving a void from which the party takes years to recover.

In contrast, trust in the collaboration of individuals within the Liberal Party broad church has served the party's electoral success far better and provided Australia with stable successful governments.

Sir Robert Menzies drew the broad church together in the shadows of World War Two. Australia today is also under attack but the enemy and the weapons are covert.

Our way of life, our social norms, our national psyche, our values are being attacked in constant and insidious ways by enemies, both foreign and domestic, who seek to end our freedom, destroy mutual trust, break up societal functionality and create adherence to a 'new normal' where we 'build back better' and create a 'great reset' of our economy.

This is totalitarianism dressed up in slogans.

The Menzies Governments, after 1949, nurtured the spirit of the individual against the then rising, rampant international socialist agenda of the period to build the modern Australia and deliver a long post World War Two economic and social boom, which attracted millions of new migrants to our shore.

The Menzies Governments galvanised the ambitions of aspirational individuals to build the modern Australia. Visionary, ambitious nation building infrastructure projects and emerging industries were designed to build national sovereignty and security. We could no longer rely on Great Britain; we needed to build our own destiny.

Too much of this is lost on younger Australians with Australia's ability to build infrastructure and sustain industries important to national sovereignty and security being heavily hampered by authoritarian process based on international standards and protocols.

Our bureaucratic addiction to processes, fees, taxes and subsidies contrived to meet international agreements, has crippled individual Australian aspiration, national security and sovereignty.

In principle, Australia needs to resist international totalitarian interference in our affairs and build what we need to succeed as a society of aspirational individuals. Australians are wanting vision based on our traditional values not international control of our lives.

Australian society has stood against totalitarianism in the past. We need to continue to reject foreign influence and covert control. Our shared values such as equality of opportunity and the fair go are worthy. They are values for which Australians have fought and died; values which have attracted people from all parts of the world to come to be part of this nation; values which have shaped our nation into the egalitarian, generous, tolerant and responsible nation we are today.

As a nation, we have always been a people of the fair go. Sir Robert Menzies saw a nation "in which living standards rise steadily as physical resources expand and ingenuity grows."

In his speech of October 1944, Menzies talked of thrift, enterprise and reward for effort. He talked of tax reform in order to help families. He talked of encouraging investment through the right types of monetary and other economic policy, of major public policy not based on 'off the cuff' pronouncements, but on underlying values which unified individuals.

Our enemies today use divisive mantra about race, religion, gender and values to attack our social norms. While there are a few racists in every country, we are not a racist nation. Menzies never saw us this way, despite his own great love, the love so many still hold, for Great Britain, Ireland and Europe.

The personal lives, religious and cultural backgrounds of individuals are respected and supported by most Australians. While we support individuals to 'be who they are', we challenge them to 'be it for Australia'.

While some want to create "victimhood" within minorities, what we have in common unites us. Most Australians realise no one leaves their country of birth for less; rather, they move here to achieve more. The impact of aspirational individual migrants has secured a stronger economy and society.

Most migrants, particularly refugees, understand as Menzies did, big government is authoritarian and dangerous.

Yet, ironically, so many younger Australians now expect government to 'provide and do'. This reliance on government is a challenge to individual trust and reward for effort.

Freedom and individualism in Australia are under genuine challenge from the permanent structures of government. Government has so many unnecessary intrusions into our lives. Government never retreats from the temptation of totalitarian intrusion, forms, fees, processes which delay and derail the efforts of individuals.

Too many politicians and government bureaucratic procedures show they do not trust us. Our elected members lack vision, while our public service is no longer fearless and frank but has become adept at admiring problems, seldom fixing them.

Our country is congealed by process and we suffer so many laws, fees, forms and taxes, all designed to restrict us, to plan our lives and to control our basic freedom.

Too many politicians forget lessons from the history of fighting on principle and against tyranny in its many forms. Too many are preoccupied by the cause célèbre and issue du jour rather than a long-term vision based on principle.

Be it climate change or coronavirus, too many politicians are so easily distracted and fooled by loud voices and false prophets. They blame the scrutiny of the 24-hour news cycle but forget such scrutiny is deserved given a paucity of vision and inconsistent values.

While there is understandable concern from the aggressive hegemony of the Chinese Communist Party (CCP), it is evident Confucius principles provide deliberate long term strategic vision better than our contemporary woke political mandarins. The CCP understands Australia's susceptibility to vulnerability better than we do.

In the post-COVID pandemic world, there needs to be a reduction in government control of individuals but power is often heady and intoxicating to the bureaucracy and their political puppets.

Australians deserve to know when pre COVID freedoms will return and what is the principled plan to build our economy and nation for the next generation to enjoy. Sadly, right now, Australians are concerned that are bequeathing an economy and society which the next generation will have to endure not enjoy.

Democracy, rule of law and free speech are bedrock principles in Australia. However, each of these bedrock principles has been weakened by codification and systemic controls.

Sadly, most Australians don't realise we are in a cultural war with international elites in Hollywood, Brussels and the United Nations which have torn apart key institutions and cultural norms.

Leadership reaffirming our core values, promoting a clear vision based on trust of the individual is needed to unite us and keep us together as a nation of individuals.

Sir Robert Menzies posed challenges we still face today. He highlighted the principles for national success. Menzies spoke, without qualification or caveat, no exclusion along class, creed or colour lines.

Menzies said what Australia should be all about:

"I see the individual and his encouragement and recognition as the prime motive force for the building of a better world."

These principles, values and vision are worth standing up for today as when Menzies observed on 13 October 1944.

"There is free thought and free speech and free association for all except the enemies of freedom."

Menzies understood the enemies of freedom would take many forms including the group think of what we now call the repressive "woke'.

Menzies earned support from what he termed 'the forgotten people', John Howard from 'the Howard battlers' and Scott Morrison from 'the quiet Australians'.

Menzies inspired the Liberal Party to set forth and create a nation where `citizens are free to choose their own way of living and of life'.

As politics is binary, there is more conflict today between long term principles and short-term immediate pragmatism which leaves so many people confused.

Too many people are unsure who to believe and who to trust, while government seems more concerned about the power they take rather than the freedom the people have.

If we don't know who we are, what we stand for, then we are lost. In many ways, right now, we are being misled on many things. Discussion of values and vision are dismissed as redundant relics of the past.

However, the old maxim 'if you stand for nothing, you'll fall for everything' seems relevant as we need to question the political 'science'.

I was once advised by a wise political type that "if you're never prepared to lose on principle, then you're never prepared to stand for things." Also, "if you stand on principle you need to know you may lose more than you'll win."

However, if politics is dominated by those who believe winning is everything, who lampoon those with principles but would rather crawl over them to the top, then the forgotten people will suffer.

The Honourable Gary Hardgrave is a highly experienced community, political and social commentator, hosting his own television program on *Sky News Australia*. He served in the Australian Parliament for 12 years representing the Queensland electorate of Moreton. During this time, he served in the Howard Government as Minister for Citizenship and Multicultural Affairs, Minister for Vocational and Technical Education and Minister Assisting the Prime Minister. He was appointed as the Administrator of the Australian External Territory of Norfolk Island from 2014 to 2017 where he spearheaded major governance reforms.

6

MODERN FEMINISM HIJACKED BY THE LEFT

Rita Panahi

The modern feminist movement has been hijacked by the Regressive Left.

Women's rights and the pursuit of equality have taken a backseat to pushing a relentlessly far-Left agenda.

For decades the bulk of the feminist movement has ignored the plight of their oppressed sisters in the Muslim world and, now, the movement is siding with radical trans activists rather than women fighting to preserve hard fought for rights and protections in the West.

Then there is the sisterhood's betrayal of conservative women who are not afforded protection against misogynist attacks from the Left.

The most unhinged, sexist vitriol I have witnessed in this country has come from feminists, male and female, who have no qualms about denigrating conservative women.

Even the Prime Minister's wife, Jenny Morrison, has been subjected to this misogyny from the very people who pretend to champion women's rights. More on that later.

For years I have spoken and written about the cowardice that sees the women's movement turn a blind eye to the plight of the world's most oppressed women; those living under Islam.

The systematic subjugation of millions of Muslim women is ignored while privileged feminists obsess over trivialities such as feminist pedestrian crossings, gendered toys and sexist air conditioning?

There are growing signs of the persecution of Muslim women right here in Australia with increasing incidence of female genital mutilation, forced marriage, forced veiling and child brides.

Yet these issues are rarely, if ever, the focus of feminists who can be callous in disregarding real suffering while painting themselves as victims.

Empowered women in the West could strike a blow against the most dehumanising misogyny inflicted on women, but instead they prefer to don "pussy hats" and march against a democratically elected president or against a centre-right Australian government.

Worse still, they tacitly approve this misogyny by admonishing those genuinely courageous women who take a stand often at considerable risk to their own safety.

Women like Ayaan Hirsi Ali who suffered FGM as a child and has spent decades campaigning for the rights of disempowered Muslim women.

Instead of being celebrated, she is criticised by feminists for enabling 'Islamaphobia' because she refuses to shy away from highlighting inconvenient truths they dare not acknowledge.

A wise man once described Islamophobia as a word "created by fascists, and used by cowards, to manipulate morons," I am yet to see a better definition.

Hirsi Ali's life has been repeatedly threatened by extremists and yet

The Age newspaper in Melbourne decided to whip a little more hate and hysteria for her Australian tour in 2017.

Their headline asked: "Why is no one protesting Ayaan Hirsi Ali's visit to Australia?" In the end, the outrage whipped up by local activists helped ensure the speaking tour was cancelled.

Australia's Leftist media echo chamber would do well to heed Hirsi Ali's words on the evils of FGM, gender apartheid and Muslim veiling which she wrote marks women as private property and non-persons.

"The veil sets women apart from men and apart from the world; it restrains them, confines them, grooms them for docility," she wrote.

The ABC, in particular, seems to have a strange fixation on hijabs even though the majority of Muslim women in Australia do not wear the garb.

The Left's fetishisation of hijabs is a truly perverse development and a sign of the vacuousness that has infected the modern feminist movement.

In 2019, we saw women in New Zealand encouraged to wear hijabs in a show of solidarity with the Muslim community after the devastating Christchurch massacre. Non-Muslim women, from police officers to reporters, newsreaders to barmaids, donned a hijab in what was a misguided, albeit well-intentioned, bit of activism.

I wonder how many of those who decided to wear the veil — including mothers who put their little girls in hijabs and posted the pictures on Instagram with a "Headscarf for Harmony" hashtag — had any understanding of what it represents.

If you are going to celebrate the hijab then you should know it is not just a garment, it is not just a fashion accessory you can put on like you're playing dress up. The hijab, and other Muslim veils, such as the niqab, burqa and chador, is imbued with deep symbolism and represents modesty culture, which requires women to cover up, marking those who don't.

At its core, modesty culture is deeply anti-women.

There is good reason why the majority of Muslim women in the West choose not to wear the hijab and why women's rights campaigners living under Islam fight, at great personal risk, against its imposition.

Women in countries such as Iran, Saudi Arabia and Qatar are required to cover up by law or social convention and there are grim repercussions for those who fail to comply.

In 2021, there are still thousands of women in the Muslim world arrested, beaten and imprisoned for protesting against compulsory veiling.

Women are not risking their life and liberty to protest against a piece of cloth, it represents much more, and we betray these brave women when we embrace the hijab as a symbol of diversity and harmony. That is the last thing it is.

Veiling was invented by men and imposed upon women to control, separate and subjugate.

To this day, it's forced upon millions of oppressed women.

It was forced on me as a child in Iran and I can only shake my head when I see women in the West celebrate these tools of oppression.

Founder of Free Hearts Free Minds, Yasmine Mohammed, who was disowned and threatened by her family when she decided to stop wearing the veil in Canada, said Western women who embraced the hijab should feel ashamed. "We all deserve freedom … not just you," she wrote. "Stop supporting our subjugation."

Anti-hijab activist, Maryam Shariatmadari, who, in the past, has been imprisoned by the Iranian regime, also hit out at privileged Western women who are wilfully blind to the symbolism of the hijab. "The

West unintentionally help fundamentalists to suppress women like me when they glorify the hijab and make it the symbol of harmony," she posted along with a picture of Jacinda Ardern in a hijab and one of herself in Iran being assaulted for not wearing the veil.

But as women who escaped Islamist tyranny complained, the media's loudest feminists uncritically praised the celebration of the hijab with no consideration of the deeper implications.

As usual, they were too preoccupied with moral posturing to worry about what message was being sent to those living under genuine patriarchal oppression.

If the plight of oppressed women mattered to feminists, we'd see regular protests outside the Saudi embassy in Canberra demanding that the country stop treating women as less than second-class citizens.

Saudi Arabia, which sits on the UN Human Rights Council, beheads women for crimes such as witchcraft and sorcery. Women still can't make key decisions about their own lives without the say so of a male guardian.

In 2021, we saw the feminist activists who dominate the media and political class in Australia take to the streets to supposedly 'march for justice' and to paint the country as systematically sexist.

The narrative from the media was that Australian women, all of us, were seething with rage and believe the country is riddled with institutional sexism. What utter nonsense.

We are a country where women are afforded every protection under the law and every opportunity to succeed, though pockets of significant disadvantage sadly persist.

Our Indigenous women are 35 times more likely to be hospitalised due to domestic violence. Where are the marches for them?

We have around 53,000 women in Australia living with FGM? But there'll be no marches for them either.

They are not useful to activists who want to target a conservative Prime Minister and paint him as an unfeeling Neanderthal.

Twisting real concerns about violence against women into a partisan issue won't advance the cause of women.

The truth is all women care about violence, sexual assault and the shortcomings of a justice system that too often re-traumatises victims, and yet the 'March4Justice' rallies we saw in early 2021 did not represent all Australian women. Far from it. What we saw was the cynical hijacking of a consequential issue that should've been above politics.

Sadly, just like the #MeToo movement, this latest "awakening" was co-opted by political operatives and grifters primarily focused on defeating their ideological opponents, rather than advancing the cause of women.

Of course, many of the women who took part in the rallies are genuinely concerned and it's sad that they are being used as pawns by those with clear political objectives that have nothing to do with women's safety, equality or justice.

It's reminiscent of the Women's March movement that began in 2017 as a response to Trump's election win, with women taking to the streets across the world including here in Australia.

It's not about women's rights but rather increasing the Left's power base and further entrenching their ideology and their people in institutions whilst pushing conservatives out of public life. That includes conservative women.

Even the First Lady is not safe from the hatemongers.

Indeed, the attacks against Australia's First Lady, Jenny Morrison, are beyond the pale — creepy, sexist and utterly unhinged abuse and lies about a woman whose only crime is being married to the Prime Minister, Scott Morrison, who leads a centre-right government.

That and that alone has earned her an enormous amount of misogynistic vitriol over the years particularly from the Twitter cesspit.

But the ugliness reached new heights in April 2021, when an image of Jenny Morrison watching on as her husband signed a condolence book for Prince Philip, sent the feral Left into fits of malignant rage.

For the record, there were also pictures of the Prime Minister looking on as Jenny signed the condolence book but they were ignored and, instead, a whole narrative about the First Lady being a submissive housewife living a 'Handmaid's Tale' existence was developed on social media.

The comic, Magda Szubanski, joined the fun, retweeting a far-Left activist that had posted the picture of Jenny Morrison and the Prime Minister with this caption: "Good morning to everyone else to whom this feels creepy, chilling, terrifying, ominous, enraging, despairing and utterly, completely f---ing depressing."

How is that a normal response to a benign picture?

To that insanity, Szubanski added: "I genuinely thought this was a photoshopped Handmaid's Tale meme. But no. It's 21st century Aussie life."

Szubanski went further, sharing an image zooming in on Jenny's hand over her daughter's wrist with the thumb and forefinger touching, "What's this little hand signal thingy??" she asked her followers.

Now, amongst the sane population, the thumb and forefinger touching is the "OK" symbol but among the loopy Left that Szubanski panders to, it is a "white supremacist" sign.

That foolishness began in 2017 as a joke on online forum, 4Chan, where users started a hoax to see if they could trick the media into believing the OK sign was a symbol of white supremacy.

Some simpletons fell for it, most laughed.

Obviously, the OK sign is not synonymous with white supremacy and any suggestion otherwise is absurd; but this is 2021 where people's paranoid fantasies must be respected and so Jenny Morrison became the target of hideous abuse from those who believe she's some closet KKK fan.

It's almost funny until you remember these people vote.

If a fraction of the abuse Jenny Morrison copped was targeted at a prominent woman from the Left, you can be sure that there'd be saturation media coverage, dozens of columns and examination of the deep-seated hatreds behind the abuse, and the sisterhood would rally around the victim; but conservative women rarely receive that sort of support and protection.

Of course, it wasn't just Szubanski "trolling" the Prime Minister's wife. There were thousands of deranged tweets from slanderous claims to commentary about her intelligence, appearance and character.

Most of the output of the tolerant, inclusive and progressive Left is too disgusting to reproduce but here is a sample of what we can publish:

> Michelle who lists #marchforwomen on her Twitter bio wrote: "I have never hated anyone as much as I hate Morrison ... and his bloody wife!!!"

> Helen, who lists "feminism", "social progress" and "support our ABC" on her bio, writes: "Is Jenny not allowed to wear anything nice, ever? She looks like the housekeeping lady".

> Rob, who no doubt identifies as a male feminist, asked: "Is

Jenny not allowed to wear make-up? Because if this is looking your best for a very important occasion, you've got problems. A potato sack? God you'd never see Anita Keating look such a mess. Or Therese Rhein (sic), Lucy Turnbull, Hazel Hawke etc." And this: "She looks more like one of the cleaning staff than wife of the Prime Minister."

Keen to show their moral superiority, the very same folk who spent weeks raging against the Morrison government for supposedly failing Australian women were poking fun at a woman's appearance.

Some of the very same activists bleating about 'March4Justice' and claiming Australia is a systematically sexist country were laying the boots into a woman not for what she has said or done, but what she looks like and who she loves.

If you need further proof that feminism is about politics, not equality, then take note of the way feminists reacted to Margaret Thatcher's passing and how they view her legacy.

Thatcher should be celebrated by feminists as a trailblazer who succeeded against insurmountable odds to lead Great Britain from financial ruin to stability, prosperity and hope.

Even now it is hard to fathom how a greengrocer's daughter overcame the "old boy network" to become leader of the Conservative Party in the 1970s, and Prime Minister from 1979 to 1990; and, she did it without ever making gender an issue.

There were no quotas, no self-serving misogyny speeches, no victimhood statements; just a determination to get the job done.

Elected after the so called "winter of discontent", Thatcher took charge of a country that was a laughing stock with crippling inflation, disintegration of public services, collapsing industries, soaring unemployment and a demoralised population.

Within a decade she had transformed the country into a successful and dynamic economy, the envy of Europe.

It is little wonder that more people voted for Thatcher in her third election win than in her first.

Thatcher faced challenges that would destroy most politicians; the IRA were trying to kill her and almost succeeded in 1984 when they set off a bomb at the Brighton hotel, killing five people and injuring another 34. And yet, through it all, the mother of two never resorted to playing the victim card.

By all accounts, despite being the most empowered women of her time, Thatcher hated feminism, once describing it as a "poison".

She was about action not rhetoric and achieved a great deal for women's rights, including substantially increasing funding for state schools, the National Health Service, as well as employment and training of women.

Sadly, modern day feminism is caught in a Leftist quagmire of irrelevance and superficiality. It is bereft of principles and too often preoccupied with semantics and trivialities.

It celebrates victimhood rather than strength and reduces empowered women in the West to lifelong victims facing enormous barriers to success.

Conservative women would do well to look at Thatcher as an enduring example of what can be achieved when one is clear-eyed, determined and with a strong sense of what is right and necessary.

As Baroness Thatcher said, "Disciplining yourself to do what you know is right and important, although difficult, is the high road to pride, self-esteem, and personal satisfaction."

Rita Panahi is a senior columnist for Melbourne's *Herald Sun* newspaper and an anchor on *Sky News Australia*. She co-hosts

the popular *Sky News Australia* Sunday program, Outsiders. Rita can also be heard regularly on *3AW* radio station in Melbourne. She grew up in Iran until her family were forced to flee after the Islamic Revolution and were granted asylum in Australia.

7

BIG AUSTRALIA: WHY POLITICIANS HAVE IT ALL WRONG

Professor Judith Sloan

"Populate or perish" – it was a favourite saying of Australian politicians in the 1950s. Against the backdrop of the Second World War, it was a common view that Australia's population needed to increase significantly so we could defend ourselves in the future. It was more about defence than economics.

These days, many politicians are still effectively shouting the same meme, although the defence rationale is seldom mentioned. Their argument is that we need to increase our population through high rates of immigration so we can slow down ageing and get the migrants to pay part of the tax bill. When Covid has run its race, we should return to levels of migrant arrivals as large as, if not larger than, we experienced in 2019.

Coincident with this pressing for a return to high migrant intakes based on a macroeconomic/fiscal rationale are the pleas from many segments of the business community, and other organisations, to open the international borders as quickly as possible so more migrants can take up difficult-to-fill jobs as well as enrol in educational institutions.

This pressuring of politicians, particularly those that make the decisions – think Prime Minister, Treasurer, Minister for Finance, Minister for Immigration, but also key State politician, is relentless and often made in public. There are several articles in the mainstream media each week about businesses finding it difficult to fill jobs, significant skill shortages and the negative consequences for our educational institutions of the decline in international student enrolments.

Of course, for many commercial interests, it is purely a numbers game. These businesses don't really care about the skill profile of newly arrived migrants. What they want are more customers to buy or rent properties, to open bank accounts and take out loans, to buy the goods and services offered by businesses. And the leaders representing these commercial interests, at least the larger ones, are very accomplished at influencing politicians.

But here's the paradox: survey after survey shows that the Australian public have been unhappy, for some time, about the high rates of population growth we experienced pre-Covid as a result of excessive migrant intakes.

Consider the surveys conducted by Newspoll, Essential Research, the Scanlon Survey and the Australian Population Research Institute: they all show support for lower migrant intakes, with the proportion of the public, including migrants themselves, with this point-of-view rising over the past several years.

The key question to answer therefore is: why does the Coalition government support high rates of immigration when voters clearly do not support this stance? Why would the government so flagrantly act in opposition to voter preference?

Before answering this question, it is worth pointing out that the federal Labor Party is also a supporter of high rates of immigration, although its attitude towards the entry of temporary workers is slightly less enthusiastic than that of the Coalition's. Labor supports higher humanitarian intakes than does the Coalition.

When it comes to the States and, even though many of the costs of migrant arrivals are borne by them, there is also widespread support for substantial migrant intakes. In particular, we have seen several States go to great lengths to facilitate the entry of international students by setting up pilot schemes and special arrangements. It is very apparent that the Vice-Chancellors have great sway on State politicians. State politicians also listen carefully to property developers.

The facts

In recent years, Australia has had one of the highest rates of population growth among developed economies. With annual growth averaging between 1.3 and 1.5 per cent per year, the only other developed economy to have similar growth rates has been New Zealand. The comparison is stark: the annual population growth rates of other countries include the UK (0.5 per cent), the US (0.7 per cent), Canada (0.8 per cent), France (0.34 per cent), Spain (0.65 per cent) and Denmark (0.44 per cent).

The principal driver of Australia's high rate of population growth has been immigration. The change in population is made up of two components: net natural increase (births minus deaths) and net overseas migration (long-term arrivals minus long-term departures).

Around the middle of the first decade of this century, migrant numbers began to climb significantly, both because of the increase in the permanent migrants and the rise in the number of temporary migrants (who often stay many years). Between 2007 and 2017, Australia's population grew by 3.7 million, with 2.25 million due to overseas migration. In other words, migration contributed around 60 per cent of population growth.

There are currently 25.7 million people living in Australia. According to the projections contained in the latest Intergenerational Report produced by the Treasury, in forty years' time, the population will have grown to between 38.8 million and 40.5 million, depending on the assumptions made about net overseas migration.

But note here: Treasury models only two immigration scenarios - high and very high. The high scenario is based on annual net overseas migration of 235,000 persons, reflecting the NOM figures that pertained, leading up to the outbreak of Covid.

The very high scenario assumes that NOM will be a fixed percentage of the population (0.82 per cent) over the next forty years. At the end of the period, NOM would be 327,000 persons per year and make up three-quarters of our population growth.

That Treasury models only these two scenarios – what about NOM at, say, 100,000 per year? One scenario has migration making up three-quarters of population growth which tells us a lot about the attitude of this central agency to the issue at hand.

In effect, Treasury has become the hand maiden of Big Australia lobbyists, providing lopsided economic research to support the case for very high rates of immigration. It is interesting to note that in other developed economies where the pace of ageing is well ahead of us, there is much less bureaucratic endorsement of high rates of immigration to boost population growth and ostensibly offset the impact of ageing.

The interesting question is: what are the forces in Australia which convince politicians to ignore the will of the people and to press on with high migrant intakes leading to high rates of population growth?

Ignoring the negative evidence

One of the ways that politicians have been able to implement policy settings that are opposed by most voters is to ignore, sometimes to dismiss, any negative evidence. This is the case in relation to migrants taking jobs from locals as well as high rates of immigration reducing wage growth.

However, there has been a distinct change of thinking in relation to the link between immigration and wage growth in recent times, with the Reserve Bank of Australia Governor now accepting that pre-Covid migrant intakes had, in part, been responsible for sluggish wage growth. By the same token, the recent closed international borders have created pressures for pay rises. This opinion has been echoed by a former RBA Governor, Bernie Fraser, and former Liberal leader, John Hewson.

This link is also consistent with a series of reports that have demonstrated that the high rates of violation of labour laws in industries with large number of temporary migrants, particularly international students. Hospitality, retailing and farm work are examples of industries with low rates of pay and recognised widespread flouting of award rates of pay and other regulations.

Clearly, this sort of evidence doesn't suit Big Australia arguments. The Department of Home Affairs (which contains the old Department of Immigration) has publicly stated that studies "consistently found no statistically significant relationship between wage growth and immigration."

Actually, there are many studies that do show such a relationship, but the fact that the department cites a piece of "research" by the Committee of Economic Development of Australia gives the game away. This polemical piece does not explicitly test the link but rather provides rhetorical support for maintaining the uncontrolled intake of temporary migrants (CEDA has always been one of the leading think-tanks supporting high migrant intakes).

In addition to the negative economic effects, both the bureaucrats and politicians go to great lengths to avoid talking about other issues related to migration that matter to voters: rising house prices, urban congestion, pressure on infrastructure, including schools and health services, social cohesion and environmental pressures.

Benefits and costs

This discussion should not be taken to imply that immigration doesn't confer benefits on the Australian economy. There are also some benefits that go well beyond economics.

The bulk of the economic studies suggest that there are small net economic benefits, although these tend to emerge only after many years. This is because the short-term effect of high immigration rates is to dilute the stock of capital and cause a fall in productivity. It is only after several decades that immigration leads to higher per capita national income and, even then, most of the worker gains actually accrue to the migrants themselves.

There is also the point that dated studies of the economic impact of immigration in Australia are of little relevance today. This is because, up to the mid-1990s, virtually all immigration to Australia was made up of permanent movements, with very little temporary migration. Many migrants who came to Australia after the Second World War hardly travelled after making Australia home. The commitment to a new country was strong and enduring.

These days, when temporary migration has come to dominate net overseas migration, the dynamics of immigration are much more complicated. While many temporary migrants can stay in the country for long periods of time – international students can secure a range of visas when they graduate – for instance, there is generally not the commitment to place that previous cohorts of migrants demonstrated. It is not uncommon, for instance, for international students/graduates from China to flit back and forth between Australia and China.

While temporary migration provides one pathway to permanent migration, it is also not always the case that permanent residents will simply reside in Australia. The second and third largest groups of overseas-born residents in Australia – from India and China – generally retain the right to reside and work in their countries of birth. And considerable proportions do just that; in some cases, leaving their families to live in Australia. Assessing the economic benefits to Australia of these types of arrangements is tricky, to say the least.

The point here is that there are both benefits and costs associated with our complicated immigration system, with its mixture of a capped permanent migrant intake and the largely uncapped temporary components, such as temporary worker, working holiday makers, international students and seasonal farm workers. In addition, there are New Zealanders who live in Australia and are free to come and go between the two countries.

While the proponents of a Big Australia like to pretend we have a mainly skilled migration program, the reality is that most migrants who enter the country are not particularly skilled and many are much less skilled than the average Australian-born person. Take the Migration Program that sets the numbers for the permanent intake. Only 27 per cent of the most recent intake (pre-COVID) of 160,000 was primary skilled migrants.

So, when the Treasurer, Josh Frydenberg, expresses the view that "a well-targeted, skills-focused migrant program can supplement our stock of working-age people, slow the transition to an older population and improve Australia's economic and fiscal outcomes," the obvious question is – is our migrant program a well-targeted, skills-focused one? Judged by the decade ending in 2019, the answer would be firmly in the negative.

The principles that should govern public policy

When it comes to establishing immigration policy settings, politicians should always heed the principle that their primary concern is to maximise the wellbeing of Australian citizens and permanent residents. The welfare of all others should be a secondary concern and not necessarily served through immigration in any case. In other words, would-be immigrants should not really figure in political decision-making.

Politicians also need to acknowledge that immigration should be about far more than economics and supporting businesses. In fact, economics really should be a secondary consideration compared with thinking about what kind of society we want and how families and individuals can live.

For politicians, particularly decision makers, to be swayed by the pleas of business leaders to increase immigration to meet skill shortages or simply to provide new customers is an abrogation of their primary duty to act to maximise the welfare of citizens and permanent residents.

While it is true that high rates of immigration will inevitably inflate GDP, it is not at all clear that they lead to higher GDP per head. This has certainly been the Australian experience of the past decade and half. An equally important aspect of immigration is the distributional impact – who gains and who loses.

The theory is very clear: the winners are the owners of capital and workers whose skills are complementary with those of migrants; the losers are the workers who compete with migrants.

The empirical literature is also clear that the gains are captured by the migrants themselves rather by Australian-born workers.

When life returns to normal after the effects of Covid have largely passed, it would be a tragedy should the *ex ante* rates of immigration be restored. What Australia needs is a return to much more modest migrant intakes (of the 1990s and early 2000s) and ones that are based much more firmly on the skill characteristics of the applicants.

The signs are not good. For instance, Treasury expects net overseas migration to return to at least 235,000 per year before the middle of the decade and the government has flagged that the (permanent) Migration Program will be increased to 190,000 per year, up from the current cap of 160,000.

What is therefore required is a very fulsome public debate on the topics of immigration and population growth – on this, there are some encouraging signs – rather than policy settings that are the result of backroom deals with rent-seeking owners of capital and other Big Australia advocates.

Professor Judith Sloan is a professional economist. She holds degrees from the University of Melbourne and the London School of Economics. She worked for many years at Flinders University of South Australia, becoming Director of the National Institute of Labour Studies. She was appointed Professor in 1988. She was honorary Professorial Fellow at the Melbourne Institute of Applied Economic and Social Research at the University of Melbourne. She has held a number of government appointments, including Commissioner of the Productivity Commission; Commissioner of the Australian Fair Pay Commission; member of the Australian Statistics Advisory Council; and Deputy Chairman of the Australian Broadcasting Corporation. She has sat on the boards of a number of companies including: Mayne Nickless; SGIO Insurance; Santos; Westfield Group and Primelife, where she was also Chairman. She is currently the Contributing Economics Editor with *The Australian* newspaper and writes regularly for *The Spectator Australia*.

8

EMPOWERING CITIZENS, COMMUNITIES AND COMPETITIVE COMMERCE

Tim Wilson MP

The continuing task of Australian liberalism is to defend the democratisation of economic, social, political, and cultural power against constant attempts to concentrate it in the hands of an elite few.

When you sit on the green leather chairs in the House of Representatives and listen to the speeches of Members of Parliament, several things stand out. First, for the highest debating Chamber of the nation there is little debate. Members normally assert, and most of the responses to one another come in the form of taunts and ridicule, with little true exchange of ideas.

Second, most people think that the divide between political parties is the solutions they offer to problems. But it isn't. The difference is how they define problems. Take industrial relations. The Labor Party defines the problem in terms of sharing wealth amongst working people and maximising their interests. It's a solution to a static problem that inevitably drives up wages for the few and makes it harder to employ more people. Liberals define the problem dynamically – how to maximise employment. The solution keeps the focus on how to get people into work and increase wages through higher standards of living for everyone.

Third, Greens and Independents measure their success in their signalling to elite opinion with no need for concrete outcomes. Liberals view their success through outcomes, focused on the success of the nation. Labor views Australia's success through outcomes beneficial to themselves.

It doesn't seem to matter the issue, there is always a narrative about Australians being saved by Labor. Apparently, Australians only have access to healthcare because the Hawke Government introduced taxpayer-funded Medicare, ignoring that a health system organised around mutuals was destroyed by a one-size-fits-all government program. Meritocratic and equitable access to tertiary education didn't exist prior to the Whitlam Government – so long as we ignore the merit-based Commonwealth scholarship system that preceded it. There's no emissions reduction, unless it was Labor's carbon tax, even though emissions have continued declining through a plan anchored around technology, not taxes.

In every case where Labor claims victory, it has been achieved through the destruction of a system that evolved organically in response to needs from citizens, families, and communities, and it's replacement by empowered Canberra, capital and corporates.

Fourth, politics is about power and, more critically, whom you empower. It is a question that Austrian economist Friedrich von Hayek understood sat at the heart of the division between liberalism and all other political ideologies. All other political ideologies seek to centralise power in the hands of the few to achieve a collective purpose, ahead of individual empowerment. For socialism it is the pursuit of equity; for fundamentalism, it is moral order; for fascism, it is order.

Conservatism is management, Liberalism requires leadership

This is what makes liberalism different. It is not a political ideology that seeks to empower Canberra or State capitals to impose solutions through conformity. Liberalism is a political ideology that seeks to build the strength of the nation from the empowerment of citizens-up. Liberalism understands that a nation's strength comes from strong citizens who form the mutual bonds of family; citizens who come together to form supportive communities and successful enterprise as the foundation for a confident Australia.

Australian liberalism is unique. Wherever liberalism has been adopted as a political ideology in other countries, it has challenged vested cultural, legal and economic interests. For example, in the United Kingdom, liberalism challenged inherited aristocracy and privilege. In the United States, it challenged economic concentration and the power of the railway and oil trusts. In both cases, conservatism was focused on protecting and entrenching centralised interests.

Australia's story is different. European settlers rejected the injustices of the past by turning their backs on religious division and inherited nobility. They chose Australia as an experiment of enlightenment, liberal values put into practice by promoting individual empowerment and social mobility. They were able to do so because they saw the continent as a blank slate for developing models of governance, but it came at the expense of Aboriginal and Torres Strait Islanders and their traditions.

Australia continues to be a liberal project anchored in empowering people and building institutions to decentralise power. This was articulated by British academic, Hugh Collins, who observed of Australia:

> Political institutions and policies are to be assessed in terms of
> the impact of their operation upon the interests of the majority
> ... not as groups or classes but as the sum of individual interests

> ... schemes for representation, legislation, and administration are a detailed exposition of the institutional means of securing that public good which maximises private interest. This individualism makes [t]his theory anti-collectivist.

One of the great cons of our modern age is for those on the centre-right to define themselves as 'conservatives' as if it were the ideological opposite of socialism. Conservatism is a disposition. The same is true of progressivism. To draw an analogy, both are speeds. Progressivism is like hitting an accelerator on a car, conservatism the break. Speed matters, the direction of the car matters more.

Social democrats seek to empower centralised political, economic and cultural institutions to impose conformity in pursuit of equity. You can believe in doing it swiftly as the left of the Labor Party and Greens do, or conservatively as the right of the Labor Party do. But either way, your direction is toward centralisation.

So too, you can be a liberal democrat that cautiously advances reforms to conserve the value of organic institutions that have evolved to temper the extremities of individual freedom or move rapidly to define change within a society – but either way, you're a liberal. Liberalism is the opposite of socialism because it focuses on democratising power.

We democratise the economy through a free and open market that responds to price signals and is built on tradable private property and, particularly, home ownership. There is limited regulation to stop needless costs that add barriers to entry and competition to fight monopoly economic vested interests.

We democratise political power through government by consent through universal franchise – with two of the greatest liberal achievements being extending full franchise to women and Aboriginal and Torres Strait Islanders – government decided through the ballot box, and competitive federalism that keeps power closest to the people it is designed to serve and away from a monopoly Canberra. It is also achieved by dividing power between an Executive, held accountable to Parliament, and independent Courts.

We democratise social and cultural power through a deference to a common law that respects people as free, unless the law prohibits otherwise; a common law which upholds their rights and freedoms, particularly the right to free and open expression while respecting organic institutions such as marriage and family, community groups and competitive institutions of centralised power in civil society, ranging from religious institutions, unions and political and social movements.

The continuing challenge for liberalism is to constantly reinvent itself for the times, keep systems open and not entrench privilege or interests.

Conformity versus individuality

We must fight for laws that respect people's individuality. In 1853, abolitionist pastor Theodore Parker identified the necessity of perspective against a background of frustration in the pursuit of a just cause, with this sermon:

> I do not pretend to understand the moral universe; the arc is a long one, my eye reaches but little ways; I cannot calculate the curve and complete the figure by the experience of sight; I can divine it by conscience. And from what I see I am sure it bends towards justice.

Parker saw the practical effect of dehumanising people into grouped classifications above their common inherent individual dignity. Identity politics is a direct repudiation of the liberal ideal of individual dignity and worth, equality through people's common humanity and seeks to undermine individual agency. As Prime Minister, Scott

Morrison, said in a speech to the United Israel Appeal:

> We must never surrender the truth that the experience and value of every human being is unique and personal. You are more, we are more, individually, more than the things others try to identify us by, you by, in this age of identity politics. You are more than your gender, you are more than your race, you are more than your sexuality, you are more than your ethnicity, you are more than your religion, your language group, your age.
>
> All of these, of course, contribute to who we may be and the incredible diversity of our society, particularly in this country and our place in the world; but, of themselves, they are not the essence of our humanity.

Contemporary 'woke' movements reconceptualise people's identity toward 'group rights' and privileges because they reduce the number of issues people feel comfortable speaking about. They deny people outside these 'groups' a voice and they narrow how people think about issues by demonising any consideration outside the left-progressive orthodoxy. Socialists have always prized the ability to constrain how people think and express themselves as a mechanism to minimise dissent and seek conformity. As American author, Andrew Sullivan, has identified, the weaponised nature of language and identity seeks to demonise people – where racism was once rightly decried as a form of social evil, it is now 'whiteness'; sexism has been replaced with 'toxic masculinity'. It turns citizen against citizen, in favour of those who write the rules.

Identity politics, however applied, is the enemy of liberal thought. It must be defeated, but opposition to identity politics must be consistent. Some who identify on the political 'right' have embraced a populist post modernism that seeks to make themselves the victims through their obligation to exercise tolerance toward others and have also resorted to grouping people on the basis of identity, principally religion. Identity politics anchored in victimhood on a religious, ethnic or cultural basis is no different from any progressive grouping on the basis of sexuality or gender – it is a focus on group over individuality and common humanity.

It is an intellectual debate that must be won through a rejection of the modern concept of 'acceptance' in favour of tolerance. Tolerance is respecting diversity. Acceptance, based on group identity, extends a person's worth based on the sanction of others. The solution to the problem is not the creation of more laws or constitutional provisions. The solution only comes from principles which live every day in the hearts and minds of all Australians.

Competitive ownership

If a cartel of interests was on trajectory to own a majority of the nation's infrastructure and the Australian Stock Exchange, any good democratic socialist would be outraged – but when it is industry superannuation funds, the Labor Party has a cognitive dissonance.

The super system already holds $3.1 trillion equating to 157 per cent of Australia's GDP. The 2021 Intergenerational Report projects that by 2061 it will be $34 trillion. In practice the super system will continue to outgrow the Australian economy while consolidating into fewer funds. Already KPMG has projected that super will be consolidated into 12 mega-funds holding 77 per cent of funds under management. That trend is only likely to continue with super funds becoming the modern equivalent of the US trusts. Super funds will dominate finance, the builders and owners or lessors of the nation's networks and infrastructure, and the ASX. While done through 'trusts' by 'trustees', in practice there is a direct fusion with political power via the trade union movement and its representation on industry super fund boards.

It's ironic that a social democratic movement is so open to the privatisation of a social welfare program, but they are wedded to super's control and ownership of the nation because they hold the reins.

All Liberals should be terrified by the concentration of economic and political power being fused through the superannuation sector. This concentrated ownership of the nation will ultimately enable private interests to impose their preferred public policy outcomes through the exercise of private capital, bypassing our democracy. Unless addressed, the law will empower capital over citizens.

That does not mean Liberals should oppose superannuation, quite the opposite. Liberals should believe in prudence and private savings as a pathway to economic empowerment in people's working life and retirement. But that does not mean there is not room for an alternative Liberal solution.

Life's biggest financial decision is home ownership because it underwrites economic opportunity and security throughout your working life and retirement. Superannuation is the second most important financial decision.

Until 1992, it was entirely logical that younger people, at the earlier stages of their income earning potential, needed access to their full wage to enable them to save for a house deposit. Super should follow second because you can save for retirement after you own a home, but not the other way around. It's on that basis that young Australians should have some pathway to utilise their superannuation to purchase their first home. This would get them onto the property ladder earlier and ultimately would be cheaper. Vested interests argue this is radical. That is absurd. It was the opportunity earlier generations had. In an act of economic social engineering these priorities were only reversed thirty years ago.

The other challenge for Liberals should be the hierarchy of default ownership and control over super. Presently default funds are allocated with an inherent bias towards industry funds. A Liberal superannuation system should default on a hierarchy of options, starting with self-managed superannuation funds (though the trustee model carries excessive regulatory and compliance burdens) or a form of shadow bank account, equivalent to the UK Individual Savings Account. After an individual account, the default should be a product in a competitive fund and after that, a default government fund as a backstop. Nowhere in a Liberal superannuation framework should a default fund be controlled by compromised interests.

To that end, Liberals should deregulate the self-managed superannuation fund sector to remove needless costs and red tape. When an employee needs to nominate a super account, their default should be a shadow account established by their bank that can only be used to trade in investment products. The complexity of a company structured trustee model for super with audit requirements should only be required if the individual owns complex or illiquid investments, such as property and art. Similarly, the government should break up the near monopoly large funds have in buying into unlisted investments, such as major infrastructure, and should establish infrastructure bonds. That way, self-managed super funds have the same capacity to compete as large funds.

Democratic climate solutions

In democratic political systems representatives rarely get to pick the issues they address, only their response. One of the follies of centralisation is that it rationalises disempowering people to impose outcomes from technocrats. There is no greater example than how the progressive-left constantly seek to weaponise climate change to bypass democracy.

Ensuring countries have sensible climate change policies to reduce greenhouse gas emissions is a critical discussion for the 21st Century, as we need to both protect the environment and decouple economic growth from emissions growth so that we can drive global prosperity and alleviate poverty. But the pursuit of climate action should not come at the expense of our democracy. Yet that is what many climate activists seek. In pursuit of 'certainty' what they want to do is bypass democracy.

For instance, a Sydney-based Independent MP has proposed a Climate Change Bill which is deliberately misleading - seeking to create a false binary conversation about being for or against climate change policy. But the real issue with the Bill is that it is designed to subvert democracy and elected representatives, and by extension voters, to create 'certainty' around climate change policy. The Bill would oblige Parliament to establish a "Commission" to set aspects of climate policy and targets. Parliament would not be able to "vary the target unless... the Commission recommends the proposed variation". In practice, this is placing the views and wishes of unelected officials above the decision making of the Parliament of Australia.

Similarly, in an example of radical judicial activism, a Federal Court found that, in approvals under the Environmental Protection and Biodiversity Conservation Act, the Minister had a 'duty of care' to children in regard to greenhouse gas emissions. While hailed by climate campaigners, in practice this is the judiciary imposing on the executive a matter that should be decided through Parliament, not imposed by Courts. This case should not surprise, there is now a large and internationally coordinated campaign to impose climate-related policies through Court rulings where advocates cannot secure them through legislative bodies.

According to aggregators of international climate change legal cases there are, as at July 2021, around 1,400 cases in the United States and around 450 in other jurisdictions, with around 115 in Australia.

The foundation of a liberal response to reducing Australia's greenhouse gas emissions should be anchored in responsibility.

First, that households, Councils, State governments and the Federal government take responsibility for their own emissions footprint to drive change. Instead, we often have Councils and State governments that set targets but have no plan of how they seek achieve the targets.

Second, to utilise technology because reducing emissions requires substitution, not absolution. Plane travel will not be replaced by people sticking to their neighbourhood; it will be replaced either through forms of emissions sequestration or new zero-carbon fuels.

Third, what measures are taken and the costs they impose should be done with a democratic mandate. The reasons are stark. Any climate change policy requires significant decoupling of one of the foundation pillars of economic growth – cheap energy. Measures to drive that transition carry some cost either through prices or the tax system. If costs are to be absorbed, they should be taken to the people. In 2010, Prime Minister Julia Gillard went to an election promising "no carbon tax under a government I lead", only for that promise to be traded away in a Labor-Greens deal for government. Regardless of your perspective on the issue, the public antagonism at this broken trust and deception led to its removal only a few short years later.

By comparison, the Coalition government took measures to buy direct emissions reduction through its emissions reduction fund to the 2013 election through a reverse auction system that was introduced and sustained. Again, the Coalition took its 2030 targets and its net zero target in the second half of the 20th Century under the Paris Target to the 2016 federal election and was re-elected cementing it as a foundational pillar for building further policy. The same is true at the 2019 federal election, coupled with action to reduce Australia's emissions by 20 per cent since 2005. In both cases sustainable policies have been advanced because they've received a democratic mandate and delivered with far more 'certainty' than manipulating our democracy ever will.

Citizens, communities and competitive commerce

These are not the only challenges facing the nation.

A foundational pillar of economic security to turn 'little platoons' into 'little capitalists' is home ownership. Yet home ownership rates are in rapid decline amongst younger Australians. No single policy will solve this problem. It requires addressing planning and zoning regulation, tax reform, interest rates and monetary policy, decentralisation and infrastructure, among others.

Similarly, we need a tax and transfer system that enables Australians to progress through all stages of life, not one that entrenches interests. But that can only be achieved by having a conversation that starts with discussing the problems of the current tax system and how it is undermining the next generation.

The capacity of Liberals to confront these challenges depends on Liberals continuing to understand the guiding principles of their beliefs – that the role of institutions is to empower citizens, communities and competitive commerce against the Labor vision to centralise collusion between Canberra, capital and corporates.

Tim Wilson MP is the Federal Liberal Member for Goldstein, serves as Chair of the House Economics Committee and is the author of *The New Social Contract: Renewing the Liberal Vision for Australia*. Tim previously served as Australia's Human Rights Commissioner. In that role, he worked with government to reform laws to stop and prevent terrorism and to improve economic opportunities for Indigenous Australians. He also stood up for marginalised communities against public harassment.

He is a strong advocate for protecting free speech and freedom of religion. Tim has postgraduate qualifications in Energy and Carbon Management from Murdoch University and a Masters of Diplomacy and Trade from Monash University, as well as a Bachelor of Arts. He has also completed executive education on climate change policy at the University of Cambridge, intellectual property at the World Intellectual Property Organisation's Worldwide Academy and global health diplomacy, trade and development from the Institut de Hautes Études Internationales et du Développement.

9

THE JOB AHEAD

Senator the Hon. Michaelia Cash

There are more than 2,700 clocks in Parliament House.

Most people who have spent some time there are very aware of the red and green lights on those clocks.

The lights flash and bells ring to call Members of the House (green) or Senators (red) to their respective chambers at the start of the day or for divisions during a sitting day. In a small way, those clocks rule the lives of Members and Senators while Parliament is sitting.

Something few people will tell you about those clocks is how loudly they tick. Sit in a quiet office with one of those clocks and the constant tick is loud and very noticeable.

I like to think of the loud ticking as a reminder to those of us elected to Parliament that time is precious and it slips away from us quickly. I also like to think of the ticking of those clocks as a reminder that the people of Australia are expecting us to get on with the job – a reminder not to waste the time we've been given to make this country a greater place.

Tick, tick, tick – get on with the job!

We presently find ourselves at a point in human history where the challenges of just getting on with the job are considerable and will remain so for some time into the future.

We've been hit by a once in a hundred year pandemic. It has spread its tentacles into every corner of the globe, destroying lives and livelihoods and creating economic and social upheaval like we have never seen before.

Those economic and health impacts have been devastating for countries around the world, including Australia.

But there is no doubt that on both economic and health measures Australia has fared much better than the majority of the developed world.

We achieved world-leading health outcomes, with fewer infections, hospitalisations and deaths than most other countries.

The Coalition Government's unprecedented emergency support provided a crucial lifeline to the economy during Australia's first recession in almost 30 years. The economy started to recover more quickly and strongly than expected. The employment recovery will be about five times faster than that of the 1990s recession.

Our nation will be better placed than most other countries in the world to meet the challenges we will face in the future. The question for government, of course, is how should we go about attacking these challenges and what should guide us at such a unique time?

The thing, as Liberals, that we have to fall back on are our values.

In our great Liberal Party we will always be guided by those values – the values that have served our Party and our nation so well for so long.

We believe in freedom, reward for effort, aspiration, a fair go for those who have a go, free enterprise and giving people a helping hand when they need it.

We believe in the innate worth of the individual, in the right to be independent, to own property and to achieve, and in the need to encourage initiative and personal responsibility.

We know that equality of opportunity is important and it gives Australians the opportunity to reach their full potential.

And we also believe that prosperity for all Australians will be driven by competitive enterprise and consumer choice.

Those values will be integral in guiding our plans for the future of this country.

They are values embedded in our party long ago – values Sir Robert Menzies espoused in his series of speeches known as the "Forgotten People" speeches.

I find it instructive to reflect on what Menzies observed in relation to those who have power and influence, and those who don't.

He observed that there were some people who "controlled great funds and enterprises".

They were those that we would now call the "business community", which he described as "able to protect themselves – though it must be said that in a political sense they have shown as a rule neither comprehension nor competence".

Other people he said were politically well-organised.

Then, as now, the labour movement has always viewed disciplined organisation as the key to applying political pressure.

He identified a third group – "salary earners, shopkeepers, skilled artisans, professional men and women, farmers", among others, who he famously described as "the forgotten people".

They were in Menzies' words: "unorganised and unselfconscious, not rich enough to wield power in its own right and too individualistic for pressure politics". And yet, they were "the backbone of the nation".

Menzies said the real life of this nation wasn't found "in great luxury hotels and the petty gossip of fashionable suburbs or in the officialdom of organised masses".

These days he might observe that the real spirit of the Australian people is not manifested in corporate boardrooms, campaigns for fashionable causes, the corridors of Canberra, hashtag activists on Twitter, or posturers on the ABC's Q&A program.

The real life of Australia was then, and is now, to be found in the homes of those who Menzies praised as "nameless and unadvertised Australians". As Prime Minister Scott Morrison has observed, "the quiet Australians".

My belief is that as a government our mission is to look after those "quiet Australians" by formulating the right policies and settings so they can pursue their dreams and aspirations. We have to give them a fair go to reap the rewards of their efforts.

The freedom of Australians to pursue those dreams, I believe, is predicated on three key priorities this government will maintain: health security; economic security and national security.

Securing the health of Australians, keeping them safe from COVID-19 has to remain a priority.

It is worth reflecting on how the pandemic crisis unfolded at the start and how the Morrison Government acted swiftly to protect Australians. In the early stages of the pandemic, we made a significant decision to impose severe restrictions on travellers who had spent time in mainland China during the previous 14 days.

The Morrison government imposed a quarantine regime on returning Australians or permanent residents and we stopped non-Australian or non-permanent residents who had spent time in China from arriving here. Closing the national border to China and then the rest of the world was the most important decision that kept Australians safe. As a result, the catastrophic loss of life seen elsewhere in the world was averted.

It is important that the government remains focused on the health security of our nation as we learn to live with the virus – because that is what we will have to do for a long time into the future – live with this virus.

No doubt, the virus will pose challenges to us. We have seen that it is very adept at mutating, but we need to meet these challenges with a clear head and a clear eye on the economic security of the country.

Economic security means many different things to different people but, for me, what sits at the core of economic security is having a job.

I have said many times that governments don't create jobs. Governments have to aim to put in place policies and settings that allow businesses of all sizes to grow and thrive and employ more people – that's how jobs are created.

When the pandemic hit, we moved swiftly to support Australian businesses and workers who were impacted by close downs and severe restrictions on their operations.

Our most important support was JobKeeper and it was designed very carefully to keep employees connected to their employers. Workers received pay cheques from their employers, not the government.

That measure kept 3.8 million Australians in their job, but it was always designed as a temporary assistance.

What we learned as JobKeeper came to an end in a planned and staged way, was that businesses had been given the time to recover and ride out the crisis and kept employing Australians. There was no jobs cliff as many had predicted.

As we continue to move out of the crisis phase and look more to the long-term as a government, we must stay focused on the things we can do to help get people into jobs.

The area that I have been passionately and directly involved in that I still absolutely believe in is skills, training and apprenticeships.

As Australia moves through its recovery from the economic impacts of COVID-19, supporting a skilled workforce has never been more important.

We have a proven track record in this area and need to continue to commit to making sure the economy has the workers it needs in the right place at the right time.

Different sectors of the economy have skills gaps at different times.

It is important that we ensure the current high standard of Australian vocational education and training is maintained and, also, that we make our skills sector more responsive to employers needs so that it can meet workforce shortages.

By providing industry with a pipeline of qualified workers, the government will help ensure businesses and individuals have the skills they need to actively participate in the workplaces of the future.

The Morrison government spent money wisely during the pandemic to keep apprentices in their jobs and to create hundreds of thousands of new apprenticeship opportunities. The value of getting apprentices into work and keeping them there should never be underestimated.

Most apprentices are young and at the start of their working lives. Helping to get them that start puts them on a path in life.

They are able to make significant purchases and it often leads to a first home purchase. The cascading benefits for the individual are many but there are big benefits for the country as well.

That is why we have worked so hard to back vocational education and training and apprenticeships and will continue to do so. Before Covid, we established the National Skills Commission to improve our skills and labour market forecasting.

We also established the National Careers Institute to elevate the status of vocational education and provide evidence-based careers advice on the vocational training pathways.

We reinvigorated apprenticeship incentives for key groups, supported foundational skills for people with low educational attainment and improved choice with clear, accessible training and career information.

Our focus will always be about supporting employers, industries, students and the broader community to be job-ready for the future.

This is how we will create opportunities for youth, at-risk communities and workers who want to be upskilled, while driving the future economic growth of Australia. Supporting Australians into careers and Australian businesses to get the staff they need will be more important than ever as we chart a path forward.

Once we get them into jobs, we are also focused on protecting them, their jobs and their rights.

As Attorney-General and Minister for Industrial Relations, one of the agencies I am responsible for is the Australian Building and Construction Commission (ABCC).

For me, that is like coming full circle as I worked hard in 2016 to reinstate the ABCC to ensure the rule of law on building sites. It was one of the two double-dissolution trigger Bills at the time.

The debate on the ABCC is often conducted in abstract terms of statistics dealing with industrial dispute levels or productivity. However, in reality, it is a story all about people, hard-working people, who have been scandalously forgotten and overlooked.

Before the ABCC was reinstated, I met and received representations from many self-employed tradies and medium-sized builders.

These were people who were subjected to the bullying, thuggery and intimidation in their industry by big building unions. The people who suffer from union lawlessness are the individual workers and small subcontractors.

Before the ABCC was reinstated, they were often too frightened of recriminations from the thuggish unions to speak up and expose how things really are in this industry.

They needed a strong voice from government and they got it and will continue to get it from me.

There is still work to be done in cleaning up the building and construction industry and we will need to be ever vigilant, but the ABCC is getting great results.

Protecting the little guys from the bullies and thugs in the union movement aligns perfectly with the values of our party – the values I believe in.

Those values are more important now, in a time of difficulty, a time of crisis, than ever before. It is the strength of our values that will drive us forward and propel this country to a better future.

Those values will give the people of Australia the best possible opportunity to get ahead and create the lives they want to create.

The Morrison government will continue to focus on the task of delivering the opportunity for job creation and keeping our country secure.

The clocks will keep ticking to remind us of the task ahead.

Senator Michaelia Cash is the Attorney-General as well as the Minister for Industrial Relations in the Morrison government. She is the Deputy Leader of the Government in the Senate. Senator Cash was elected to the Senate as a Liberal Senator for Western Australia in 2007. In 2015, Senator Cash was appointed to the Cabinet as the Minister for Employment, the Minister for Women and the Minister Assisting the Prime Minster for the Public Service. In 2017, she was appointed the Minister for Jobs and Innovation and, in 2018, was the Minister for Employment, Skills, Small and Family Business. Prior to entering Parliament, Senator Cash was a senior lawyer at law firm Freehills practicing employment and industrial law. She holds an Honours Degree in Law from the University of London and a Bachelor of Arts (Social Science) from Curtin University in Perth, graduating with a triple major in public relations, politics and journalism. In addition, she holds a Graduate Diploma in Legal Practice from the University of Western Australia.

10

BOILED FROGS:
THE GREAT RESET
Dr Maurice Newman AC

In his 1960s bestseller, *The Naked Communist*, former FBI agent, W. Cleon Skousen, lays bare the post-war Marxist manifesto. He identified 46 goals ranging from re-ordering Western values and institutions to a one-world government under the United Nations.

A major objective was the capture of one or both of the major American political parties. Marxists would use the courts to weaken American institutions through technical decisions based on human rights. Schools would become transmission belts for socialist propaganda and, by softening the curriculum, teachers' associations would carry the party line in required-reading textbooks. Loyalty oaths would be abolished.

They aimed to infiltrate the media and control editorial writing, book reviews and student newspapers. Where possible, key positions in radio, television and film would be filled with sympathetic presenters, actors and producers.

"Cultural Marxism" would target all laws governing obscenity by calling them "censorship". Lower cultural standards of morality would be encouraged through wider acceptance of pornography and obscenity in books, magazines, motion pictures, radio and TV. Degeneracy and promiscuity were to be presented as "normal, natural and healthy". Even churches would be targeted. Traditional religion would be replaced with "social" religion. The aim was to discredit the Bible and mock those who saw need for a "religious crutch".

While the United States was the primary target, the mission was to aggressively spread the word to all parts of the Western world.

And so it came to pass.

Australia was an early adopter with post-war Labor Prime Minister Ben Chifley promoting a welfare state and pushing bank nationalisation. In the 1970s, Prime Minister Gough Whitlam took Australia further to the Left using his opposition to the Vietnam War to support anti-capitalist intellectuals as they infiltrated campuses and workplaces. Radical intellectuals in search of "big structural change" were given authority.

Post the Howard government and, with the exception of Prime Minister Tony Abbott, whom the Left quickly dispatched, Australia has been led by a succession of left-wing Labor and Coalition governments. Prime Minister Scott Morrison admits no interest in the debate about Australia's growing "wokeness", declaring, "There's a lot of talk about all this ... and, if (people) are woke enough or they're not woke enough or, they're too woke ... who cares?"

But it is at the State level where the Left has made the greatest inroads. It is here where there has been either active encouragement or ambivalence to the radicalisation of important public institutions. It is here where Critical Race Theory, and anti-capitalist teachings form part of the school curriculum and, where indoctrinated children are allowed to take school days off to protest at Black Lives Matter and climate change.

Universities, where once open debate flourished, now actively discourage unfashionable views, their champions shut down and persecuted. Aside from a grumble or two, the ruling class condones this intolerance.

In today's brave new world, politicians in robes get appointed to courtrooms, delivering judgements which they know will influence public policy from the Left. They bully critics into silence and, in sentencing, often show leniency to convicted minorities who they judge to be victims of an unjust or, racist, society.

But it is within the media where Marxists have had their most striking victory. When Black Lives Matter rioters caused widespread bloodshed, looting and property damage, the world's media characterised them as mostly peaceful and justified.

Social media monopolies like Twitter and Facebook are in the vanguard. While leveraging their platforms to promote their radically partisan agenda, they randomly censor anything which offends it. Major mastheads also strongly identify with the Left, not least, Australia's taxpayer-funded ABC. It abandoned accuracy and impartiality long ago, making truth secondary to dogma. Yet shareholder ministers do nothing.

Even the West's military, including Australia's armed forces, have been deeply penetrated by cultural Marxists. To meet gender equity benchmarks, the army's elite units modified fitness tests. The Navy now focusses on all aspects of diversity, while Australian Defence Force personnel reached the epitome of wokeness by marking the International Day Against Homophobia and related prejudices. These preoccupations suggest the top brass considers combat training a lower order priority.

Once a defender of capitalism, business has abjectly surrendered to the harassment of activists, social media and woke fund managers. It, too, has embraced identity politics and progressive causes like climate change. human resources departments ensure their bosses' boardroom virtue is codified into corporate culture, ensuring "diverse" and "politically correct" employees are preferred in hiring and promotion. Profits now give way to "stakeholder obligations".

This corporate behaviour is eerily reminiscent of Germany in the 1930s. In his secret diary, journalist Sebastian Haffner, wrote "There are few things as odd as the calm, superior indifference with which I and those like me, watched the beginnings of the Nazi revolution in Germany, as if from a box at the theatre". Like today's managerial class, Haffner observed that when an organisation's future is inexorably linked to being on one political side, close attention is paid to the new doctrine. John Donahue, the CEO of Nike talks of a commitment to an inclusive culture and breaking down barriers for athletes around the world. Yet, without seeing the extreme irony, he enthusiastically supports gross human rights abuser, China, saying "Nike is a brand that is of China and for China".

This is no aberration. Most of the Marxist goals identified by Skousen 60 years ago have been achieved. It has taken meticulous planning, patience, determination and, relentless indoctrination. Like boiling frogs, the public has offered little resistance. Relentless propaganda has persuaded voters that governments must play a bigger role in their lives as the sensible trade-off between freedom and security. They have also realised it is safer to join the chorus than remain silent about perceived injustices. After all, to argue against the mob, is to side with the oppressors. It takes rare courage to risk being stigmatised as a bigot, a racist or, a member of the alt-right. The thrust of this self-hating groupthink, is to reward minorities with a superior status vis-a-vis what is now referred to as the "dominant culture".

Like a slow growing cancer, Marxism has silently invaded society's healthy cells and vital organs, leaving tolerant liberal democracies vulnerable to existential threats from inside and without.

COVID-19 has demonstrated just how susceptible they have become.

Not only has this pandemic exposed Western leadership to be weak and unprepared from the start, it has revealed a ruling class eager to seize control and willing to cynically politicise science to frighten the public into meekly accepting harsh "emergency" measures. Once-empowered, sadistic health bureaucrats have distorted evidence and callously refused the most reasonable requests. A mere handful of infections can result in lockdowns and closed borders. If police brutality is involved, authorities ignore it. Reflecting the totalitarian within, any easing of restrictions is presented as a generous dispensation, not the rightful restoration of the people's inalienable liberty.

China's agency in spreading this malignancy should not be underestimated. For decades it has supported anti-capitalist activists while simultaneously embarking on a massive charm offensive. It invested heavily in strategic infrastructure abroad, recruiting foreign nationals to Chinese company boards and government bodies and, at times, resorting to outright bribery.

This purposeful, influence-peddling, proved particularly effective inside the United Nations, enabling President Xi Jinping to fashion it into a tool to suit his own authoritarian priorities. It allowed Beijing, with its record of blatant human rights abuses, to join the UN Human Rights Council. And, notwithstanding it being the world's second largest economy, the worst carbon dioxide emitter, having the biggest standing army and achieving a Mars landing, China continues to be accepted as a "developing nation". This status exempts Beijing from meeting the economically ruinous emissions reduction targets that its developed adversaries must meet.

So dominant is China's UN influence, that the World Health Organisation cravenly collaborated in downplaying the severity of the coronavirus epidemic, right up to declaring it a pandemic. While COVID-19 was running rampant around the world, the WHO's sycophantic repeating of Beijing's disinformation bought China time to hoard medical supplies and cover its tracks.

No matter, President Xi had a global army of influential fifth columnists willing to run interference for his shameless and heartless regime.

Professor Klaus Schwab, founder of the World Economic Forum is among those in China's Marxist/Leninist thrall. He argues "The pandemic represents a rare but narrow window of opportunity to reflect, reimagine and, reset our world". Using climate change as the driver, he believes, "All aspects of our societies and economies must be revamped, from education, to social contracts and working conditions." He calls this the "Great Reset of capitalism" and argues that governments will need to intervene (coerce) more, to ensure "better and fairer outcomes". The World Economic Forum has a "strategic partnership framework" with the UN and supports the concept of a one-world government.

China may well appeal to the world's ego-driven intelligentsia. That Beijing presides over one of the world's highest levels of income inequality and, a widening wealth gap worse than America's, matters little. Nor does a 2016 Beijing University study which found the richest one per cent of households hold a third of the country's wealth, while the poorest 25 per cent account for only one per cent of wealth. For them, "better and fairer" are in the eyes of the beholder.

Such a mindset excuses as "cultural" the reality that, after 72 years of Marxist/Leninist control, 70 percent of the CCP's nearly 92 million members, are men. And its "culture" which justifies today's pervasive anti-black sentiment in China. The Western world's critics would rather focus on racism in white societies.

Of course, these Sinophiles must accept Beijing's assurances that the gross mistreatment of its more than one million Uyghurs, Kazakhs and other Muslim minorities and, the organ harvesting from Falun Gong detainees, (admitted to privately by doctors from leading

Chinese hospitals), are nothing but "rumour-mongering through and through and, bare faced lies".

To the West, these practices are abhorrent, yet are too inconvenient a subject to warrant raising at the UN, the WEF or, among the multitude of self-righteous critics of Western values. How to control the masses through supra-national governments takes priority over risking Xi Jinping's displeasure.

Of course, the Left strongly holds to the view that "cultural Marxism" is a conspiracy theory dreamt up by the Right. However, it matters little whether the international spread of Marxist/Leninist doctrine is a spontaneous coalition of authoritarians coming together in a common cause or, an organised movement headed by an Orwellian Big Brother. What matters is that the 46 Marxist goals described by Skousen in the 1960s have all but been achieved and freedom is rapidly slipping from the West's grasp.

The argument goes that today's complex problems are incapable of being solved by self-interested individuals. That big governments, run by superior intellectuals, can plan our lives better than we can. Yet the most important lesson to be learned from the pandemic, is the sheer perfidy and incompetence of governments. Whether it be international political groupthink, egomaniacal leadership, or, unprepared, disingenuous, health officials, the impact of the pandemic has been far worse than it should have been. However, thanks to centralised control, there is no accountability.

Will the lesson be learnt in time? As the West careers down the road to serfdom, driven by ever more reckless governments, the opportunity for a U-turn becomes more difficult. Indeed, liberal, free-market democracies, which are relatively new and unique in history, may well become a fleeting experiment in the evolution of human affairs.

Yet, there are signs that the boiling frogs are stirring. China's increased truculence appears to be highlighting the true perils of totalitarian rule. Parents have begun pushing back on the insidious indoctrination of their children, leading some American States to reflect this by outlawing the teaching of critical race theory in their schools. Former climate change warriors are making films and writing bestsellers, debunking global warming orthodoxy. And, prominent people in the Black community are calling out positive discrimination as perpetuating the cycle of misery already prevalent in America's big cities. Conservative networks like *Fox News*, *Sky News Australia* and the newly launched *GB News* in Britain, are dominating the important time slots favoured by advertisers.

Perhaps these will prove straws in the wind? After all, the Marxist collective won't easily surrender its hard-won gains. And it remains to be seen whether Western democracies, having lost so much ground, are prepared to pay a price which may inevitably involve blood sacrifices.

Dr Maurice Newman AC is the former Chairman of Deutsche Bank Australia & New Zealand, Australian Securities Exchange (ASX), and Australian Broadcasting Corporation, and Chancellor of Macquarie University. His career spans over 50 years in stockbroking and investment banking. Dr Newman has chaired a number of Asian business alliances and has been an adviser to Australian governments, State and Federal. He is currently Chairman of Melon Pastoral Pty Ltd; SCG Heritage Trust; Chamber of Australia-India Trade & Investment; M Value Capital Advisory Board; and The Australian Fathers' Day Council. He is a Director of O'Connell Street Associates Pty Limited; Senior Corporate Advisor to the Marsh & McLennan Companies; Member, SCG Members Advisory Committee; Member, ADC Advisory Council; Member, Advisory Council Advance Australia; Member, CEDA Leadership Council; and Honorary Life Trustee of CEDA. He was appointed Chairman of the Prime Minister's Business Advisory Council in 2013; and Honorary Professor in

Public Diplomacy at the Soft Power Advocacy & Research Centre, Macquarie University in September 2012. Dr Newman served as a Trustee, Sydney Cricket & Sports Ground Trust and Chairman of the Bradman Foundation.

11

NEW VISION, NEW HOPE
Gemma Tognini

In the Old Testament of the Christian Bible, the prophet Zechariah decrees a command to the Israelites, "Return to your stronghold, oh prisoners of hope."

The words are musical, lyrical. They're beautiful. But their beauty belies the contradiction within. The marriage of hope and imprisonment, two concepts not typically united in such a way. It's an unusual construct, the idea that hope may be a form or tool of captivity.

Some scholars believe the answer lies in a wrestle between past glories and things spoken of but not yet seen, that the Israelites are in fact held captive by a hope misplaced. For the Jewish people, at the time living under Persian control, and indeed having spent much of their existence in various forms of captivity and subjugation, hope in the idea of past victories, in the memory of them, could easily have become a prison, a prison where they are locked into old ways, redundant ways of doing, thinking, warring and being; old ways of viewing the world and engaging with it; a prison-like mentality where hearts and minds remain captive to a hope in ways of the past.

When I reflect on this story, it speaks to me of the Australia we see today. More specifically, it speaks to a place where conservative politics finds itself, challenged externally and from within, searching for meaningful identity in an environment that doesn't reflect or accommodate the ways of old. We have spent the past decade lurching along, fighting within ourselves, struggling to be the signal above the noise, grappling with how to preserve the fundamental strengths of our values system, while being able to adapt and grow in pace with the changing expectations of communities we seek to serve; and yes, amidst all of this, eyes fixed on the rear vision mirror, hope placed in the safety and comfort of the past, without a clear vision for the future.

Conservative politics in Australia are inextricably linked to the Menzies era, his leadership, his legacy, his ways. These values have been a foundation, a compass and point of reference, serving Australia well for generations.

Likewise, the 13 years of the Howard Government set the benchmark in modern Australia for leadership that was highly prudent, fiscally responsible and not afraid of reform. It was captive to neither the hard-line right nor left of the party. It was the Toyota Corolla of governments, the not showy, ostentatious, or egotistical but sturdy, reliable, affordable and damned good value.

When Menzies delivered his Forgotten People speech in 1942, Australia was at war, cut off from the rest of the world, her sons in their hundreds of thousands, fighting tyranny on foreign shores. Australia was on the cusp of massive socioeconomic and cultural change.

As I write this, our country is once again cut off and isolated from the rest of the world; not just at war with a virus but in many ways, at war with itself, suffering an identity crisis of sorts, badly fractured and losing itself in the midst of significant social transition.

It would be simplistic to just blame policy, a lack of discipline or an electorate that's tuned out, though these are all factors to a degree.

I believe something significantly less tangible, though equally if not more powerful, is behind the current malaise – vision. Conservatives in Australia have failed to articulate, let alone communicate, a vision for this country.

Oh, we're okay at stating our case in specific areas of policy and the like, but when it come to the thread which weaves it all together, we're lacking.

We lack clear vision and it's my view that we no longer offer hope for a better future; instead, we are prisoners of a hope which is anchored in the past, afraid to turn our eyes to the horizon and dream.

If the dream alone is simply to govern, to hold power, it is a bankrupt dream indeed.

Menzies and Howard were leaders who lead with purpose and with vision. They understood and they heard the generations they were elected to serve. It's been said that nobody understood the electorate better than Howard, nobody took the time to listen and understand the way he did. Few since have had a similarly honest relationship with the Australian people.

He offered vision and hope in equal measure. He abandoned the role of a conservative warrior in order to lead for all.

Slowly and by degrees, the ability to communicate vision has waned. Slowly and by degrees conservatives have been talking more than listening. Slowly and by degrees we have abandoned vision for political ambition; real hope for the election cycle; and the service of community for service of self.

If people perish for a lack of vision, the same can be said of Governments, a hundred times over.

Some of you will take offence at my views and perhaps that is unintended validation because being reluctant to accept one's own shortcomings and being resistant to change are both symptoms of the problem I'm describing.

Some of you will contend that conservative values don't change and certainly should not adjust to reflect the times. Think again. When my mother married my father (both raised in conservative families based on middle class, conservative values) it was the social expectation that a breath after saying "I do", she quit her job to keep house or something. That is what she did.

Today, that idea is archaic and unimaginable. Women are encouraged to pursue the life of their choosing, be that as a stay-at-home mum or in the workforce. Conservative values prioritise choice.

The example I've offered is what it looks like to adapt these values to a new social context, rather than abandon them all together.

Conservatives must find and articulate fresh vision that builds on the past, rather than tries to replicate it.

This is particularly critical when it comes to the challenge of generational change. This is our dark horse, the sleeping giant. The much-maligned millennials and Gen-Z, cohorts that could be forgiven for feeling that they've been treated by conservatives as an afterthought or an inconvenience.

When we speak of the Howard legacy, it is wise to remember that the generation now engaging with politics, a generation that turns elections, wasn't alive when terrorists flew their planes into the Twin Towers. This generation isn't just flirting with socialist principles, they're dating and it's getting serious. The fall of the Berlin Wall does not represent an indelible mark in their social narrative. They've never known a world in which choice was denied. Financial pressures are different for them. Their wages have long stagnated while the cost of living has not.

Consulting firm Deloitte conducts an annual survey of millennial sentiment. It is comprehensive in size and scale. Its 2020 report tells us Millennials and Gen Z have little hope for a future. Their socio-political optimism is at record lows. They have no faith in traditional institutions. They are pessimistic about the future. So, what are conservatives doing to convince them otherwise?

Conservatives, the world over, have failed to engage with this cohort and Australia is no exception. Here, unless they're part of the party machine itself, we've simply told them they're wrong and that they don't get a say. They have rewarded this disdain with disengagement. They've simply gone elsewhere.

Do you blame them? Why engage with a party that offers no vision for a future they will inherit?

This is a problem of manner over matter, as much as anything else because the fundamental drivers remain the same, it's simply the vehicle that's different.

The challenge is making the same liberal, conservative values that so powerfully served Australia under the likes of Menzies and Howard, culturally relevant to a new generation. Bringing them into a new social context, bringing the next generation meaningfully into the conversation and being able to clearly spell out a vision for the future. Their future.

For example, what does a conversation around the cost of living look like to a 35-year-old single person, trying to build a life for himself/herself living in Sydney or Melbourne? Maybe they're working part time in one job and toughing it out in the gig economy after hours. Maybe their partner is doing the same thing and they still can't get ahead. What does a conversation about smaller government look and sound like? Why should they care?

How well do we understand what the next generation of voters needs to have the freedom to build the life of their choosing, and understand the role that conservative values play in delivering that? How do we do this when our only points of reference are decades in the past?

It's not enough to say things like, smaller government and greater personal responsibility. It's not enough to say that higher taxes are bad, that renewables are too expensive, and that unrealistic green targets risk plunging people into energy poverty. It's not enough to just say that this is the way it is because this is the way conservative politics operates.

For nearly two decades, I have employed and continue to employ a cohort of young people who would mostly fall into the centre or centre-right of politics. They are smart, ambitious, driven and engaged. They have a clear vision for the Australia they want to see thrive. They can articulate it.

There are days where I keenly feel the intergenerational disconnect, but there are many elements that bridge the gap in years – a shared and healthy distaste for the vanity of internal politics and factional bickering; a robust lack of interest in constant, meaningless obsession with self; neither do we care for the institutionalised pettiness that has so weakened our standing; we're not interested in ideological warriors; we want to remind the political class who they work for, who pays their wages. These are the distractions that come from having no clear compass beyond an election date somewhere in the near future.

The fact is, the world outside politics has moved on and the political class has failed to recognise this, conservatives in some ways more so. Look no further than how we have framed conversations around women, the environment and innovation. There are expectations in the community that have simply not been met and continue to fall short.

If conservatives continue to frame everything through the lens of the past, and obsess about an imaginary voter base, they will be throwing away the party's future.

It wasn't some notion of a political base that delivered government to John Howard and kept him there for more than a decade. It was his battlers. They were the 1990's version of the "Forgotten People".

It's important for all reading this to understand that the observations I'm offering are not born of political ambition, nor from any deep knowledge of the inner workings of the Liberal Party. I'm a life-long conservative voter, a business owner, a writer of sorts, a holder of opinions, a pretty good listener to the world around me and the people in it. I've been looking at the party I've voted for all my life and waiting for them to catch up with the rest of us.

For 18 years, I have been an employer of the very people the party I support is losing and failing to engage. To labour the point, there's nothing in it for me in terms of personal gain. I offer these views earnestly and with honesty of motive.

What it means to be conservative looks very different today and will continue to look different into the future. Millennials, Generation Y and Z – they are the ground conservatives are refusing to cultivate and nurture. How do you engage them, inspire them, fill them with hope and a vision for their future? From the outside looking in, this is the conversation the Liberal Party is refusing to have with itself.

Oh, the irony that so many pride themselves on being able to read the room politically, but can't discern the times we're in.

It is a fool's errand to continue to try to define vision through the successes of the past.

The values so core to our identity – freedom of choice, smaller government, individual responsibility, freedom and ability to build and live a life that is rich and fulfilled – these cannot be taken for granted. They resonate now as they once did, especially for so many for whom there has been no meaningful individual point of reference.

Giving them new voice, telling the story afresh and through a new paradigm, writing the vision, making it plain so that everyone who reads it can run with it, this is the heart of vision, and vision must be at the heart of our future.

Gemma Tognini is the Founder and Executive Director of GT Communications, a strategic communications, corporate affairs, public relations and reputation management firm. She is also an opinion columnist with for _The Australian_, _West Australian_, and Sydney's _Daily Telegraph_, as well as a contributor on _Sky News Australia_. Gemma was the 2014 Business Owner of the Year in the prestigious Telstra Business Women's Awards and a finalist in the Entrepreneur of the Year category in 2017. She has served as a non-executive director of Surf Life Saving WA, The Salvation Army of WA and The Starlight Children's Foundation.

12

LIBERAL BACK IN LIBERAL
Jason Falinski MP

The purpose of a Liberal government is to give the better angels of our nature a chance, to empower the working men and women of this country, and to expand opportunities for all. It is not to tell people how to lead their lives nor how to think.

For those who have forgotten the example of post war eastern Europe, this is not a partisan political point, but an historical fact. The East Germans did not build the Berlin wall to keep west out but their own citizens in.

Robert Menzies founded the Liberal Party to be the political embodiment of the Forgotten People. Today, Australia is divided into three classes: the welfare class, the talking class and the working class. The talking class towers over this nation as none before it has. They dominate our politics, government, public service and media. The Forgotten People of the 21st Century are the working class who fund this edifice. The Liberal Party was founded to give voice to their hopes, ambitions and dreams.

The Liberal Party is at its best when making the lives of working men and women better. We must focus on delivering what Howard and his Treasurer, Peter Costello, achieved for so many years – real, sustainable wage increases.

To accomplish this, we need productivity rates like those of the 1990s and 2000s. Productivity is the key to making the lives of working Australians better. It is the metric we should focus on because it also prohibits cronyism.

Cronyism is the antithesis of merit. It rewards people for whom they know not what they do. It is the ultimate road to rewarding undeserving elites. For too long, this toxic mix of crony insiders has imposed its values on others forcing them to pay for the privilege with increasing taxes and levies like the Superannuation Guarantee.

As the party that wants to improve the lives of the workers and undermine the culture of cronyism, the only question that should consume us is, how do we lift productivity so the people, on whose shoulders this nation's future rests, can get a better deal.

We must answer why companies do not employ the best workers in the world? Why do they outsource, import and divest Australian talent? Why do so many small businesses move their companies overseas once they are successful?

The root causes of this problem would be familiar to Menzies. Australians are over-regulated, over-taxed, live in constant fear of being sued and rely on an education system not delivering for our children, parents or the nation.

It is too easy and misleading to blame greed. We pass law after law. I have given up counting the number of times we introduce legislation to fix problems created by previous legislation. It is a unique form of national masochism.

British philosopher, Karl Popper, put it bluntly: the greatest troubles come from our impatience to better the lot of those around us. Well-meaning schemes get all the attention and noise while genuine freedom strains to be heard.

If you want to improve working peoples' lives through productivity look no further than class action law reform. There is too much litigation in Australia, forcing small businesses to hire an army of lawyers to protect themselves from frivolous lawsuits filed by predatory lawyers.

Too many of our laws benefit no one but class action lawyers. In 2020, the Parliamentary Joint Committee on Corporations chaired by Senator James Paterson and assisted by Celia Hammond MP conducted a six-week review of litigation funders. What the committee found was truly disturbing. An entire system has evolved designed to pervert the justice system against the people it is meant to protect.

Class action law firms have little interest in justice, but a lot of interest in profits. Litigation funders are so overrun by investors that they can afford to turn away investments of of USD $1 million. In Australia, investments in litigation funders have average returns of 580 per cent.

The exemplar of this is the Banksia Case. It revealed how the justice system has utterly failed to supervise these tax-dodging spivs. Lawyers were sending e-mails encouraging one other to over-charge so they could keep more for themselves. Everyone, except those suffering, were in on it.

The Committee uncovered that Maurice Blackburn, a class action law firm, met with Jill Hennessy, the Victorian Attorney-General, on the morning she announced that the Victorian Andrews Government was introducing contingency fees – a financial windfall for class action lawyers of untold millions. This coincidence would normally raise eyebrows. Clearly not. Later that day, Maurice Blackburn brazenly donated $100,000 to the Labor Party. No one from the talking class, especially its "investigative journalists", have said a word.

Insurers are leaving the Australian market en masse. Small and medium sized companies cannot get insurance; large companies are seeing their premiums increase 500 to 900 per cent. On average, fewer than 30 per cent of this money finds its way to the victims.

As the behaviour of big super's IFM in Tandem shows, Australia is at real risk of becoming a nation of class action lawyers, leaving their investors, big super, to pick over the carcasses of once thriving businesses, forcing the ones who survive to leave the country, taking their jobs, investments and intellectual property with them.

When Australian small businesses are not too busy looking for insurance to protect themselves, they are filling out forms that no one reads, no one needs and no one cares about. Over-regulation is the talking class' weapon of choice.

There is always some inequity that needs fixing. This inequity is greatest when it can be highlighted with emotionally compelling pictures and members of a pre-ordained marginalised community who fit into its woke narrative. These stories are usually promoted by taxpayer-funded advocates who profit from it. No one ever cares about the facts, especially when they do not add up.

In the last Parliament there were over 55,000 new pieces of regulation, like the Responsible Lending Act introduced by the Rudd Government. Kevin Rudd wanted to fix home lending the United States way. It was that delusional. Its application to Australia's circumstances were non-existent, because we already have one of the most regulated financial service sectors in the world. There are virtually no similarities between the Australian and US residential mortgage market. The law resulted in unintended negative consequences – reduced lending, increased costs, more paperwork, choking off credit to small business and, as recent court cases have shown, increased credit defaults.

ASIC used the law to fine financial institutions tens of millions of dollars which they then funnelled to advocates. As the Federal Court later found, virtually none of these fines were legal. Advocates like the

Financial Counselling Service, the Consumer Rights Legal Centre, Financial Rights Legal Centre, Super Consumers Australia, Choice and others were the real winners.

These advocates have profited from this law and are the most vocal opponents of reform that would increase credit to small businesses, reduce borrowing costs and credit defaults. These groups are the most prominent campaigners against conflicted remuneration. We now know why. They don't want the competition.

The advocates have systemically worked to stop Australians getting independent advice by turning their partisan, crony-funded attacks on financial planners. There were 28,000 financial planners in 2019, helping working Australians navigate one of the most sophisticated financial systems in the world, ensuring they got advice that would help them become financially secure and holding big super to account. Industry super hates them and they put the advocates to work to destroy them.

As of 2021, over-regulation and misuse of ASIC's powers had seen 10,000 planners give up, some committing suicide. Those who remain, openly state that the cost of regulation and ASIC fees are so high that they cannot take on new clients unless they have $1 million in investible assets. This means the vast majority of Australians are defenceless against big supers' rapacious cost structure. Australians spend more on superannuation fees than they do on energy. Regulation is the talking class's favoured tool to get money out of workers while doing nothing in return.

The talking class' regulations do not just deny working Australians affordable credit or financial advice, they also ensure that the next generation of Australians is cut-off from ever owning a home. Over-regulation has created the most expensive housing market in the world.

Australia is the least densely populated continent in the world (except for the South Pole), with the highest wages in the world, and, still, we have the world's least affordable homes. Home prices are more aligned with the land-constrained city states of Singapore and Hong Kong than they are with the open prairies of Kansas.

At the beginning of 2021, just as demand for housing surged, NSW building approvals decreased by 33 per cent. This reduction had only one possible outcome, a surge in prices. Over the next six months, house prices in NSW reached record highs.

The Economist reported at the end of 2019 on the example of Japan. After the property crash of 1989, the Japanese Government tried to stimulate the economy through deficit spending. One of the favourite causes of the talking class is government-owned housing, marketed as social housing. The Japanese government spent billions on government housing.

Predictably, masses of new government housing did not shift the dial on homelessness. In fact, the problem got worse. Meanwhile the Tokyo City Government decided to reform planning laws in 2004. Over the next ten years, homelessness dropped 80 per cent, home ownership went up and prices moderated. Australia's unaffordable housing has everything to do with the talking class's regulatory program aimed at protecting themselves, without caring whom it hurts.

This lack of care extends to our tax system. A good taxation system should be simple, easy, productive and fair. Australia's is almost the opposite, constantly used to advance woke social policy rather than promoting productivity. It is the complexity of our system that drives companies to hire expensive lawyers instead of researchers. Tax lawyers advise our companies to relocate overseas. Researchers create products that the world demands enabling businesses to expand job opportunities here.

Australia's education system should be producing the researchers and engineers of the future, not tax accountants and lawyers who swell the ranks of the talking class.

We have one of the best funded education systems in the world, but we produce too many graduates in critical theory and not enough in critical sciences. We have managed this feat of high-cost education delivering unwanted skills by trenchantly ignoring best practice evidence.

At the very time that global education systems were letting local schools make decisions to better tailor their classrooms to the needs of their students, Australia was centralising our system to better match the needs of our unions. In Germany and Switzerland, about 80 per cent of their students attend technical schools that are highly integrated with industry. This has helped create low youth unemployment, high wage manufacturing jobs, and an innovative manufacturing sector, the envy of the world. In Australia, we do the opposite – forcing over 50 per cent of our high school graduates into university courses that it is doubtful many want to do, which do not provide an education for a lifetime of engaging, fulfilling work.

What is needed to improve the lives of working Australians has been obvious for a long time – reform litigation, regulation, taxation and education. Why is it so easy to say, but so hard to do? Because these systems are supported by a cartel of advocates, regulators, class action lawyers, unions and big super trillion-dollar fund managers. Put together, this cartel acts as the tentacles of a giant vampire squid rapped around the face of working Australians that will not let go until it has sucked us dry.

The Liberal Party should not let this battle be framed as more government versus less government. This battle is about better government for the people, by the people and of the people versus crony government that feeds the vampire squid.

The great work of the Liberal Party is only just beginning. It is up to us, in the here and now, to continue the journey that others so bravely began towards a more perfect nation, a nation that guarantees the freedom of all because no imprisoned group has ever created a fair and equal society.

We must embark on a journey that builds on equality based on equal opportunity because only when our opportunities are bountiful, can justice be assured. There is a truth that will not die, that compassion comes, not from the hands of a government bureaucrat, but from a network of loving and caring friends, families and neighbours. Together these networks create a thousand points of light that cross our continent shining the way for all. This will build an even more open and tolerant society that will continue to be the envy of the world. These things we fight for because they matter and are worth preserving.

Jason Falinski MP is the Federal Member for Mackellar. First elected to Parliament in 2016, Jason is now the Chair of the House of Representatives Standing Committee on Tax and Revenue. He has over 25 years' experience in business, including founding his own company in 2004 designing and manufacturing health care equipment and furniture for aged care homes and hospitals. Prior to this he worked in roles in financial services, banking and corporate governance. Jason served on the former Warringah Council for 4 years and is passionate about improving the lives of residents on Sydney's Northern Beaches. He holds an MBA from the Australian Graduate School of Management, a Graduate Diploma of Applied Finance from the Securities Institute of Australia and a Bachelor of Agricultural Economics from the University of Sydney.

13

HUMAN RIGHTS
IN A POST-COVID ERA
Adam Creighton

The coronavirus pandemic ushered in the most profound restrictions on basic human rights by any democracies since at least the Second World War.

Rights of association, assembly, movement, even speech, were suspended, throughout most western nations, and not for short periods, in the name of the "public good". The UK was in various stages of "lockdown" for 480 days.

As the pandemic reaches its final stage (let's hope), it's timely to ask if these impositions were reasonable and, if not, how might we prevent their reimposition.

I argue they weren't, and make some modest suggestions to limit the possibility.

After the end of the Second World War, the words democracy and freedom were typically used interchangeably. Free countries were by definition democracies, so the thinking went.

This was understandable because victorious democracies, led by the United States, had prevailed over various forms of tyranny in Germany and Japan, and their people were indeed free by any historical standard or absolute standard.

The triumph against Soviet tyranny, decades later, only underscored, in the public mind, this winning combination, the idea that democracy and freedom went hand in hand.

The coronavirus pandemic has starkly illustrated the tension between democracy and freedom. While democracy might be a necessary condition for a free society, it might not be sufficient. That requires additional constraints.

Freedom relates to the rights of individuals, or groups of individuals, within a society; democracy, simplistically, is a system of government, where the majority make the rules.

Spelt out in that manner, then, it's clear to see how tension can arise.

The tyranny of the majority, as philosophers from ancient Greece onwards have recognised, could undermine individual freedom putting unreasonable burdens on a minority. What is popular isn't necessarily good or right.

That's why few constitutions avoid 'direct democracy', where voters through referenda-style votes decide policy questions directly.

Members of parliament, as Edmund Burke once said, are meant to follow their conscience as much as they should their electors' desires.

We have seen how democracy can't function in an atmosphere of hysteria, delusion and misinformation.

Surveys showed American and British voters, for instance, believed COVID-19 was at least ten times more dangerous than it actually was; and the belief is widespread that the virus leads to "long Covid" in those who survived, despite only anecdotal evidence.

The pandemic response should prompt some awkward reflection

among those, myself included, who had played down concerns that democracies wouldn't adequately safeguard individual rights.

Popularly elected representatives would not, for long, permit governments to deny basic human rights, because they would lose office, the thinking went. Moreover, "bills of rights" were a recipe for "lawyers' picnics" and empowered activist judges to twist the words of any set of rights, however reasonable, to suit whatever the fashionable political fashions of the day.

These are powerful arguments, and they are no less correct now than they were before coronavirus emerged.

But the pandemic has revealed how, in conditions of widespread fear, however irrational, governments can and will impose extreme arbitrary "measures", without little resistance from parliaments.

The human rights "industry" also offered little protection too. Since the 1980s, governments have charged various human rights agencies with the specific task of advocating in favour of human rights and highlighting transgressions by governments, business and individuals.

Australia's Human Rights Commission (AHRC), established in 1986, for instance, has over 100 employees and a budget in excess of $20 million a year.

Other jurisdictions have similar bodies, such as the Equal Opportunity and Human Rights Commissions in Victoria and a similar body in the UK.

There is barely a mention, let alone a single substantive piece of analysis, on the AHRC's website relating to the pandemic, which led to the most severe restrictions on human rights in peace time.

Even if commissioners privately agreed with the measures, a thoughtful analysis of why they were justified would seem to be within the remit – and certainly the resourcing – of the AHRC.

The United Nations Declaration of Human Rights for instance, proclaimed in 1948, includes the right to "freedom of peaceful assembly and association", "to work, to free choice of employment" and "to freely participate in the cultural life of the community, to enjoy the arts."

It also enshrined the right "to freedom of movement and residence within the borders of each state and the right to leave any country, including his own, and to return to his country", rights trampled on in Australia perhaps more than any other nation.

Victoria, uniquely among Australian States even has its own human rights "Charter" that includes rights to "freedom of expression" along with many rights listed in the UN Charter; yet a Victorian woman was arrested in her home during the pandemic for posting on social media, her support of a rally intending to protest against lockdowns.

The Charter even has a protection against "degrading treatment", yet it forced sentient adults to wear pieces of cloth on their face for more than six months when outside. Evidently, these rights aren't worth the paper they are written on when voters are scared.

As English barrister Francis Hoar pointed out last year, European governments, too, ignored the European Declaration of Human Rights. That document provided for member states to apply for exemptions in certain grave emergencies, but no government wanted to make COVID-19 an emergency.

All this should be troubling for genuine human rights advocates, and even for those who use "human rights" as a vehicle and banner to push progressive agendas.

Once the hysteria subsides, it's possible the public won't take demands for "more rights" for disabled or trans people, for instance, so seriously when their advocates were practically silent for 16 months about incursions on basic fundamental rights that were far greater, and affected a far larger share of the population.

Sweden stood out in Europe for not following China's response to the pandemic – shutting almost all businesses and requiring people to stay in their homes with limited exemptions.

This response to some degree stemmed from the Swedish Constitution, which guarantees freedom of movement for Swedish citizens, in turn making lockdown legislation or regulations prima facie illegal.

Moreover, some public agencies, including the health authorities, had the right to set policy independent of government, making it easier for experts who weren't caught up in hysteria themselves, or cynically enjoying the limelight, to make rules more calmly.

It was a similar situation in Japan, where the US-drafted post-war constitution stressed individual rights and made lockdowns by central government difficult. The Japanese government declared various "states of emergency" throughout the pandemic, but these only included recommendations to stay home and for some businesses to close.

The US, arguably with the most well-known constitutional bill of rights in the world, also offers an instructive case. Certainly, most US states enacted at least one lockdown during the pandemic, but many states and territories did not.

In September 2020, for instance, in a case in Pennsylvania, a judge ruled against lockdowns and arbitrary business closures on constitutional grounds.

"Good intentions toward a laudable end are not alone enough to uphold governmental action against a constitutional challenge. Indeed, the greatest threats to our system of constitutional liberties may arise when the ends are laudable and the intent is good, especially in a time of emergency," Judge William Stickman wrote.

"There have never previously been lockdowns of entire populations – much less for lengthy and indefinite periods of time," he added.

The decision was ultimately overturned by a higher court, but the reasoning and decision stand forever for other judges to reference.

More recently a Florida court in a 2-1 decision upheld a complaint against compulsory masking.

"A person reasonably can expect not to be forced by the government to put something on his own face against his will," Judge Adam Tanenbaum wrote. Florida's own constitution has a "guarantee of personal inviolability" which, the judge reasoned, "must include the inviolability of something so intimate as one's own face".

Unfortunately, Australia's own High Court did not strike down inter-state border closures, despite Australia's constitution declaring that "trade, commerce and intercourse among the states shall be absolutely free".

As all political philosophers understand rights conflict with one another. John Stuart Mill's famous dictum that men and women should be free to do whatever so long as their actions don't harm others isn't as simple as it might sound.

What is harm, and how far should the state go to stamp it out? Free speech is typically limited in circumstances where it could, for example, incite violence.

Some political philosophers distinguish between positive and negative rights. The latter tend to protect individuals from the exercise of government power, typically enshrining the right to free speech, movement, property. They typically don't "cost" money, beyond funding the police and courts.

Positive rights emerged much later in the 20th Century and, typically, bestow rights to something, such as education, welfare, healthcare, or even "respect". Naturally these rights require a mix of taxation, or even requiring others to do something against their will.

The right "not to be infected by COVID-19" could be considered a positive right, fulfilment of which has called for a massive encroachment on more traditional negative rights.

Leaders need to balance rights against one other.

It is far from clear that balance was struck correctly in Australia, and the wider western world, during the COVID-19 pandemic. What appeared to work in Wuhan, China, might not be appropriate in nations founded on liberal democratic principles; and it's still not clear the measures taken have, in fact, at least in an obvious way, protected people from catching coronavirus. The international evidence is increasingly clear on that point. States like Florida and California in the US, despite pursuing wildly different strategies, have broadly the same outcome. The same can be said for Sweden and the rest of Europe.

The question remains, then, what changes can we make to protect individual rights in the future?

First, one shouldn't be so dismissive of bills of rights, as many conservatives have been. As the US case has illustrated, some judges, even if a minority, will not bow to public pressure during a "crisis" and will interpret rights as the original drafters intended.

It is true the Victorian Bill of Rights wasn't worth the paper it was written on; but that doesn't mean in other States, in other contexts, a Bill or Rights wouldn't at least make it more difficult, politically and legally, for governments to invade people's homes for posting on social media about walking in the park.

Perhaps Liberals should consider proposing a referendum to add a short Bill of Rights to the Australian Constitution. The history of referenda in Australia suggests strongly such a move would fail, but in making the case, the public would be far better informed about their own rights, or lack thereof.

Few Australians would realise, for instance, that State Constitutions contain essentially no restraints on their parliament's power, meaning, in theory, they could do whatever happened to be popular, however reprehensible.

Any Bill of Rights should require super majorities of Parliament to override. Of course, no Parliament can tie the hands of future Parliaments. But again, creating additional political and legal hurdles reduces the likelihood of bad outcomes.

Any such Bill should be short and restricted only to "negative rights", which are easier to understand and implement.

Finally, retired judges should be encouraged rather than censured for speaking out on issues of human rights. The common law is founded ultimately on principles of individual rights and, for want of a better expression, basic common sense.

In the UK, retired Supreme Court judge and historian, Jonathan Sumption, frequently criticised UK government pandemic measures as fundamentally contrary to English common law. His arguments failed to sway the majority but his erudite contributions must have changed at least a few minds.

In the broad sweep of history, COVID-19 will be seen as a moderate pandemic, a highly contagious virus with a tiny infection fatality rate. Had it emerged half a century ago, it's doubtful it would have been noticed.

The response, however, has been anything but moderate.

Proponents of authoritarian disease control have argued temporary suspensions of human rights, enacted by informed officials acting in the public interest, were justified to "save lives".

While ultimately there's no "right" answer, a growing body of evidence, statistical and medical, is showing the costs of the lockdown and other measures have far outweighed the benefits, rendering them incorrect on a utilitarian calculus alone.

Even if they did "work" in net terms, it's still not clear they were justified. No-one would kill a person if he or she happened to have organs that could save the lives of five other people. Some rights should be sacred.

Moreover, the decision to pursue measures unprecedented in disease control have fuelled significant social discord and political rage, which isn't likely to subside for a generation.

Nevertheless, precedents have been set now that make lockdowns more likely when "COVID-21" arrives or, even, for other reasons of the "public good" such as climate change. The conventional wisdom emerging is that "earlier, harder, and longer" lockdowns are the correct response.

For human rights advocates, this isn't a rosy future.

Adam Creighton has been Washington Correspondent for *The Australian* since April 2021, having been the newspaper's Economics Editor before that. He is an award-winning journalist with a special interest in tax and financial policy. He was a Journalist in Residence at the University of Chicago's Booth School of Business in 2019. He has written for *The Economist* and *The Wall Street Journal* from London and Washington DC, and authored book chapters on superannuation for Oxford University Press. He started his career at the Reserve Bank of Australia and the Australian Prudential Regulation Authority. He holds a Bachelor of Economics with First Class Honours from the University of New South Wales, and Master of Philosophy in Economics from Balliol College, Oxford, where he was a Commonwealth Scholar.

14

THE CRISIS IN WESTERN POLITICAL LEADERSHIP

Alan Jones AO

In a time of political upheaval in the 17th Century, John Milton, the English poet and intellectual, wrote his pastoral elegy, "Lycidas".

He argued, "The hungry sheep look up and are not fed; but, swoll'n with wind and the rank mist they draw, rot inwardly and foul contagion spread."

One of Milton's themes was the widening gap between those in power and those governed who can be compared to "the hungry sheep."

Therein lies the metaphor of current political leadership.

Without it, the "foul contagion" of surrender to the other side beckons.

This prompts the simple question, what is leadership if not a real skill, exhibited by individuals or a group, to lead or influence or guide others, whether they be teams or organisations. It also involves the art of motivating people to act towards a common policy goal.

In political parties, it can mean persuading and encouraging membership and would-be members, with a clearly articulated strategy, to meet the future objectives of the organisation.

This leads to a significant problem.

If the only objective of the organisation is to gain power by whatever means; and the only objective of the individual is to be part of that power structure, no matter how bereft of ideas, philosophy or ability an individual might be, then political success will prove elusive.

It was Lewis Carroll who wrote, "If you don't know where you are going, any road will get you there." That feeling of disillusionment pervades the young conservatives.

My dearly departed friend, Sir James Killen, represented the seat of Moreton, in Queensland, from 1955 to 1983. He witnessed politicians of varying abilities come and go. He was a worldly man, a man for all seasons.

When, in 1961, he retained the seat of Moreton on Communist preferences, the irony did not escape Menzies' critics; ten years earlier, Menzies had sought, by referendum, to ban the Communist Party, but was more than happy to take the Killen victory, which enabled his government to be re-elected with a majority of only two.

The one sentiment of Sir James Killen that has always stayed with me was his injunction, "Alan, always remember. Not all the good players are in the one team."

Coincidentally, the leadership and ideological crisis we face today is not unlike that faced by Gough Whitlam when he became leader of the ALP, following its landslide defeat at the November 1966 election.

I prefer to regard the non-socialist forces as radical conservatives – radical enough to know what to change and conservative enough to know what to keep.

Whitlam recognised that in a speech that he made in Melbourne on June 9, 1967, when he unapologetically challenged his Party to reform itself internally and renovate its policy platform.

That is where we must start.

Whitlam was speaking in Victoria which, in 1955, had recorded the lowest vote "at any time since Australia became a Nation."

He argued, "We construct a philosophy of failure which finds, in defeat, a form of justification and proof of the purity of our principles. Certainly, the impotent are pure."

The conservative forces today face a similar challenge.

In the West Australian State election of 2021, the Liberal result was worse than that of Labor in Victoria in 1955.

The Liberal Party was decimated, two seats out of 59; and the big policy idea was closing down all coal-fired power plants by 2025.

This corresponded with a published study, at the same time, that the Coalition had lost more than two million primary votes in the 19 Federal and State elections since Tony Abbott returned the conservative party to power in 2013 – 2,105,000 to be exact.

Only a fool would argue that this has nothing to do, apparently, with the conservative "better economic managers" heading towards a trillion dollars of debt; and the fact that the previous architects of private sector wealth and enterprise have not built a dam or a coal-fired power plant; nor does their philosophical commitment require them to stand up to Black Lives Matter or school children protesting climate change.

Rank and file conservatives are wanting leaders to get into the ring and prosecute the conservative case. Or don't they have one?

Fancy in 1967, a Labor leader arguing, "Under the present Government, more and more of our assets are falling into foreign hands ... the Australian employees of vast corporate overseas empires are finding increasingly that employment policies are determined, not in Geelong, Melbourne or Sydney, but in the Boardrooms of the parent company overseas. Some of these companies have resources and assets greater than those of our greatest States."

These sentiments are being echoed in 2021.

So where to from here?

Edward de Bono passed away in June 2021.

He was identified with the concept of "lateral thinking" which, he believed, far outweighed the traditional "vertical thinking model" which limits people and organisations.

De Bono thought tyranny was a world devoid of creative thinking.

We have to think creatively or get left behind.

Another important concept, tangentially related to the Edward de Bono principle, found expression in the 1989 film, "Field of Dreams."

Kevin Costner plays the role of the farmer, Ray Kinsella, who hears a voice and builds a baseball field in the middle of his cornfield.

The voice said, "Build it and they will come."

That is precisely what the conservative political forces now must do. Where do we start?

The answer is simple, in the classroom.

How much longer do we stand by and watch our students falling behind those in comparable countries on the best international measures of education performance.

This is what Whitlam was talking about when he argued that Labor had to renovate its policy platform.

How can we have growing Education Budgets, year upon year, with no adequate evaluation of what they're producing.

Each year we have thousands and thousands of students who don't learn the foundational concepts of arithmetic, geometry, literature, syntax, punctuation and spelling.

We need to focus less on academic research and theory and more on what happens in the classroom – on what we teach, how we teach and how we assess learning.

We don't want to because we are terrified of the results.

The situation is even worse than that.

Emile Durkheim was a French sociologist who argued that schools were essential for imprinting shared social values into the minds of children; and he rightly believed schools would play a central role in forming modern societies.

The opposite is happening.

Durkheim believed that education should transmit "the shared values of society, as well as providing specialised skills for an economy increasingly based on specialisation."

The opposite is happening.

The classroom has become a vehicle for standing "shared social values" on their head; yet Durkheim believed that "society can survive only if there exists, among its members, a sufficient degree of homogeneity; education perpetuates and reinforces this homogeneity by fixing in the mind of the child, from the beginning, the essential similarities that social life demands;" and that education does this by instilling a sense of social solidarity in the individual, a sense of belonging to a wider society, a sense of commitment to the importance of working towards society's goals and "a feeling that the society is more important than the individual."

The opposite is happening.

Education has been replaced by indoctrination and the teaching of content that bears little relationship to the "shared social values" about which Durkheim is speaking; and bears little relationship to the shared values of the home.

Indeed, Durkheim argued "Education, and in particular the teaching of history, provides the link between the individual and society. If history is taught effectively it "comes alive" for children, linking them to their social past and developing in them a sense of commitment to the social group."

The opposite is happening.

Children today are taught that the social group into which they will transition has betrayed them because we are either racist or because we are allowing the world to be destroyed by climate change.

Durkheim argued that education should provide secondary socialisation; the primary socialisation is delivered by the family, which passes on particular norms and values.

Secondary socialisation passes on universal norms and values that are shared by the broader society.

That is not happening.

Once we can be confident of securing the proper education of our children, and that will be a monumental task, but not impossible, we have to be sure, through the way we practice our conservative values to leave the world a better place for those who follow.

We must, by our philosophy, our ideas, our policies and our values, create economic growth.

Two policy positions are central to that, water policy and energy policy.

It is a dishonest argument that our nation is short of water; and we have some of the most magnificent and productive agricultural land in the world. Water it and we could feed Asia and secure our wealth.

But, as with government generally, the dominant feature of water policy is waste.

We use about 6 per cent of our available water. For example, Lake Argyle in Western Australia releases 50 tonnes of water a second. Only 10 per cent of it is used in the Ord irrigation system.

Forty-five tonnes per second, four billion litres a day, is pushed into the Timor Sea; yet the catchment area of the Fitzroy River is 50 per cent greater than that of the Ord.

Queensland's Northeast has four times the water of the Murray Darling basin.

The total flow down the Murray Darling basin is fewer than 23,000 gigalitres; in the Northeast coastal region of Queensland, 70,000 gigalitres flow into the sea.

You have to wonder whether we haven't left our brains behind.

Go west and the Gulf of Carpentaria has 130,000 available gigalitres; as well, more than 400 billion litres of sewage, much of it untreated, goes into the ocean off Sydney every year.

But if we can't build dams, we can't harvest water.

Jack Beale was a Minister in the NSW Government in the 1940s.

Almost 80 years ago, he proposed the development of the Clarence basin in Northern NSW to create a giant water and power project that would dwarf the Snowy Mountains scheme.

Under the plan, 14 storage dams, linked by cuttings, tunnels and pipelines, would divert inland five million megalitres of water, or ten Sydney Harbours, which flow into the ocean from the Clarence River system each year.

Jack Beale wrote, all those years ago, "Surplus coastal water is the logical future source of arid inland development and electricity generation."

He argued the water captured under his scheme could be diverted to Queensland and into the Murray Darling, doubling the flow of the Murray Darling and minimising its salinity.

He said prophetically, "A nation can't afford to let resources remain idle, even if it has to build pyramids."

Beale argued that with sufficient will, all this would be underway by 1988, completed by 2001, the centenary of Federation.

The hungry sheep look up and are not fed.

The 1983 Fraser Government approved four million dollars to investigate Beale's idea; the incoming Hawke Government cancelled the approval.

The flip side of water is, of course, energy, cheap energy which would return productivity and manufacturing to Australia.

Instead, political leadership sponsors the national economic suicide note, zero-carbon dioxide emissions, when carbon dioxide is 0.04 per cent of the atmosphere.

Human beings worldwide, in all we do, are responsible for 3 per cent of that; and of the 3 per cent, little Australia is responsible of 1.3 per cent.

Michael Shellenberger, a world-renowned environmental activist, apologised, in July 2020, for peddling climate alarmism.

He admitted he wanted to, "Formally apologise for the climate scare we created over the past thirty years ... I have been a climate activist for twenty years and an environmentalist for thirty ... I feel an obligation to apologise for how badly we environmentalists have misled the public."

Bjorn Lomborg, a recognised world authority on climate change, has argued the Paris Agreement will be the most expensive treaty in history and that President Biden's climate alarmism is "almost entirely wrong."

Further, when we are talking about economic growth, he observed that if we followed the policies of the Paris Agreement we will "fix little at a high cost;" indeed, our contribution to atmospheric carbon dioxide is 0.0196 particles per million or, two parts per billion; but the cost to our economy of Paris, according to Lomborg, would be $250 billion a year.

One of the world's leading researchers on the subject of climate change is the Czech Canadian, Vaclav Smil, who has said, "The great hope for a quick and sweeping transition into renewable energy is wishful thinking."

Who prosecutes these untruths? Very few.

This is the crisis in political leadership.

Then there is nuclear energy.

Thirty countries in the world operating at least 450 nuclear reactors for energy generation; over 60 nuclear power plants under construction in 15 countries; more than half the world has access to some electricity generated by nuclear power, but it is illegal to operate a nuclear reactor in Australia, even though we have over 40 per cent of the world's uranium reserves and export the stuff so that other countries can have cheap, clean energy.

As the Chief Scientific Advisor to Barack Obama, no less, Professor Steven Koonin, argued in 2021, "Leaders talk about existential threats, climate emergency, disaster, crisis, but in fact, when you actually read the literature, there is no support for that kind of hysteria."

A self-declared Democrat, Professor Koonin said he is "increasingly dismayed by climate alarmism."

These three issues, the propaganda in the classroom, the failure to harvest water, the intellectually dishonest arguments about carbon dioxide and climate change are all metaphors of the problem.

Our so-called political leaders are not leaders but "followers", marching in step down the wrong road.

Where then do tomorrow's leaders come from?

The answer is, from the generation that is being betrayed, yet there are outstanding, thoughtful and idealistic young people to whom we must appeal.

They baulk at putting their hand up to represent the new direction that conservative forces must take because of factional control of political parties, on all sides, determining, mostly for all the wrong reasons, who should make it into the halls of decision making.

There, we need significant reform.

Conservative parties need to encourage a commitment from young people to offer themselves for public office.

There should be an independent body of distinguished conservative figures to act as a Nomination Secretariat.

Individuals would offer their nomination and their credentials to this body and, in so doing, indicate their geographical preference for a seat.

These applications would be reviewed and each applicant would be required to submit a piece of writing outlining their philosophical beliefs and policy areas to which they could contribute.

These would be assessed by the Secretariat.

These names would then go forward to a nominated electorate for a plebiscite of all paid up members, with appropriate endorsement from the Nomination Secretariat.

Such a system would, I believe, encourage the brightest and the best to offer themselves, knowing that there is a better chance than currently exists for them to avoid the political snake-pit of factional bullyboys.

Gough Whitlam was right in 1967, when he argued that he confronted a battle to reform his Party internally and renovate its policy platform.

That is true today of us.

Without this, the hungry conservative sheep will remain unnourished and uninterested.

Alan Jones AO is one of Australia's most influential broadcasters, currently covering television and print media. He hosts a primetime program on *Sky News Australia* which boasts millions of viewers online through social media platforms. He formerly hosted *The Alan Jones Breakfast Show*, which was the number one radio program in Australia for more than 30 years, winning a record-breaking 226 consecutive radio surveys on Sydney's *2UE* and *2GB* radio stations with more than two million listeners every day across Australia. Alan writes weekly for *The Australian* as a rugby columnist. He is regarded as one of the most successful rugby union coaches in the history of the game, leading the Australian national team to 89 victories in 103 matches, which included a European Grand Slam and the only Wallaby side to win the Bledisloe Cup in a series in New Zealand. Alan also coached the Balmain Tigers and South Sydney Rabbitohs in the NSW rugby league competition. He was previously Deputy Chairman of the Australian Institute of Sport and, before the merger, was the longest serving Trust member in the history of the Sydney Cricket Ground. He now serves on the Venues NSW Board. Prior to his broadcasting and radio success, Alan was the Senior Advisor

and speechwriter to the then Prime Minister Malcolm Fraser. He is one of Australia's most prominent advocates for the causes of rural Australia and its farmers. Alan is a graduate of Queensland and Oxford Universities, with majors in English and French language and literature and education. He has University Blues from both Queensland and Oxford in tennis.

15

NEW BATTLELINES TO BE DRAWN

The Hon. Tony Abbott AC

For the advocates of big government, the pandemic has turned out to be the very best of times; not so for those who prefer smaller government to bigger, and less public spending to more. Not only have most people willingly accepted unprecedented government spending and unimaginably intrusive government controls, supposedly "for their own good", but the pandemic seems to have reinforced the catastrophe narrative and the injustice narrative driving climate alarmism, identity politics, and political correctness more generally. Even worse, the pandemic has given everyone involved with politics an excuse to focus on nothing else, even though the challenges facing Australia are mounting all the time.

The long-term risk is that the pandemic will confirm bigger government plus cultural Marxism as the standard response to every problem. So perhaps the centre-right's most pressing task is to examine what went wrong, as well as what went right, including: why it took 18 months for any level of government to plan a way forward; how so much of our response was dictated by the so-called expert opinion of unelected and unaccountable officials; whether the daily drum call of cases and deaths (even though most had serious co-morbidities) promoted public panic over health outcomes; and how "lives and livelihoods" rhetoric notwithstanding, the only real consideration has been to try to eliminate this one disease, never mind the cost.

At least as important as protecting his announced pathway-from-lockdowns, from grandstanding premiers and over-cautious experts, Prime Minister Scott Morrison should have a royal commission into our pandemic response, to try to ensure that we don't over-react to the next one. It should compare our approach with others', including Sweden's, that maintained the old pandemic policy of slowing the spread, ramping up the health system, and protecting the vulnerable, rather than forcibly minimising activity until "herd immunity" or effective vaccines rendered Covid no more dangerous than the standard seasonal flu.

The question would be whether lockdowns were more severe or more prolonged than they needed to be and whether governments surreptitiously shifted from an initially necessary suppression strategy to an unrealistic elimination one, dressed up as "zero community transmission", without the full public debate that should accompany any big and consequential policy shift. In the meantime, the government should turbocharge the vaccination programme and announce the date when everyone should have had the chance of a jab, after which all domestic restrictions should cease and restrictions on vaccinated returning travellers should drastically reduce. Marking out a definite end to this crisis should mean that we can start to focus once more on the things that will determine our long-term prosperity and safety.

Any government that wants to be effective should identify the problems it wants to tackle, specify what it's going to do about them, effectively implement the relevant policies, and then carry a majority of the public with it. For instance, in the run up to the 2013 federal election, the key issues then facing our country were: prosperity-sapping new taxes, out-of-control people smuggling, log-jammed big cities, and governments that were spending too much for too little return. Hence the 2013 election mantra: "stop the boats, scrap the taxes, build the roads, and balance the budget". And with Operation Sovereign Borders, the abolition of the carbon and mining taxes, the big urban road projects that had been identified and largely agreed with State governments, and the measures in the 2014 budget, there were programmes to get all this done.

Back then, we were "a great country let down by a bad government". Alas, the issues today are more fundamental. Leaving aside the Covid crisis, our economic and security challenges are much deeper; and are compounded by an underlying cultural self-doubt, exemplified by state governments allowing Black Lives Matter protests to go ahead, in defiance of health orders, while relentlessly cracking down on citizens socialising in parks. Even so, the key problems to be tackled still need to be identified and explained; and any specific measures of improvement still need to be decided upon and justified.

The characterisation of the Liberal Party as the political custodian, in this country, of the liberal tradition of J.S. Mill and the conservative tradition of Edmund Burke still holds. As liberals, our preference is for smaller government, lower taxes and great freedom; and as conservatives we support the family, small business and institutions that have stood the test of time. But as well as being the freedom party and the tradition party, we should also be the patriotic party: the party that can be relied upon to stand up for Australia, not to defer to global bodies; and to make our country stronger based on what we know to work. For conservatives, context is critical. Every person counts but individuals are only fully realised through the communities and ultimately the country that's shaped us.

Australia's biggest long-term challenge is this notion of national illegitimacy based on our dispossession of Aboriginal people, and our supposedly on-going racism, sexism, and environmental despoliation. Wittingly or not, this is being fed by schools that are required to teach every subject, from Latin to PE, from an indigenous,

Asian, and sustainability perspective. There's not that much that the federal government realistically can do to produce principal-led, parent-responsive, academically rigorous schools with teachers who are well-paid and professionally respected, but it could at least help to avoid making a bad situation worse by vetoing the proposed draft national curriculum. It's almost impossible to overstate the importance of challenging the "black armband" brigade at every turn, even while continuing to focus on "bread and butter" issues.

Lower wages, higher house prices and more clogged urban infrastructure have been the unavoidable consequence of doubled immigration averaging a quarter-million-a-year for the past decade and a half. For universities and businesses, very high immigration has become the lazy way to higher revenue and lower costs. It's not enough that immigration increase overall GDP; it's got to increase GDP per person if it's to make Australians more prosperous, and not just the newcomers. Of course, newcomers determined to join Team Australia should be welcome here; but that should normally mean doing a job that Australians can't. Spouses and dependent children of permanent residents and relatively small numbers of genuine refugees aside, our immigration programme should comprise people who have a job-to-go-to-from-day-one at market wages with an employer-paid foreign worker tax. Not having the 160,000 a year typically admitted on "spec" as "skilled migrants", but who rarely end up working in their area of supposed skill, should help to take migration back to Howard era-levels. It would also help to end the somewhat demeaning notion that migrants are needed to boost our cultural diversity and to overcome Australians' lack of skills.

Over the past two decades, Australia has gone from having some of the world's lowest to some of the world's highest energy prices, largely because our power system has been run to reduce emissions rather than to produce affordable and reliable electricity. In the process, our manufacturing sector has shrunk and, with it, our strategic self-reliance. There should be no new subsidies for intermittent wind and solar power and the ability to supply 24/7 should be a condition of selling into the grid. If Snowy Hydro can build a gas peaking plant in the Hunter to help keep the lights on, it could also build a new low-emission coal plant to help supply base load power. And in a system based on "engineering and economics", rather than ideology, of course, the Howard-era sop-to-the-Greens nuclear ban should be scrapped.

Political correctness has become entrenched in big public companies, in part, because union-super funds are major shareholders. Superannuation contributions are our money, not the government's or the funds'. On top of all the other taxes, we shouldn't have to pay a 12 per cent superannuation tax so that the government can one day reduce its pension bill. At the very least, a centre-right government should not further increase compulsory super contributions, and it should allow younger people to use their super savings as a deposit on a home, given that owning your own home is the best guarantee of security in retirement.

Getting the budget back to surplus is not just an economic imperative but a moral one too, given that governments should not habitually live beyond their means and put today's bills on tomorrow's taxpayers. Because getting any spending restraint through the Senate tends to be mission impossible, if the budget is to be restored any time soon, a centre-right government should commit to no new spending, other than on national security and economic infrastructure.

With the world once more in an era of great power competition, pitting liberal democracies against Beijing-led dictatorships, we can't be content with a naval build-up that might be our biggest in history but is undoubtedly our slowest. We can't afford to wait decades for new submarines given that they're our most important strategic strike capability. There must be a Plan B to the French deal and that should include asking Britain and America whether we could buy an off-the-shelf nuclear-powered sub.

As the Hawke/Howard era showed, good governments can effect change for the better despite the need to work with the States and to get legislation through the Senate. On the other hand, senators now regard themselves as having "mandates" of their own and more and more programmes (the NDIS is a good example) are not accountable to any one level of government. The main reason why the Abbott government was so readily able to stop the boats (aside from having the will do so) was that this could be done by executive action without requiring any "say so" from the Senate or the States.

For conservatives, institutional change should be a last resort, and invariably "restoration" rather than "reform". Rather than seeking more "cooperative" federal-state structures, a centre-right government should be trying to disentangle the Commonwealth's responsibilities from State ones so that it's clearer who's in charge and who's to blame when things go wrong. This was my intention in commissioning the tax and federation reform white papers (subsequently scrapped). A constitutional amendment to turn the Senate from a "house of rejection" to the house of review it was always supposed to be should be considered. Alternatively, the Senate voting system or the Senate's size could be changed to make it easier for the government of the day to get a majority. At the very least, no new entities that further complicate governance should be created and the "national cabinet" should be renamed given that its decisions aren't binding.

Ending Covid restrictions, scrapping the national curriculum, cutting back immigration, restoring super to you, building coal-fired power, no new spending, getting nuclear subs, and making government simpler: here's a series of specific steps that would make our country stronger, our citizens freer, and our government smaller and more accountable. I reckon that's a politically saleable, instinctively appealing agenda for the centre-right and hope that coming from a former Prime Minister doesn't make it harder to adopt!

The Honourable Tony Abbott AC served as the 28th Prime Minister of Australia between 2013 and 2015, defeating Kevin Rudd in the 2013 federal election. He served as the member for Warringah in the Federal Parliament between 1994 and 2019; and leader of the Liberal Party of Australia from 2009 to 2015. Prior to entering Parliament, he was a journalist with *The Australian*, a Senior Adviser to Opposition Leader John Hewson, and director of Australians for Constitutional Monarchy. He has degrees in economics and law from Sydney University and in politics and philosophy from Oxford where he attended as a Rhodes Scholar. Since 1998, he has convened the Pollie Pedal annual bike ride which has raised nearly $7 million for organisations such as Soldier On, Carers Australia and other charities. Currently, he is a director of the Ramsay Centre for Western Civilisation, serves on the council of the Australian War Memorial, and is an adviser to the UK Board of Trade. He's patron to several charities, including Soldier On, the International Sports Promotion Society, and Worldwide Support for Development.

16

WHATEVER IT TAKES: FIGHT LIKE LABOR

Peter Gleeson

Like never before in this country's rich and fabled history, Australia needs a strong and unified conservative voice.

The alternative is a country which consigns itself to mediocrity. A banana republic indeed, haunting words once echoed by federal Labor's last good Prime Minister, Paul Keating.

Australia is not just at the crossroads. We are way beyond that. Australia is in the fight of its ideological life. One false move, one soaring Labor vote, and Australia risks a Chile, Argentina or Peru-like fiscal catastrophe.

We're hanging by a thread.

Labor's obsession with climate change and zero net emissions will shut down the economy. They don't care. It is written in the stars for Labor.

The problem is that the conservative movement in this country has put the white flag up to the woke brigade and cancel culture. True leadership is about standing for something. Weak, lily-livered policy backflips are for the birds. It's time we were led.

Australia's stance against China is a great example of how we have championed to the world why China is a major problem.

We need more of it. We are a resilient nation. We are the best in the business at so many things. We must stand on our own feet. The rest of the world waits for nobody, especially in the furnace-like geo-political environment of a pandemic.

To cede power at federal and state level to the Labor-Greens alliance will spell generational change we just can't afford. Make no mistake, Labor and the Greens are running an ideological campaign to shift the country's political axis to the extreme Left.

Woke is here. It is real. It is in our schools, our business boardrooms and among our sporting elite. Only the conservative parties have the mettle and understanding to stave off this cancer. It has been bubbling along in our schools and particularly universities for at least 30 years – and the day of judgment is fast approaching.

The problem for the Liberal-National Party is that the far-Left, the Socialists, treat politics as a matter of life and death. They have the killer instinct. They stop at nothing. They have no problem mixing their messaging with untruths and misleading material.

As the famous federal Labor Minister Graham Richardson always quips – in politics, you do whatever it takes.

That's the attitude we see among the radical Left and the Greens in this country. They have a sole purpose to reform and radicalise the Australian economy and people. Reaching net-zero emissions by 2050 is just the tip of the iceberg. The only answer to this demonisation of the national economic narrative is to have a strong and united LNP.

It is important for this piece of work that we characterise the challenge facing the conservative movement by addressing the *modus operandi* of the radical Left of the Labor Party and the Greens.

By doing so, identifying what makes them tick and their own challenges will deliver the blueprint for the conservative narrative. Let's not forget, the Labor Party was founded on the great shearers' strike in the Queensland bush more than century ago.

Now, Labor is turning its back on miners. It, too, has lost the plot. In identifying the Labor Left and Greens alliance as a threat to our national economy, security and future prosperity, the pathway forward for the conservative movement becomes much clearer.

Much has been made of Prime Minister Scott Morrison's last election victory, where the "quiet" Australians backed him over Bill Shorten. This is the most crucial part of any conservative renaissance in the Labor states such as Western Australia, Victoria and Queensland.

The national narrative is important, especially with a federal election looming in the next six months, but the key to the conservative ascension is in the states.

A former high-profile Labor premier once told me that Queenslanders would "never vote for a Socialist leader", when asked if former Queensland deputy premier, Jackie Trad, was electable as a premier.

That rationale rings true, particularly at federal level. Anthony Albanese is from the Left. It's an albatross around his neck.

Most Australians are honest, hard-working people who believe in a fair day's pay for a fair day's work. They are aspirational and still believe strongly that a house is a man's castle, and that castle is well and truly worth striving for.

With housing affordability, a massive issue in 21st Century Australia, policy framework that gives hard-working Australians a leg up is crucial. The Berejiklian Government in NSW – a conservative government – is trying to phase out stamp duty to give first home buyers a shot at securing property. It's innovative policy.

Federal Treasurer Josh Frydenberg has deftly navigated the policy course during the COVID-19 pandemic, juggling essential welfare support with ensuring that there is still enough incentive in policy to make people want to get back to work. The results have been nothing short of spectacular, with unemployment now around 5 per cent. Let's not forget it was tipped to be 15 per cent this time last year yet the economy bounced back with renewed gusto.

The challenge now for the Commonwealth is to ensure that the massive handbrake on the economy – red and green tape – is jettisoned. Now is the time for federal, state and local government to open the floodgates to developer investment in big projects. Councils and state environmental authorities have a responsibility to clear the decks of ideological fantasy, engineered by daft bureaucrats.

The problem for the Labor-Left and Greens alliance is that it wants to kill jobs rather than foster and encourage them; it wants to close coal-fired power plants, instead re-skilling miners to become baristas. It wants to chase crazy renewable targets which will send the country broke, while other big emitters like China, just laugh at our stupidity.

Chinese president Xi Jinping has committed to a zero emissions target for China by 2060. How convenient. He'll be dead by then, as will most people in decision-making roles right now. If China has zero greenhouse emissions by 2060, if I'm alive, I'll join the Greens. Not going to happen.

And therein lies the conservative movement's biggest advantage going forward – it's the Labor Party and the Greens and the lessons to be learned from both.

Firstly, the lesson from the Greens is simple. Whatever they say or do, enact the opposite. They are a rabble and, except for delusional, easily influenced millennials, they have nothing to offer.

They are a great advertisement for voting conservative and Morrison's "quiet" Australians are awake to their wokeism.

It is becoming increasingly clear that the Left faction of the Labor Party has become the party's dominant influence. Its cosy relationship with the union movement is a terrible look. While Labor bans donations from developers to political parties, it takes tens of millions of dollars from union thugs who run rampant on construction sites. The mob in New York in the 1980s did the same thing until they were caught on hundreds of hours of wire transcripts detailing how the Mafia Commission ran the city.

Again, private enterprise and voters who think about their politics are awake to this nonsense. Only the darlings of Twitter, dumbed down by their own idiocy, fall for this ruse.

Fundamentally, the conservative movement in this country has much to offer. Morrison could be less reactive to the ABC and *The Guardian*, especially when they start throwing around mud. But, in general, he has done a reasonable job.

Not so his State counterparts, particularly in Western Australia, Victoria and Queensland. Poor performance and internal squabbling has led to three Labor Governments in those States who have no conception of proper governance.

But here's where the LNP must learn from the "spin and win" ways of Mark McGowan, Daniel Andrews and Annastacia Palaszczuk. They are masters of political chicanery but the tragedy for Australia is that a lot of people buy this blustering bulldust.

Stockholm Syndrome is alive and well in the Labor States. It seems people would rather be punished during these times of pandemic by Labor Governments, fiscally and mentally, than cop a conservative administration with little or no talent.

Again, to improve the LNP's performance and standing, it is essential to look at the way Labor operates and learn.

In the socialist States, Labor grows the bureaucracy, knowing full well that most vote for them because they will never cut the numbers.

Labor also appoints the best journalists in the State to amplify its messaging. They have teams of journalists whose explicit job is to send out messaging that paints the government in a positive light. The media teams are unapologetically Labor acolytes and they play a crucial role in formulating policy and executing messaging going into the next election.

They lie and obfuscate and shroud policy in secrecy because they know the truth will not play out well among the "quiet" Australians; but while the "quiet" Australians buy conservative policies at Commonwealth level, they are happy to swallow Labor's rhetoric in the socialist States.

The fact the LNP has been a rabble in the three Socialist states for some time is not lost on voters.

Earlier this year, the internal dysfunction in Queensland was laid bare in a series of Courier Mail and Sunday Mail exposes which depicted a party in organisational crisis. Moves are being made to fix this and they must be led by the Queensland LNP leader, David Crisafulli. That same level of dysfunction exists in Victoria and Western Australia.

Where the Labor machine really excels at State level is in mounting an election campaign. With selective amnesia, Labor glosses over its poor economic performance, its scandals and its being a captive of the unions to portray a State with stability and confidence. Nothing could be further from the truth but using the "whatever it takes" mantra, they spin their way into office.

The LNP needs to get hungry and angry. It needs to treat elections and policy reform like as Labor does, a matter of life or death.

Labor hates losing and it confines its internal squabbles, mostly to behind closed doors. When it doesn't, like the Joel Fitzgibbon coal-fired power saga, it ostracises the main characters and gets on with the job of attacking the Tories.

This brings me to the Craig Bellamy strategy. If the LNP wants to win back states like Queensland, WA and Victoria, they need to adopt the Bellamy game plan.

Craig Bellamy is arguably the best club coach of the National Rugby League modern era. He has guided the Melbourne Storm to five NRL premierships, and is the NRL's most-winning coach, with a win/percentage record of 69 per cent, extraordinary. He has wonderful assistant coaches around him, has a brilliant player recruitment structure and plans meticulously for each game.

Bellamy knows when his team runs onto the field they are perfectly prepared for whatever may arise. The fact he had Cameron Smith, Billy Slater and Cooper Cronk as his "spine", for many years, ensured Melbourne were always competitive.

The lesson from the pre-game planning is clear. The Liberals have to be all on the same page, all day, every day, plan meticulously and be ready for anything.

Division is death. At the first sign of enmity or division, the perpetrator must be banished; and the most important component of the Bellamy strategy is that the team must win, at all costs.

It is not surprising that the Melbourne Storm was the team to perfect the grapple tackle, aimed at keeping opposition players on the ground for longer so that defensive structures could be set.

It is no surprise that Melbourne flirted with the salary cap. It is no surprise that Cameron Smith influenced the referee, like no other player. It all adds up to the "edge" needed to win. And take a look at Bellamy in the coach's box when his team plays poorly or is the recipient of a bad refereeing decision.

The bloke wants to win. He has to win. That's the way Craig Bellamy operates.

Labor has that mindset going into most elections. When they get complacent as they did with Bill Shorten, they lose.

The time has come for the LNP to use every trick in the book to win elections. Just like Labor does, just like Craig Bellamy does. Like the NRL, politics is brutal. Only the fittest and fastest survive. Australia needs a strong, conservative political movement, right now, because the tide is turning, quickly.

Australia is in danger of becoming a nation of leaners not lifters, rewarding mediocrity not excellence.

The game plan is simple. Exploit the Labor and Greens alliance and its ridiculous economy-wrecking policies and get fair dinkum about taking Labor head-on.

Nothing is more important in this country right now.

Peter Gleeson is the Queensland Editor for *Sky News Australia* **and a columnist for Queensland's** *Courier Mail* **and** *The Sunday Mail.* **He is the former editor of** *The Sunday Mail, Gold Coast Bulletin* **and** *Townsville Bulletin.* **He has also worked at** *The Times* **in London. Beginning his 40-year journalism career in Grafton with a cadetship for** *The Daily Examiner,* **Peter went on to write for the** *Gladstone Observer,* **after which his career in writing for metro mastheads in Brisbane began where he is now arguably the most-read opinion columnist in Queensland. He has a passion for thoroughbred and greyhound racing.**

17

TYRANNY OF TRIBALISM: WHY IDEAS TRUMP IDENTITY

Alex Dore

When a black man was killed by police in Minneapolis, the global Black Lives Matter movement erupted – riots, protests, violence, outrage, social media posts and wall-to-wall coverage; yet professional sportspeople "take the knee" to signal their deference.

US police are twice as likely to shoot a black person as a white person, but it goes mostly unmentioned that they are 20 times more likely to shoot a male than a female. In Australia, men are 10 times more likely to be imprisoned. They are 18 times more likely to die in custody.

So why do we focus on race but not gender? Why do we care about the possibility of one bias, but not another? The truth is that these statistics run against the preferred oppression hierarchy of the Left. This is the irrationality at the heart of modern identity politics.

In their book, *The Boy Crisis*, Dr Warren Farrell and Dr John Gray propose an answer, "To win wars, we had to train our sons to be disposable. We honoured boys if they died so we could live. We called them heroes." How else could we accept the new age gender wisdom that the world is – and always has been – run by and for the benefit of men; that we have had a system of "male privilege" since time immemorial, even though a boy born in 1900 faced a future of national conscription and economic depression. In fact, from a population of just 5 million, over 400,000 Australian males enlisted to fight in WW1; over 60,000 of them died and over 150,000 more ended up wounded or captured. Though an elite few men subsequently served in Parliament and ran large companies, masses of young men were dying on an industrial scale. How can we possibly call this "male privilege"?

The simplistic narrative of male privilege may defy common sense, but it is exactly the image painted by identity activists today. We are told that Australia has a "male history"; that we are hopelessly affected by "unconscious bias" and "toxic masculinity" perpetuated by a "patriarchy". We're warned of "mansplaining" and "manterrupting" by "angry white men" and told that merit, science, Australia, AFL, and even algorithms are actually sexist.

This essay challenges these claims. In doing so, it explains how identity politics is contributing to cultural and institutional decay and how this ideological battle is not a break-point, but a continuation of the conflict between collectivism and individualism. It seeks to understand why the Right has fallen for the trap and how our leaders can start fighting it; and, in doing so, it seeks to prove that the contest of ideas still trumps the politics of identity.

The Left is resurrecting a failed experiment

Identity politics contends that we should treat people on the basis of their "group identity" – attributes like race, gender, sexuality, class – rather than their individual merits, aspirations, and capabilities. Old collectivists, motivated by the work of Karl Marx, saw the world through the lens of social class. People were to be treated on the basis of their relationship to the means of production, as proletariat or working class, bourgeoisie or capital class. New collectivists retain many of these assumptions but view social structures as a product of race, sexuality, gender, and other identity attributes.

Yet from the Soviet Union to Cambodia, China to Zimbabwe, human history is littered with the ruins of this ideology. Over 10 million were sent to forced labour-camps or 'gulags' in the Soviet Union. In *The Gulag Archipelago*, Aleksandr Solzhenitsyn recounts how a person's suspected class alone was proof warranting punishment, with state-owned newspapers openly declaring:

> "We are not fighting against single individuals. We are exterminating the bourgeoisie as a class. It is not necessary during the interrogation to look for evidence proving that the accused opposed the Soviets by word or action. The first question which you should ask him is what class does he belong to ... These are the questions which will determine the fate of the accused."

This was formalised discrimination aimed, so its proponents claimed, at overcoming historical injustice by one group against another. In practice, it became a mechanism of categorising and then delegitimising political opponents.

When collectivism was applied to race, as in Zimbabwe and South Africa, where land and property reforms were instigated to evict white farmers, two burgeoning nations, with promising futures, imploded. We now see two economies in tatters and their societies ravaged by division and poverty. This is the destructive conclusion of identity politics.

Even in democratic India, deciding social outcomes according to immovable identity groups (in this case, by caste) has stymied growth. In *The Narrow Corridor*, Daron Acemoglu and James Robinson explain:

> "The caste system has produced a society fragmented against itself and a state that lacks capacity, which is nonetheless unaccountable as the fragmented society remains immobilised and powerless ... Just as Ambedkar pointed out, society is divided against itself."

This caste-approach is described as "economically irrational" because "it involves an attempt to appoint tasks to individuals in advance, selected not on the basis of trained original capacities, but on that of the social status of the parent." The "dogma of predestination" is like building "a palace on a dung heap". This division is not the means unto itself. By dividing people into groups, the Left seeks social reengineering, second-guessing individual choice.

Yet for all their differences, both the old and new collectivism involve the dehumanisation of the individual, stripping back the complexity and nuance of a person and instead treating that person on the basis of class or tribe. This is exactly what gender activists seek to do. Where first-wave feminism had a liberal heart, focused on universal rights like suffrage, property rights, and employment, new-age feminists demand redistribution, tribalisation by identity, and voting based upon and policies directed towards these tribes.

Any evidence that defies the simplistic gender-war assumption is dismissed and ignored. People are defined merely by their category; a tyrannical world view because it robs the individual of the ability to break free from these constraints. As Jordan Peterson explains, "You don't know anything about my background You don't know anything about where I came from. And it doesn't matter to you. Because fundamentally to you, I'm a mean white man."

This tribalism has infected our institutions

And yet, right across the West, we are falling for this rhetoric. Many have given in. Employers now openly practice discriminatory hiring practices on the basis of gender and race (Queensland's Crime and Corruption Commission labels it "corrupt manipulation"). Corporates openly impose "targets" – quotas in disguise – on their promotion processes. We impose compulsory diversity training and we talk of people's "lived experience" as a precondition for having an opinion on an issue. We've even changed language to enable "preferred pronouns" like they/them and "zem/zey", alongside a new list of 54 genders.

Schools now promote this ideology, painting young boys as prospective domestic violence abusers. At one school, boys are asked to stand before a school assembly and apologise to the girls simply because of how they were born. Soldiers, Nobel laureates, Oscar winners and even barristers now face gender selection and that's not to mention the hidden discrimination like government procurement policies, which require female employment targets, even when building a hospital or school. Everywhere we look, gender politics is afoot.

'Woke' gender politics does not work

Despite all the talk of "inclusion", the folly of the gender crusade is that it drives people further apart. It creates a zero-sum game of adversarial and competing interests, insisting that in order for women to win, men must lose. This diminishes all of us and inevitably invites counter-cultural pushback. Their claims are easily dismantled.

Gender warriors are misleadingly selective when it comes to the facts. We hear about female under-representation on boards and in parliament. AICD Chair, Elizabeth Proust, has gone so far as to threaten, "The boards of our largest companies have 10 months to prove to the community that they take the issue of gender diversity seriously." But we hear no mention of other disparities: that men die younger (by an average of 4.1 years, a bigger gap than even 100 years ago), are more likely to die at work (consistently > 95% of work-related fatalities are men), are less likely to go to university (~60% of domestic university students are female), are more likely to commit suicide (a rate 3 times higher for men), and fill jobs most likely to be impacted by automation (for example, 89% of people employed as machinery operators or drivers are men). Truth is more complicated than the gender narrative can admit, but by dividing people into categories and insisting their category is determinative, activists seek to create a self-fulfilling prophecy.

Female quotas are imposed by almost all large corporations, despite 60% of industries recording a hiring bias in favour of women. In these industries, the proportion of women employed was higher than the proportion of women in the respective labour pool for that industry. A study by the Australian Public Service yielded similar results. It found that when references to gender were removed from resumés, male candidates were more likely to be hired than when their gender was known. These are not outlier examples. In the NSW Liberal Party, for example, where activists consistently demand gender quotas, the evidence suggests no measurable bias against women in the selection process. In fact, since 2016, 48% of candidates were women, but they accounted for 56% of preselection winners. These are inconvenient truths for woke gender warriors.

All of this creates an incredible dilemma. Not only is it morally wrong to treat someone on the basis of their 'group identity' – on the basis of an attribute out of which they cannot break – it also leads to bad outcomes. People of merit miss out on positions, creating an outcome that is less efficient and meritorious. This worsens division and feeds resentment, creating an in-group and an out-group, a group of winners and a group of losers.

Perhaps the critical flaw in identity politics is its inability to reflect human nature. Despite its rhetoric of "empowerment", it ignores that when empowered to make a choice – free of formal barriers – men and women tend to choose differently. Consider that there are no formal barriers to entry for men in teaching. Men can choose this profession and yet a mere 15% of primary school teachers and fewer than 2% of early childcare staff are male. Were the proportions reversed, a preferred tool of gender activists would be rigid gender quotas – but how would that work here, given analysts predict a teacher shortage by 2030 of between 11-14 thousand teachers in NSW alone, and to make matters worse, teacher quality is dropping with fewer high-ATAR students selecting teaching as a first choice? While programs to incentivise entry may ameliorate the problem, a quota would merely reduce quality unless the supply of male teachers was to increase. In other words, it requires people to make different choices. Far from 'empowering' individuals, a quota presupposes that they should be choosing differently – that women should choose subjects like engineering and mathematics, and men should choose teaching. The modern gender war is still delineated by equality of opportunity versus equality of outcome.

Other woke assertions are made-up entirely. We constantly hear about the 'gender pay gap'. The *Workplace Gender Equality Agency* (WGEA) reports an average gap of 13.5% between men and women. This is curious given the ironclad laws that make it illegal to pay men and women differently for the same work. In fact, when we compare like-for-like – the same hours, work, tenure, education, and industry – the gap disappears. Take the case of Uber. A study of 2 million Uber drivers found that while men were paid 7% more than women, this entire difference was due to differences in driving location, experience and speed, not a bias in the gender-blind algorithm. Gender activists don't have a solution to this "pay gap" because they can't even correctly identify it – and why would they, when their existence depends upon the presence of a problem.

Perhaps the most insidious assertion of gender warriors, is that a person needs "lived experience" to voice a view on "female or male-issues"; that opinions and ideas should be discounted, or dismissed, based on the "privilege" and "identity" of the speaker. This absurd oppression Olympics assumes that only people who belong to a particular "tribe" could ever hope to understand them – it has dispensed with empathy. As NSW Upper House MP, Natasha Maclaren Jones MLC explains:

> "[I]t implies that only men can represent men, only seniors can represent seniors, only children can represent children, and so on. Ultimately it will create a situation where other groups claim representation based on religion or age. The fact remains that as elected representatives, our role is to represent our constituents regardless of age, gender or race."

It is impossible to seriously confront bad ideas on their merits under such rules. And so, the tyranny of tribalism risks overtaking the law of logic.

The Right has not been immune

Such has been the force of the new collectivist movements that even centre-right politicians have swanned to the siren song. This has manifested itself in two distinct responses. There are the appeasers who have adopted the rhetoric of the Left, promoting specific "women's budgets", introducing radical "affirmative" consent laws, despite legal consensus that this would unfairly shift the onus of proof to an accused, and proposing gender quotas in political parties. The Liberal Party now diverts money to a campaign fund solely for female candidates, ignoring the fact that in an environment of scarce resources, a rational political party should direct funds to the seat where it'll make the most impact.

Then there is the counter-cultural Right, which has tended to adopt its own exclusionary identity politics, focused on white working-class men. In her book, *Political Tribes*, Harvard Professor Amy Chua observes that:

> "For decades, the Right has claimed to be a bastion of individualism, a place where those who rejected the divisive identity politics of the Left found a home. For this reason, conservatives typically paint the emergence of white identity as having been forced on them by the tactics of the Left... this leaves the United States in a perilous new situation: with nearly

no one standing up for an America without identity politics, for
an American identity that transcends and unites the identities
of all the country's many subgroups."

On all sides, this gender politics is creating real and lasting damage.
It is creating formalised discrimination. It is encouraging division
and it is promoting the idea that your label matters more than your
merits.

Politicians should show bravery

As institutions cascade under the pressure of identity politics, there
is cause for hope. Increasingly, Australians understand that this
gender activism may be causing harm. Consider a national survey of
two thousand Australians by the 2030 Foundation. It showed that
46% of Australian men believe that gender equality measures do not
take them into account and 42% believe that men and boys are being
increasingly excluded from measures to improve gender equality.
Stunningly, millennials, a generation subjected to a relentless stream
of political correctness in schools and universities, reported being
more likely than any other generation to feel that men are excluded
from these measures.

An IPSOS poll reiterated this astounding sentiment, finding that just
25 per cent of Australian men and a minority of Australian women
say they identify as a "feminist". Contrast this with the media or
academia, where you would struggle to find a single person with this
opinion, driving home the massive gulf between ordinary Australians
and the 'elites' in the media.

This is a truth of great importance and inconvenience for the Left.
Dividing people by gender and age is difficult in a society that
values the family unit, because these building blocks transcend the
group identities. It is difficult to turn a mother against her sons
and a grandson against his grandparents. Identity politics might be

undergoing institutional creep, but it has not yet captured the hearts and minds of the mainstream.

The solution is time-tested

Today, amidst the ascendency of loud demands for "inclusion", politics is more tribal and balkanised than ever before. Gender is just one of the special attributes being weaponised by the Left. But the Right has a tested and compelling antidote to this political tribalism, a unifying response to the societal fragmentation stoked by identity politics.

By incentivising creativity, inventiveness and hard-work, liberalism has lifted hundreds of millions out of poverty, promoted freedom all around the world and actually empowered civil rights movements. It looks at people as individuals, rather than labels, and therefore sits in natural partnership with meritocracy. This is a critical partnership, because reward based on merit encourages aspiration and social mobility.

By revitalising our message and confidently reclaiming the debate and by reiterating our unwavering belief in the power, potential and dignity of the individual, we can prove that liberalism is still the most enduring, progressive, and decent organising force in human history. And we should shout, from the rooftops that the contest of ideas will always trump the politics of identity.

Alex Dore convenes Liberals for Merit and sits on the State Executive of the NSW Liberal Party. He is a management consultant at a global professional services firm, and previously served as President of the NSW Young Liberals. Alex is a Non-Executive Director of a national sporting organisation and Youth Ambassador for Australians for Constitutional Monarchy. He holds a postgraduate law degree and a Bachelor Degree in Economic

Theory and Public Policy from Sydney University. He is a life member and the longest-serving former President of the Sydney University Liberal Club.

18

BIG PICTURE IDEAS: THE INFRASTRUCTURE DILEMMA

John Alexander OAM MP

Australia is the 'lucky' country, or so we are told. Looking at how we survived through 2020, perhaps that is right; but looking at the inequalities peppered through our society, it is clear that luck is not shared equally across this country.

Recent inquiries conducted by the Parliamentary Standing Committee that I have had the good fortune to Chair, exposed huge sums of taxpayer money being pocketed by lucky landowners. As alarming as the evidence is, we are embarking on a course of even greater injustice.

Essentially, the evidence of our inquiry *Fairer Funding and Financing of Faster Rail*, revealed that in the entrenching of land-based inequality that could easily be seen as a modern-day equivalent of the feudal system of Lords and tenant serfs, the government has a duty to ensure that all Australians pay their fair share of tax and, equally, when they invest taxpayers' funds, there should be a fair return on that investment.

In the normal course of development, land is bought with a plan to gain rezoning on the back of the developer putting in the required infrastructure – including roads, water, and power – to provide for the subdivision of the land. The developer will often build houses or may just sell the improved sites. All costs are born by the developer and, if successful, are deducted from revenues with the resulting profits taxable.

I should point out that the "developer infrastructure" is different from government/taxpayer-funded infrastructure, things like post offices, schools, a very fast train, an inland rail and, dare I say, an airport. And here is the rub.

The question is what should happen to landowners/speculators when they are provided with taxpayer-funded infrastructure and favourable zonings by government which then deliver enormous profits from infrastructure paid for by the government/taxpayer?

For example, the evidence before this inquiry cited the dramatic impact on land values, in the region of the proposed Western Sydney Airport. In short, the government is investing tens of billions of taxpayer funds into a new international airport and supporting facilities. Lands impacted, which previously were dairy farms and the like, will now be transformed into mixed residential, industrial and CBD commercial centres adjacent to transport hubs. Those who bought all this land, years ago, now enjoy unconscionable profit.

Australians getting rich on real estate is not new. It is a sad historical truth that Australians, to a greater degree than that of any other country, have become rich from real estate. While the British empire became rich from trade, the United States from entrepreneurial innovators, and the Chinese from cheap and efficient manufacturing, from the earliest colonial times, right through to today, the gaining of wealth through land has proved our stock in trade. Our early mercantile heroes are not entrepreneurs like Henry Ford or Thomas Edison. They are exploiters of free land grants like John Macarthur and that says a lot about how we have made money since.

Donald Horne coined the phrase "the lucky country" as an indictment of our reliance on our inheritance and in order to make a call to do better. The overuse of the phrase has hidden its true meaning but we are not just the "lucky country" because we are fortunate; we are the "lucky country" because we rely on our good fortune rather than on hard work and intelligence to get ahead. Our wealth is lucky but it is also lazy.

This fortunate wealth is today reaching new heights. Dairy lands in the area around the new Western Sydney Airport have moved in value since the announcement of the airport, from around $2,000 per acre to over $10 million per acre because they are close to a proposed metro rail station with high rise development approved. This stupendous uplift, caused wholly by taxpayer funded infrastructure nearby, has been entirely pocketed by the lucky landholder.

The lucky country has presented many with very good luck but as things are, the current small generation of superstars of good luck will only be exceeded by their next, more elite iteration. If the taxpayer has been the funder of this good luck, should not the taxpayer participate in the spoils?

What are the alternatives? Around the world, the simplest solution seems to be value capture mechanisms that ensure those who benefit from infrastructure contribute to the infrastructure that made them wealthy. Our inquiry heard evidence from officials representing the Republic of Korea detailing how they fund their high-speed rail network, and MTR who develop and operate the Hong Kong metro rail. Both these organisations explained that they fund their infrastructure by hypothecating the funds they earn from selling land or leasing buildings near the infrastructure itself, utilising the huge uplift in value created by the provision of this infrastructure. For decades, Japan has also funded its Shinkansen high-speed rail in a very similar way.

We also have examples here in Australia. In the ACT, when a

developer seeks a lease variation there is an impost of 75% of the increase in value. By way of example, the Medic brothers bought land at Badgerys Creek for $3.5 million and, reportedly, recently sold it for $500 million. Under the ACT structure, 75% of the $500 million, minus the purchase price, would come back to the government/taxpayer. The Medic brothers would still have walked away with $125 million, $122 million more than their initial investment. Hardly an unfair proposal. Meanwhile, the taxpayer gets reimbursed $375 million which can go into the provision of the infrastructure, freeing up other funds that can strengthen our welfare, education or health budgets and put downward pressure on taxes. At the current rate, as this region grows, in time, all the cost of the infrastructure would be met by this just, equitable and fair impost on the lucky.

Other States are also getting involved. Just this year, Victoria has proposed a windfall gains tax which demands extra tax contributions when a home is sold following rezoning and the home has thereby gained more than $100,000 in value. In the NSW budget of 2021, there was an announcement of an infrastructure contributions system. This is even better than the Victorian system in that it applies to new infrastructure as well as rezoning, ensuring taxpayer funds are recouped for taxpayer-funded infrastructure.

These State-based systems are fine but not as efficient as a federal version could be. Indeed, it could be said that the states have been forced to create these new systems to compensate for the lack of action from the Federal Government. While State action is good, imagine how great federal involvement could be if the uplift from light rail lines and metros that move people dozens of kilometres could raise such huge sums.

What about High-Speed Rail lines traveling hundreds of kilometres to open up our regions, or freight airports that connect the inland rail with the world?

A Federal Value Capture System could access capital gains taxes as well as further contributions. In the Medic case, a capital gains tax would be paid on the difference between his gross $125 million and the original price of $3.5 million. Working closely with State and Local Government, the Federal Government could collect these funds and redistribute them to the States as it does with the GST. To work, it would need close co-operation with all three levels of government, which would certainly be a silver lining for everyone.

Detractors raise two issues, both of them spurious; one of fair value and one of taxation.

Many people complain that for this system to work, the value of land before announcement must be known in order to correctly attribute the growth created by the infrastructure. This much is true. But they go on to raise concerns that there is no way of having this certainty. This is a patently ridiculous claim, defying the good work of the Valuer General, data collectors and the system by which councils charge rates. Purveyors of this argument are clearly trying to throw up arguments to defend the indefensible.

The second issue can be thornier as it is the issue of politics. It is regularly pointed out that any party that puts this forward would be attacked by the other as raising an unfair tax. This is, of course, rubbish. What could be fairer than asking for a portion of the funds that made an individual wealthy to be returned to those who created the source of the newly found wealth? Besides, if your house rises in value, without rezoning or infrastructure, you would keep the capital gain. But where there is politics, there is mischief, which is why it was so pleasing to see all parties agree to the recommendations from our latest inquiry into these matters. I hope this bipartisan vision can continue to deliver on such an important work.

Bipartisanship is important here because this could set up a vision and plan for Australia that will outlast any term of government. If we want to shape Australia for tomorrow, we'll need more infrastructure and we'll need a way to pay for it.

Which brings us to today and the need to invest, in the Treasurer Josh Frydenberg's words, "phenomenal amounts into infrastructure" which will ultimately be funded out of debt and future taxpayers in order to pay for the "phenomenal amounts into infrastructure". This must raise serious alarm.

If we continue to fail those who elect us to govern in a just, equitable and fair fashion, the grossly inequitable scenarios that have played out in Western Sydney will be repeated time and again with the lucky getting rich beyond belief and the taxpayer footing the bill with interest.

Will we again take from the taxpayer and give to the select rich or will we seize this opportunity to install a fair and equitable distribution of the wealth created as we relieve our major cities of the entire load of growth and endow our regions with a fair share while sustainably funding the essential infrastructure to achieve this great vision? If we fail to seize this opportunity, the Commonwealth of Australia will be replaced by a kingdom replete with Lords and impoverished serf tenants, destined to never own their own home.

A great leader would mine this for all it is worth and would ride to each successive election on its back to the cheers of the great majority.

Or do we opt for the lucky for some country?

John Alexander OAM MP is a former professional touring tennis player and currently the Federal Member for Bennelong. He was first elected to the Australian Parliament in 2010 and serves as Chair of the Standing Committee on Infrastructure, Transport and Cities. During his tennis career, he was the youngest player to represent Australia in the Davis Cup and one of Australia's longest-serving Davis Cup players, representing the country from

1968 to 1983. In December 1975, John achieved a career best singles ranking of World No. 8. He served as captain of the Australian Fed Cup team and worked as a sports commentator for *Channel 7* and British television networks for over 20 years. He is known for his extensive knowledge of tennis, both in historical terms and technical. Prior to entering Parliament, John was Managing Director of Next Generation Clubs Australia and also managed a variety of small businesses in the retail and sporting sectors.

19

STAYING THE COURSE:

THE CASE FOR SKILLED MIGRATION

Julian Leeser MP

Australia's migration success

Migration has been a feature of Australia's story since Europeans stumbled ashore from the boats of the First Fleet. Through the contribution of their knowledge, enterprise and initiative, migrants have helped to build the prosperous and successful society Australia has become.

Australia remains one of the most attractive countries in the world in which to live. Australia is one of the world's oldest continuous, democracies, a stable, free society with the rule of law; a successful multicultural nation free of social unrest with natural beauty and a temperate climate. Australia's response to the Covid-19 pandemic has also demonstrated that we have good leadership and systems that work.

Former Prime Minister Tony Abbott was fond of saying, "To be born in Australia is to win the lottery of life."

It is little wonder that people would want to migrate here.

We will decide who comes to this country

We have never been a country of open borders but we have always been a country which seeks to use our migration program to help build the human capital needed to boost our nation's economy, skills base and defence and strategic interests.

Public confidence in Australia's migration policy is vital to its success. If people think the program is well managed and Australia is getting the right people, there will be greater support for the program. Support tends to diminish when people feel we have lost control of our borders or hard-working Australians are being taken for a ride by people trying to game the system.

This was the case during the Rudd/Gillard/Rudd Years where people smugglers tried to bring 50,000 people to Australia on 800 boats leading to the loss of 1,200 lives at sea. It was also the case during the Hawke/Keating years when the migration program was dominated by family reunion with more than one in three migrants being dependent on welfare. In both instances, this led to a loss of public support for the migration program.

Australia's migration tradition is not the American tradition of "give us your poor, your weak, your huddled masses, yearning to breathe free." Australia has always believed in a migration policy which serves our national interests; this was best encapsulated in former Prime Minister John Howard's immortal phrase: "We will decide who comes to this country and the circumstances in which they come."

While the Left have spent decades trying to tell us we are a nation of racists, the truth is that Australia has successfully integrated one of the largest and most diverse migrant populations on earth and it is the rigour of our migration system that has enabled this. There is nothing enlightened about implementing a careless migration program and then failing to integrate migrant communities. To do so is to create fertile ground for racial tension to grow. Much of Europe now battles with those mistakes.

Unlike the Left who have ignored the importance of integration, the Morrison Government's interventions in settlement services and reforms to the Adult Migrant English Program to ensure that migrants can speak English, are designed to create a more integrated and unified Australia. Without English, a migrant can, to paraphrase Jonathan Sacks, be physically here but mentally elsewhere. We cannot be a successful society if nearly 1 million people have little or no English especially when only 13 percent of those who don't have English are in work.

Australia has been unashamedly committed to a migration program that has been selective, methodical, and rigorous and that has ensured that those who arrive are most likely to integrate. Selection of migrants has been at the heart of our integration project.

The big change in our migration policy occurred in the years after 1996 where the program switched from being 70 percent family migration to 70 percent skilled migration. This enabled the program to not only find people who would work and contribute meaningfully, but fill gaps we otherwise could not fill ourselves. Migration became a tool for upskilling the Australian population as a whole.

Migration makes a positive contribution

Today around half the Australian population was either born overseas or had at least one parent born overseas. Our migrant communities have contributed to the social and economic fabric of Australian life, setting high standards for contribution and achievement.

Speaking in 2006, John Howard put it well when he said:

> "No country has absorbed as many people from as many nations and as many cultures as Australia and done it so well.

The strength of a culturally diverse community, united by an overriding and unifying commitment to Australia, is one of our greatest achievements and one of our great national assets."

Australian support for migration is extremely high. According to the latest Scanlon Report, 90 percent of Australians believe that "someone who was born outside of Australia is just as likely to be a good citizen as someone born in Australia." Seventy-one percent of us think "accepting immigrants from many different countries makes Australia stronger" and 62 percent believe the migration intake is "about right or too low."

Recent figures from the Department of Home Affairs illustrate the strong economic performance of skilled migrants compared with the rest of the Australian population. In terms of employment rates, 18 months after arrival, 94.3 percent of all skilled stream migrants were employed compared to 62.3 percent of the Australian population. Participation rates for skilled migrants were 96.7 percent compared to 65.6 percent for the Australian population.

The children of migrants are also likely to perform better in school than those of non-migrant parents; and migrants who have become Australian citizens are less likely to be unemployed than the rest of the population.

The economic benefits of migration for Australia are beyond doubt.

A 2016 Lowy Institute report found "Economic immigration to Australia has produced net economic benefits in terms of helping to offset population ageing, contributing to higher levels of GDP growth per capita, and improving labour productivity." While the 2018 *Shaping a Nation* report from the Departments of Home Affairs and Treasury, found migrants, particularly skilled migrants, are a net fiscal benefit to the economy.

Today, our immigration system is being studied worldwide by other nations who are dealing with ghettos and racial tension that threaten the cohesion of their country.

It is in regional Australia where migration is having the greatest positive impact.

The Regional Australia Institute analysed the 2016 Census figures and found that in the preceding four years, 151 of 175 regional Local Government Areas "increased their overseas-born and decreased their Australian-born population. In other words, for 151 LGAs, their population increase was solely due to international migration."

Skilled migrants are providing vital services in regional communities which are needed to support the very existence of those communities. For instance, at Shepparton base hospital, 75-80 percent of their medical staff are skilled migrants. Despite this, the hospital still deals with staff shortages and needs more skilled workers.

It is therefore no surprise that there is a very high level of support for migration in regional areas.

In some regional communities, unemployment is well below the national average and so migration to those areas is vital for the sustainability of regional communities. Without migration to regional communities, ultimately there will be a capital flight from those communities and their future will be bleak.

Skilled migration benefits Australia

While Australia's migration project has been extraordinarily successful, there is growing ambivalence about the future of the program.

In recent years, concerns about the liveability of cities and the concentration of migrants in particular locations have sparked reasonable questions about whether large-scale migration has run its course and have led to calls for a shrinking of Australia's migrant intake.

Familiar opposition is also being mounted by those on the far-Left and the far-Right who believe that migrants take Australian jobs and that if we bring in migrants we stop investing in Australians.

Australia's productivity is not threatened by the arrival of migrants who are entrepreneurial and skilled. On the contrary, those skilled migrants are what will place us in the best possible position to develop greater productivity and to grow. Those migrants need to be welcomed and encouraged to make Australia their home. As other countries follow Australia's lead and become more selective about who they take in, we are in a global competition for the best talent from around the world. We would be foolish to shut up shop and turn in on ourselves.

Harold Holt was Australia's second longest serving Immigration Minister and, as Prime Minister, dismantled the White Australia Policy. Delivering the Monash Lecture in 1967, he suggested that Australia's migration program had five key benefits. The Migration program he said:

a. Underwrites the future growth of consumption demand for a wide range of products and acts as an insurance against under-employment.

b. Enlarges the domestic market by allowing economies of larger-scale production.

c. Speeds up technical progress and an increased supply of skilled workers to manufacturing industry on which the onus rests to help bridge the gap between import spending and export income.

d. Stimulates a high rate of capital formation and a widening capital base.

e. Assists the supply of labour in areas and industries to which native born Australians are least attracted.

These benefits are as true now as they were then.

Staying the course

Our path forward needs to be one of ongoing commitment to a migration program that is designed to serve Australia's interests.

Australia's comparative success in handling the Covid-19 pandemic has also presented us with an opportunity to focus on attracting highly talented individuals and businesses to Australia. This is an opportunity we will never get again and we need to ensure Australia gets those settings right.

Because of the closed borders resulting from the Covid-19 Pandemic, an exodus of 500,000 temporary visa holders many of whom were skilled migrants, and failures of Australia's education system over a generation, Australia is now facing significant skills shortages.

Our unemployment rate is now 5.1 percent, 1 percent below pre-Covid unemployment in March 2020; job vacancies are at a record 362,500, the highest since the ABS began measuring them in 1979.

The skills shortage is a problem which is reflected in more than just the effects of Covid. Australia's low birth rate will also put a strain on Australia's economic performance. As the 2021 Intergenerational Report demonstrated, Australia's fertility rates will continue to decline in every State and Territory over the next decade as the population continues to age. Our working-age population will increasingly be under strain as the ratio of taxpayers to non-taxpayers declines. Put simply, we need more workers to support our ageing population.

Unfortunately, for a generation, Australians have failed to undertake study in technical trades and hard sciences and engineering. The effect of discouraging people to pursue careers in the trades and away from Science, Technology, Engineering and Maths, has caused persistent skills shortages for a range of occupations including mechanics, carpenters and electricians, nurses and other allied health professionals, doctors, vets, a range of engineers and workers for the digital economy. These professions have all been placed on the Priority Migration Skilled Occupations List.

The National Skills Commission recently put out their Skills Priority List, identifying Australia's national skills needs. There are 57 occupations the NSC identified as having a national shortage with strong future demand for the occupation. There are a further 86 occupations they identified as having a national shortage with a moderate future demand for that occupation.

Part of a longer-term solution will be to reorient Australis's education system to better meet our skill needs. However, that won't solve the problems today or tomorrow and it will never provide all the workers Australia will need at the level of experience to meet business needs. In some areas like nursing, there is a global shortage causing fierce competition to attract and retain nurses in Australia's health care system.

This is why a migration program, with skilled migrants as its focus, remains vital to Australia's future. Skilled migrants create Australian jobs. Australia's employers prefer to employ Australians over migrants – they understand the culture of the country, do not incur the costs associated with employing migrants and can fill vacancies more quickly. However, there are not always Australians available with the skills needed. Skilled migrants are not replacing Australian graduates, nor are they replacing unskilled unemployed Australians, but they fill the missing middle of our economy, including people who can train Australians and whose presence in a business can create more Australian jobs.

For decades, Australia's migration program has positioned us in an enviable position globally. We know how to ensure migration is a net-positive for the country and we must continue to be unapologetic about proceeding with a program that works economically and socially.

I hope that for decades more, Australia will be enhanced by those who arrive, ready to contribute, and with a commitment to our values, institutions and future.

Julian Leeser MP is the Federal Member for Berowra and Chair of the Parliamentary Joint Committee on Migration. Prior to his election, Julian was a senior executive at Australian Catholic University. He served on several Boards including Mercy Health, Teach for Australia and Playwriting Australia. Julian was previously Executive Director of the Menzies Research Centre. He also worked as a lawyer at Mallesons Stephen Jacques (now King & Wood Mallesons) and was an associate to High Court Justice Ian Callinan AC. Julian was the youngest councillor in Australia when he was elected to Woollahra Council at age 19. Julian was also an elected delegate to the Constitutional Convention in 1998 as part of the No-Republic ACM team. Julian has degrees in Arts and Law from the University of NSW and is a Graduate of the Australian Institute of Company Directors. He spent 2006-2007 as a Visiting Fellow at the Taubman Centre at the John F Kennedy School of Government at Harvard University. He has co-authored or edited a series of publications including, *An Australian Declaration of Recognition (2016), State of the Nation (2013), Don't Leave Us with the Bill: The Case Against an Australian Bill of Rights (2009) and State Policy Perspectives (2006).*

20

THE SIDE OF OPPORTUNITY
David Crisafulli MP

In 1960, a man known as Frank took the biggest leap of faith in his life. At age 40, he rolled the dice and left his homeland of Sicily to head to our country without knowing a word of English. He was one of the late movers to North Queensland after a bold decision by successive Queensland governments to expand the sugar industry. Words were not his strong point but hard work was and he found success with each swing of a cane knife, forging a future for his family. Frank was my grandfather, a man short in stature but big on ticker.

As with many people, my philosophy on life was shaped heavily by the early influences of my family experience. Whether it be the stories of my grandparents coming to this country with nothing and building a life for their family, or the immeasurable work ethic of my parents that continued the dream, I learned that anything was possible. Australia was truly the land of opportunity.

While I didn't realise it at the time, these early experiences pushed me towards the Liberal National Party when my interest in politics developed. The protection and promotion of the individual is a core belief of the LNP. What does this mean to me? It means that government should facilitate an environment where any person, regardless of their situation, has the opportunity to realise his/her dreams, large or small.

Economy for purpose

The Liberal and National Parties of Australia have a hard-earned reputation for being responsible economic managers. While we should be proud of this reputation, it sometimes gives the impression that we are devoted to the bottom line rather than people. Responsible management of the economy is merely a tool to achieve our core mission – to provide people with the opportunity to live their lives, raise a family and fulfill their dreams. For the next three and a half years, as Opposition Leader, and beyond then as Premier, this is what I will seek when I talk about the economy.

The mistaken theme is that managing an economy is all about money; in truth, it is much more complex than that. Governments often shout about record spends, but that is the easy part. The great example of this is the ongoing crisis in Queensland Health. Ambulance ramping has seen people wait over 10 hours to get to hospital after suffering serious medical episodes. Tragically we have been told stories of people dying in the arms of family members because they haven't been able to get into a hospital to receive the life-saving care they needed. The Queensland Government's response has been to trumpet the record spend on health despite the fact they are losing control of delivery of service. This situation outlines that an economy that focuses on inputs rather than people will rarely achieve what must be the ultimate goal – policy outcomes that create a better life for people tomorrow than the one they have today.

My focus is not merely on the economy, but rather on an economy for purpose. Often our side of politics will talk about a strong economy that can provide engineering masterpieces in the form of local roads and bridges.

Why is that important? It is important because the time saved on the drive home allows people more time with their loved ones, or more time for small and family businesses to get their product to market, or for emergency services to have the best chance of getting patients to hospital. For business, time is money. Any small business owner will tell you that if you are sitting in a traffic jam, you are not making a dollar.

It is time for leaders to dream big on infrastructure, as we did in the era of the migrant success stories of my late grandfather. It was under Frank Nicklin that state development took on a whole new meaning with the doubling of roads and the doubling of irrigated land, while mining truly found its feet. Nicklin was proof of the value of humility and respect for the then Public Service. The standards he set for his team are a benchmark we must follow today. Similarly, a strong economy can deliver positive results for law and order. But again, what does that mean for the person in the street? It means that people in Townsville can drive through an intersection without the fear of a stolen car smashing into them. It means the tradie in Pine Rivers doesn't get up in the morning for work, only to find his tools have been stolen. The seemingly intractable problem of today is that offences are being committed by a cohort of criminals who see crime as a recreational activity, a game, a joke. They refuse to take responsibility for their actions and believe that society should simply carry the burden of their existence. Lines in a budget alone will not fix this. It needs the changing of laws and the knowledge of those who wear a blue uniform that the government has got their backs. Again, it is not just the dollars but rather a focus on creating a better life for the community.

Small Business vs. Big Business

It has been a great frustration of mine that, in some quarters, our Party is seen as the one for big business. This belief is counterintuitive to me. As someone who is unashamedly dedicated to creating a better life for the people I serve and to protect individuals from the excessive power of large organisations, both corporate and government, my focus is squarely on small and family businesses. Of course, I support big business insofar as they provide jobs and security for individuals; but the soul of any vibrant community is a beating small and family business heart.

They've been the forgotten people of the lockdowns we have seen during COVID. Decisions taken with apparent disregard for the greater community good have left many with stock they can't sell, staff they can't keep and dreams they can't cling to.

Transparency

Transparency and accountability matter. There is a reason I named a Shadow Minister for Integrity. Government conducted in the dark is fundamentally wrong. It is essentially saying to the people you serve that you do not trust them with the information to make decisions about their own life. The more sinister manifestation of a lack of transparency is deliberate deception.

I believe if we care and value individuals, we must share information with them that impacts them. We must trust them with information that allows them to make informed decisions. A government should value this transparency and the trust it engenders.

I believe that democracy is served well when voters go to an election informed. Appropriately, there is always pressure on political parties to provide robust costings for their election policies. The claims and counter claims of political actors about each side, do nothing for the cause of democracy; it only adds to the confusion of the process.

In a unicameral parliament, transparency matters even more. The Queensland Parliamentary Committee System is not as robust as it was designed to be. The Budget Estimates process has become a protection racket for underperforming Ministers and scrutiny on policy costings is paper thin.

I have committed to establish a Parliamentary Budget Office and start the journey towards transparency. This is a small investment in a large shift in the way we respect our democratic process. The Parliamentary Budget Office will produce an intergenerational report that sets out a long-term strategy for Queensland. It will provide a vision and a road to get there. It will ensure Queenslanders know the truth at election time by producing a pre-election economic financial outlook to be delivered six weeks before the start of the election period. It should be available to the leaders of all political parties.

Conclusion

These are just a few of my thoughts on what effective, centre-right, government looks like. I have tried to make this about process not people and policy not politics. Where I have used examples, it has been to illustrate the values and consequences of differing approaches.

I support a customer service, focused style of government; a government that prioritises service delivery for its people. In 1960, that meant more government buildings, today it's the ability to get timely resources through a phone app.

I support a government that puts small and family business front and centre when reforming the regulatory agenda. In 1960, that meant extra land under cropping; today it means new trading opportunities in a global world.

I support a government that values transparency. In 1960, that meant standing on a soap box on a street corner; today it means releasing your data every month to drive cultural change.

In the end, that's the only way we are going to open up opportunities for the next generation of "Franks" keen to take a leap of faith and see our great nation as the land of opportunity.

David Crisafulli MP is the Leader of the Opposition in the Queensland Parliament and State Member for Broadwater. First elected to the Queensland Parliament in 2012, David was one of just three members of that parliament who were appointed to Cabinet at the start of their first term. In the Queensland Newman Government, David served as Minister for Local Government, Community Recovery and Resilience until 2015. Following the 2015 State election, David established a small business offering planning and government strategy advice and relocated his family to the Northern Gold Coast. Prior to entering Parliament, he worked for *WIN News* in North Queensland and was appointed Chief of Staff of the Townsville newsroom in 2002. David was also a correspondent for *The Australian* and *Sunday Mail* newspapers before working as a Townsville-based adviser to the Federal Government. In 2004, he became the youngest person elected to the Townsville City Council; serving on the Council for almost eight years, including nearly four years as Deputy Mayor from 2008. He was the Council's Planning and Development Chairman. Born and bred in Ingham in North Queensland, David and his family now reside on the Gold Coast.

21

A SEPARATION OF CHURCH AND STATE, OR RELIGION AND POLITICS?

Senator the Hon. Alex Antic

When Prime Minister Scott Morrison spoke at a Pentecostal conference in early 2021 about being called by God to his role, many in the mainstream media, and on social media, criticised him for violating the principle of the separation of Church and State. According to critics, the Prime Minister was striving to transform Australia into a theocracy, with himself as the great high priest.

One commonly hears this objection whenever controversial policy clashes with religious convictions, for example, in debates about abortion or euthanasia. Advocates of these ideas argue that Australia is a secular country and that, while everyone is entitled to their own private religious views, religious convictions are a private matter and should not play a role in shaping public policy.

This is strange given that, according to the 2016 census, roughly 60% of Australians identify as religious – 52% of those as Christian. It is therefore inaccurate to apply 'secular' to Australian society as a blanket description, as though Australians are not a religious people.

Saying that religion is a private matter amounts to saying that being religious is fine, so long as one's religious views don't affect one's behaviour at all. If an individual expresses a religious conviction or attempts to persuade someone else to adopt their position, they run the risk of being accused of "forcing" their views onto another. Religious convictions on morality and identity are generally construed as harmful by the radical Left.

Did Australia's founding fathers envision a hostility towards Christian perspectives when they drafted the Constitution? Some of those draftsmen spoke of a secular government, while others described Australia as religious. There are several factors to consider.

Firstly, it is worth noting that the term "Separation of Church and State" does not appear anywhere in the Constitution. What does appear, however, is a reference to "Almighty God":

> WHEREAS the people of New South Wales, Victoria, South Australia, Queensland, and Tasmania, humbly relying on the blessing of Almighty God, have agreed to unite in one indissoluble Federal Commonwealth under the Crown of the United Kingdom of Great Britain and Ireland, and under the Constitution hereby established... .

Whether a reference to God should be included was debated by the founding fathers, who ultimately concluded that God should be referred to because religion was important to the Australian people.

Secondly, when people refer to the Separation of Church and State in the Constitution, they are usually referring to Section 116, which reads:

> The Commonwealth shall not make any law for establishing any religion, or for imposing any religious observance, or for prohibiting the free exercise of any religion, and no religious test shall be required as a qualification for any office or public trust under the Commonwealth.

In other words, the government may not create an established state Church, like the Church of England; require that anyone practise a particular religion; prevent you from practising your religion, or discriminate against anyone based on their religion.

Unpacking each of these provisions is more than this brief essay can accomplish; but suffice to say that the Constitution, in no way, states that religion is not welcome in public life; rather, it seeks to protect peoples' basic freedom to practise (or not to practice) a religion.

Furthermore, many simply misunderstand what the term "secular" meant to the founding fathers. For them, 'secular' did not mean a repudiation of religion in public life but instead it meant a different way of living out the virtues inherited from a Christian tradition.

Academic historian Dr Stephen Chavura, in his interview with former Deputy Prime Minister John Anderson, describes a census undertaken in 1867 by the Victorian government, in the lead-up to the *Education Act 1872* which removed state funding of non-government schools which posed this question to Victorians: "How do you understand the word 'secular?'" This is what was reported back to the committee:

> If they [Victorians] are spoken to about secular instruction, they will tell you they are in favour of it. But they mean by that that they are always to have a chapter of the Bible read every morning. I find this is their understanding of the term "secular instruction".

This sentiment was common in Australia at the time, yet these words would appear virtually nonsensical to most contemporary Australians, especially those who insist that secularism means keeping religion out of politics altogether.

Dr Chavura explains that the purpose of Australian secularism was not the suppression of religion but avoiding sectarianism by not favouring one Christian denomination over any others. Dr Chavura writes:

> Ultimately the question [of whether the state or churches should be primarily responsible for education] hinged on whether general religious education could be substantial enough to teach the essential tenets of Christianity and also nonsectarian enough so as not to alienate any Christian denomination (Catholics in particular).

The term "secular" is derived from the Latin for "of this age." If etymology is anything to go by, a secular political system is one that is concerned with temporal matters – things which affect people in this life such as freedom, individual rights, and law and order in order to create a flourishing society, rather than eternal matters such as what happens to the soul after death.

Of course, according to the logic of many Australians during the nineteenth century, to create a flourishing society, there must be a common moral ground upon which citizens can stand, or else it runs the risk of collapsing because people cannot agree on what constitutes the good life.

The founding fathers were British men who were profoundly shaped by their Christian heritage. To them, the basis for morality was Christianity or, at least, the existence of God. If you had told the founding fathers, or many Australians, up until roughly the 1960s, that religion has no place in politics, you might as well have said that morality has no place in politics.

Contemporary Australians derive their moral principles from Christianity far less than in previous generations. Perhaps the West's moral turmoil and confusion over basic questions such as "what is gender?" is the fruit of this spiritual erosion.

As Carl Trueman writes in his book *The Rise and Triumph of the Modern Self*, "moral discourse today is so fruitless because it lacks any commonly accepted basis on which moral differences can be discussed and assessed." We were once more united in that vision, but now there is little common ground between conservatives and progressives.

However, Australians still derive their morality from Christianity far more than they realise. So much so, in fact, that we forget that many of the moral principles which we take for granted are not the natural state of things but rather the result of centuries of tradition and philosophy that we hastily dispose of at our own peril.

We forget that, prior to the emergence of the Church in the ancient world, slavery and military conquest were commonplace (rulers had no qualms about utterly annihilating their opponents). Women were deemed inferior to men and there was no such concept as universal basic human rights. The notion that all people were equally endowed with dignity, regardless of their social status, was simply unheard of.

The Christian religion changed all that and as Christianity spread across the globe, slavery eventually became untenable. The charge to abolish the slave trade in Britain was led by an evangelical Member of Parliament, William Wilberforce.

Those who claim that the West was built on slavery while also deeming Christianity harmful or oppressive would do well to remember that it was the doctrine of the image of God that led to the end of slavery in Europe and was the theological basis for those words which the American abolitionists relied on – "We hold these truths to be self-evident, that all men are created equal, that they are endowed by their Creator with certain unalienable Rights, that among these are Life, Liberty and the pursuit of Happiness." We should also remember that slavery is far from dead in places where Christianity has not been so influential.

Because of Christianity, women came to be afforded dignity and respect. In fact, there may have been more women in the early Church than men because Christianity afforded them rights, dignity, purpose, and safety that was previously unknown to them.

It is ironic that many of the same people who wish to keep religion out of politics usually adopt a distorted vision of human rights, often predicated on a Marxist concept of class struggle, that is cut off from the theological convictions that gave rise to the concept.

People often talk about a separation of Church and State, but what they are describing is a separation of religion and politics. The fact is, everyone brings their religious views to the table, whether they realise it or not. We all have views about God, the human person, the soul, what happens after death, good and evil, the good life, and what makes a flourishing nation.

Would those who wish to keep religion out of politics dispense with all the virtues and accomplishments that Christianity has given to our society?

So next time someone tells you that religion has no place in politics, remind them that without religion virtually all the moral principles that they take for granted would not exist. Without religion, Australia would not have become the great nation that it is; and without religion, Australia will become much less than it can be.

Senator the Honourable Alex Antic is a Liberal Senator representing South Australia in the Federal Parliament. Before entering Parliament, Senator Antic completed a Law Degree at the University of Adelaide, worked as a commercial lawyer from 2002 to 2019 and served as a Councillor on the Adelaide City Council from 2014 to 2018. He is the Chair of the Senate Standing Committee on Publications and a member of the committees for: Foreign Affairs, Defence and Trade, Rural and Regional Affairs and Transport, Law Enforcement, Australian Commission for Law Enforcement and Integrity and National Broadband Network.

22

HOW TO SAVE THE NATION
Professor David Flint AM

This Commonwealth of Australia, the singularly advanced democracy our forebears bequeathed to the safekeeping of this and future generations, is in a serious state of decline. What we are losing are the promises of federation. Already the home of some of the most advanced democracies the world had ever seen, federation was to unleash a proud nation intended to become a leading, wealthy, technologically advanced, civilised and benevolent world power on the patterns set uniquely by the United Kingdom and the emerging United States, with a mission to support liberty and freedom across the world.

Corowa Plan

A politician at and before federation was far more likely to be acting on what the great Edmund Burke said he owes the electors, his independent judgement. Dare he do that today, he will be consigned to the back bench or forced out of the party.

Yet even then, the politicians were unable to deliver federation.

When it seemed that the blueprint had been achieved by the first appointed convention in 1891, the politicians bickered over its proposals with the process "broken down hopelessly". It was clear they would never agree. The solution was to come from a people's conference at Corowa where Sir John Quick proposed a plan to hand the question over to the Australian people to resolve.

Once that plan was put into operation, federation was achieved with the widest involvement of the people. This was done through a mainly elected convention, one which consulted widely and, through referendums in the states (in most States two referendums), obtained the approval of the people.

That was not all.

The premiers, or most of them, then took the long sea voyage to London to shepherd the Constitution, as Imperial legislation, through both houses of the Imperial Parliament at Westminster and then to obtain the Royal Assent of the revered Queen-Empress, Victoria.

This was done with neither computers, jet aeroplanes nor armies of advisors and consultants.

The creation of this new great nation, from the convention election through to the Proclamation on 17 September 1900 by Queen Victoria at Balmoral signifying that she was satisfied the Western Australians wished to join and then bringing the new nation into existence on 1 January 1901, took less than four years.

Using essentially 19th Century technology today, we were unable, in four years, to lay a tram track down George Street, Sydney or build what we desperately need, dams and coal fired or nuclear power stations, much less obtain a fleet of outdated submarines.

It is well-established that the reasons for the success of some countries and the failure of others is neither race nor, as Venezuela demonstrates, even the rich resources they may enjoy. It is sound institutions.

Australia was fortunate to have sound institutions inherited from Britain and mixed with those of the United States. A significant number of our institutions have since been captured by various elites, too often for the advancement of unworthy purposes.

What Australia needs today is a second Corowa Plan.

Decline

The second decade of this, the twenty first century, has seen a remarkable decline.

Changing the great advantage of having the lowest electricity prices in the world to not only the dearest but also, in an increasingly unreliable system – endorsing the transfer of manufacturing in a naive belief in the advantages of abandoning protection unilaterally; and in the allegedly free trade practiced by a hostile genocidal communist dictatorship, presiding over an economy registering significantly lower growth rates than the rising economies to the North; rushing to adopt every new fashionable dogma released by American Neo-Marxists; presiding over a dramatic fall in educational standards; a criminal justice system which seems more concerned with the criminal than with the victim; creating increasing dependency by persecuting farmers and self-funded retirees; making droughts and floods far worse than they should be; refusing to engage in a vigorous plan to harvest water across the country; insisting on a massive immigration intake which adds to the overcrowding and unbearable expense of housing especially in the capitals; running up massive debts; raiding the defence budget to buy votes, needlessly undermining the morale not only of our soldiers, sailors and airmen but also of those who would enlist – our politicians seem determined to turn Australia into, if not the Venezuela, the Argentina of the South Seas.

It is difficult to think of any one problem confronting Australia which, if it were not created by the politicians, has not been made significantly worse by them.

And in these endeavours, the politicians are supported increasingly by the elites who have replaced the ancient values of our Judeo-Christianity with the dogmas of a new and alien religion.

Reasons for decline

Our core institution, a federal representative democracy, has been seriously damaged by the emergence of a rigorously controlled two-party system captured by cabals of powerbrokers, factional leaders and lobbyists.

How did this come about?

The reasons are interrelated.

First, a little noticed but continuing judicial coup d'état which has, contrary to the original intention of our Founders and of the Australian people then, and in every referendum put to them, turned the Commonwealth into the most centralised federation among comparable countries.

Second, the formation of what might as well be called an Anti-Australian Alliance between party powerbrokers and the proponents of a new and alien religion.

Continuing judicial coup d'état

In the nineties, when Australians for Constitutional Monarchy were running the NO Case in the republic referendum, I was asked to advise on the likelihood of a rejected referendum being approved in a subsequent vote.

I found that whenever Australians were asked to vote again on an issue they had previously rejected, they always voted No. Sometimes they had been asked up to five times.

But then I noticed something extraordinary. In those referendums seeking the transfer of more power to Canberra, that is most of them, not one would be needed today by the power-hungry in Canberra. For all intents and purposes, they already enjoy those powers. This has been effected by the High Court giving provisions in the Constitution a meaning intended neither by the Founders nor by the people who approved them, nor indeed by the Australian people when subsequently asked to agree to a transfer of that power.

This is unacceptable in a democracy.

The Founders biggest mistake was not to turn us into some politicians' republic. Nor was it not to 'recognise' the Aboriginal people according to whatever the latest fashionable version of 'recognition' is.

The Founders biggest mistake was to copy the United States institution, the Supreme Court, uncontrolled by any checks and balances.

The Founders, who were well versed in the US Constitution, would have been well aware of the notorious Supreme Court decision, Dred Scott v. Sandford. Some believe it caused the Civil War. Deciding that the Constitution protected slavery and that slaves and descendants of slaves could never be citizens, the court struck down the modus vivendi, the political compromise, between free and slave-owning states, the Missouri Compromise.

Perhaps the Founders thought that by making the Australian High Court the nation's general court of appeal, which the US Supreme Court is not, they would ensure the Australian judges did not take to judicial activism.

In any event, they compounded their error in allowing an absolute power to the judges to interpret the Constitution as they wished, by vesting the sole power to appoint judges effectively in the Federal Cabinet. The result was predictable. Judges would tend to be chosen from those who could be expected to see the Constitution, consciously or unconsciously, through Canberra's centralist eyes.

The Founders could have also spelt out clearly what everyone, including the High Court until the 1920 coup, assumed was the constitutional intent. This was that any power not specifically listed as a Commonwealth power, exclusive or shared, was obviously reserved to the states.

That 1920 decision has gradually made Canberra more powerful and taking a greater proportion of taxes than any other central government in any comparable federation.

The result has been to turn our federation into the most fiscally centralised in the world with Canberra collecting a vastly higher proportion of the nation's taxes, more than 80%, than in any other comparable federation. About one third is handed to the states with a good slice of that, about one third, being grants subject to conditions allowing Canberra to intrude into state powers.

There have been at least four disastrous consequences for the country.

First, instead of state governments having to justify how they spent state taxes to their electorates, which is a fundamental principle of federalism, they escape responsibility by blaming Canberra for any problem, thus confusing the electorate as to who is responsible.

Second, the resulting massive duplication and waste costs Australians, on one authoritative estimate, over 10% of GDP. This is AUD $185 billion, not once but every year, money poured down the drain.

Third, with both Canberra and the states trying to run the same power, the resulting confusion leads to serious mismanagement. In the case of education, this has been infiltrated by Neo-Marxists who are indoctrinating children with an alien agenda. At the same time, they are seriously running down standards which have fallen significantly below those of other countries.

Fourth, Canberra pays inadequate attention to some of the most important powers given to them by the Constitution, especially the most important one, defence. It is not too much to say the result is that Canberra has left the nation next to defenceless.

Alliance between party powerbrokers and the elites

The second reason for our decline is that our once strong institutions have been compromised by the power brokers who control the major political parties and therefore representative democracy to an extent unknown in any other comparable democracy.

Rather than most candidates being chosen on merit, more and more candidates are chosen from a class of apprentice politicians. We are then represented by politicians who have done little more in life than live and work in the political world. There they have learnt the arts of manipulation, lying and backstabbing and the need for a patron or patron powerbrokers who will hopefully deliver a safe electorate to them.

What Australia needs – what Australia once had – were politicians previously successful in their work in the real world, including trades, professions, farming and small business, and who were guided by strong ethical principles and common sense. They did not see politics as a life-long career culminating in an early retirement into some well-funded sinecure, even one funded by a hostile genocidal communist power.

Australia's establishment or ruling class is made up of those politicians coming together with all the elites who today dominate so many of our institutions, from big business, the various national organisations who claim to represent groups from business to farming, and as well the academy and much of the mainstream media, especially the taxpayer-funded segment. This ruling class has become an Anti-Australian Alliance which is, brick by brick, bringing the nation down.

Among this ruling class, religion has not declined, as is so often claimed. What has happened is that our Judaeo-Christian religion, which so successfully provided the values of our civil society, has been replaced by a new religion manifested by a succession of increasingly outrageous dogmas to which the rest of us are all immediately expected to bend the knee. These dogmas are all discredited theories ranging from man-made global warming to those monstrosities, critical race theory and critical gender theory. They are all designed to ensure the self-destruction of our nation and all of the West.

These dogmas emanate from the new and fashionable religion which is Neo-Marxism. This form of Marxism tries to fill the vacuum created by Marx's greatest error, that the workers of the world would rise up to bring in a communist utopia. They never did.

From Lenin himself, new ways had to be found to take power. Realising Lenin's coup d'état could not be easily copied, Gramsci proposed a takeover from inside, a long march through the institutions. With this, Marcuse proposed the takeover of culture and the identification of break-away groups to imagine discrimination and destroy those democracies by disunion from within. The long march has been so successful, it is now often difficult to determine, from what governments actually do in office, to see much difference between the politicians of the major parties.

A second Corowa Plan to save the nation

To those who ask whether it is too late to save the nation, the answer must be a firm NO. Think of the achievements of the Magna Carta, the Glorious or Bloodless Revolution of 1688 and the American Declaration of Independence. What Australia needs is a bloodless revolution based on the precedent born at Corowa. The fact is that our Constitution, now aged over 120 years, has never been the subject of general review by the people. They have only been asked by politicians to approve changes which they usually realised would only damage it.

It is more than time for a second Corowa Plan under which the people would elect delegates ☐ neither unpaid nor endorsed by any political party — to a convention to review the Constitution. After the convention developed a draft there would be a decent period for public consultation and debate. With the benefit of that, the convention would then adopt a final version with a series of questions to be put to the people in referendums to be held soon after.

The politicians will only agree to a second Corowa Plan and actually put the referendums if there is very strong support for change.

Australians have tried everything else, changing the government, voting for new parties, petitioning the Parliament. A second Corowa Plan would be a revolution but one which is necessary if we can have any hope of saving the nation.

I would hope that the convention would complete the Constitution by what was begun with the referendum provision, making the politicians truly accountable and not just in confected elections with candidates preselected by the powerbrokers, but by introducing control by the people through the tools of direct democracy, as in other countries and especially Switzerland.

This could be done through the Convention adopting what can be called the five Rs: Returning to the Constitution, Reducing Canberra's powers and its excessive taxation, Reforming the political parties and as well, including Recall elections and Referendums initiated by the people.

Australia cannot but decline even more if we continue under the rule of the political class and other elites.

Professor David Flint AM, an Emeritus Professor of Law, read law and economics at Universities of Sydney, London and Paris. He is the author of books and chapters in books on politics, law and economics and comments frequently in the media. He remains National Convenor of Australians for Constitutional Monarchy which led the NO Case in the republic referendum and previously chaired the Australian Press Council, the Australian Broadcasting Authority, the Committee of Australian Law Deans and World Association of Press Councils. In 1991, he received a World Jurist Association award as World Outstanding Legal Scholar. He is a Member of the Order of Australia and a Grand Officer of the Order of the Star of Ethiopia.

23

BACKING THE FORGOTTEN PEOPLE
Campbell Newman AO

The recent publication of the Fifth Intergenerational Report painted a bleak outlook for Australia's economic future. Its release, in the middle of the Covid-19 pandemic, meant it quickly disappeared from the news cycle – which was most unfortunate given the sobering projections that it contained. The scenario of lower growth, higher government spending, ongoing deficits, increased government debt and slower population growth should have been cause for significant reflection and public debate.

The economy is forecast to grow more slowly with growth at 2.6% per annum over the next 40 years compared to 3% over the previous four decades. Now, the economists may be saying that, but I don't actually believe it needs to be so – more on that in a moment.

Nevertheless, for the realists out there, the message is clear that the next generation of Australians will be dealing with lower incomes and living standards and potentially higher taxes and reduced services. Clearly there is a major challenge for our political leaders and their parties but, if the past 15 years are any guide, it currently seems unlikely that they will rise to the reform challenge.

During the pandemic, the move to big government and economic intervention has accelerated. Rather than adopt a mantra of personal responsibility and resilience, the message has been that government has all the answers. The response from a Coalition Federal government has particularly eroded its traditional strength as the home of small government, balanced budgets, lower government spending and low debt.

Sadly, I am convinced that the past 18 months has fundamentally damaged the Liberal Party and its long-term credibility. However, I am also of the view that the "white ants" had already infested the structure long before the pandemic. For two decades, despite positive wins at Federal and State level, there has been a drift from the Liberal and the National parties to minor parties and independents. The primary vote at elections and ongoing polling demonstrates this decline. Added to this is the decline in membership numbers and the aging demographic of the party.

I reflect that the Labor Party faces its own challenges but this essay is not about them per se. Nevertheless, in a recent article in The Australian, Troy Bramston quoted Paul Keating in 2016 lamenting that the ALP had failed to capture the votes of the middle class that had benefited from the reforms instituted during the 1980s and early 1990s. Labor needs to win votes in the centre ground of politics – the aspirational middle class – but it has not been able to develop a policy agenda that can appeal to them.

At face value some consider this to be all bad news for the ALP and good news for the Coalition.

However, a more strategic look at what has been happening in Australia and other western democracies is offered by Thomas Piketty, the French economist. Essentially, he has pointed to a strong trend for the highly educated in the community to support the centre-left with those without tertiary qualifications to vote for centre-right parties. Older, well-educated progressives vote for the ALP while young inner-city professionals have gravitated to the Greens.

The numbers are stark – only 15% of the 18-24 age group and only 27% of the 25-34 age group vote for the Coalition. In contrast, 55% of the 65-plus demographic support the Coalition.

It is therefore time to recognise that the Liberal Party is facing a crisis with its support evaporating and particularly worrying that the young in the community have abandoned the party in droves.

I believe that the problem has arisen for the following key reasons:

- A failure to be true to the stated values of the party and to explain and defend those values;

- The dominance of the Left within the primary, secondary and tertiary components of the education system and its impact on young people;

- The rise and dominance of the professional "political class" that are former political staffers or employees of peak representative bodies. People who don't come from a true business background; and

- The introduction of public election funding which has reduced the need for parties and politicians to fundraise and, therefore, engage with and listen to small business.

It is not good enough to say that you are better than the Labor Party. That is not a compelling pitch for electoral success and breeds cynicism and resentment amongst those that could be genuinely won over. I believe it's this that has led to the fragmentation of the centre-right vote and the drift away from the Liberal and National parties.

So, what's to be done?

Well, at a time of crisis for the centre-right and the Liberal Party, it's helpful to reach back to the words of Sir Robert Menzies. In his iconic "Forgotten People" address of 22 May 1942 he says some things that, 80 years on, still speak with great resonance.

Firstly, he defines the middle class as:

> " ... the kind if people I myself represent in Parliament – salary earners, shopkeepers, skilled artisans, professional men and women, farmers, and so on."

And makes the point that:

> "They are taken for granted by each political party in turn" and yet "they are the backbone of the nation".

He warned that:

> "The great vice of democracy – a vice which is exacting a bitter retribution – is that for a generation we have been busy getting ourselves on to the list of beneficiaries and removing ourselves from the list of contributors, as if somewhere there was somebody else's wealth and somebody else's effort on which we could thrive."

And, in a comment that is remarkedly prescient considering the current response to Covid-19:

> " ... under the pressures of war we may, if we are not careful – if we are not as thoughtful as the times will permit us to be – inflict a fatal injury on our own backbone."

Most importantly:

> "If the new world is to be a world of men, we must be not pallid and bloodless ghosts, but a community of people whose motto shall be, 'To strive, to seek, to find and not to yield'. Individual enterprise must drive us forward."

Based on the expression of these values by the founder, and reflecting on what has been happening, I cannot help but come to the conclusion that impostors have taken over the Liberal Party. They mouth platitudes about their support for the aspirational voters and private enterprise but, when in government, they don't deliver. In short, particularly for small business, they have taken them for granted.

To those serving politicians in the Liberal Party who object to this and say I'm wrong – I say, as someone in small business, you have absolutely no idea and you actually don't want to know. Since leaving politics in 2015, I have watched as you talked "cutting red tape" whilst your government instituted even more.

Again – you are imposters!

Anyway, don't just take my word for it. Bill Lang from Small Business Australia essentially said this on *Sky News Australia* on 1 July 2021.

So, when I stand back and review all the above factors, the conclusion I come to is quite clear. The Liberal Party should reaffirm its traditional values, be true to them again, and relentlessly focus on an agenda to totally support the "Forgotten People" or those who, perhaps, should be called the Disregarded Toilers.

Such an agenda could totally capture the middle ground for a generation, build membership of the Liberal Party, re-establish trust with small business and deliver electoral success.

Such an agenda is true to those voters, particularly older people who support the Liberal Party, as well as restoring faith with those in small business, but it gives the greatest prospect of boosting support amongst the young creatives who are thirsting to get ahead.

Critically, this agenda is strongly differentiated from that of the Labor Party and the Greens.

Here are some initiatives that would make that difference:

1.   Be the party of free enterprise:

Create a comprehensive, national framework for the establishment and operation of small business.

Reverse the insidious erosion of the protection afforded by the "corporate veil" and the imposition of criminal liability on Directors.

Get regulators, such as ASIC under control, by putting in place supervisory Boards with significant small business representation.

Constrain the ATO and put in place a supervisory Board to curb their excesses.

Ensure strong small business representation on the Board of Infrastructure Australia.

Legislate to ensure that the primary objective of the national electricity market is to deliver reliable low-cost power that is benchmarked against our international competitors.

Lock in ongoing accelerated depreciation/instant asset write off for small businesses.

Allow cash-strapped, start-up firms, to issue shares in lieu of cash that are totally exempt from tax until they are actually sold.

Commit to red tape reduction and vigorously resist new forms of regulation.

Have as rule number one that you will always, as a default position, back small business before backing the public servants.

Require local government to approve or reject development applications for small business strictly within 30 days.

Legislate that the key objective of council town planning departments is to support the economic development of Australia.

Bolster competition policy to protect small business from predatory pricing behaviour from large firms and ensure access to low cost, streamlined redress grievance procedures.

Reform employment law to make it easy and straightforward to employ people, under flexible agreements that work for employer and employee and enable people to be safely terminated for misconduct or non-performance.

Legislate to prevent large companies arbitrarily imposing extended payment terms or disregarding commercial agreements with small business and provide access to affordable redress mechanisms.

Reform to law/legal procedures to allow standard, streamlined procedures for electronic execution/lodgement of all legal and contract documents and interaction with government.

Require the heads of government departments to demonstrate that they, personally, are across their website and that anyone of reasonable skills and intelligence can effectively interact with them without the need for specialist assistance.

Ensure that the call centre wait times for regulators such as ASIC, APRA, ATO etc. are kept to below 10 minutes and that staff are required to provide direct contact details if an issue has to be followed up.

Fast track harmonisation of mutual recognition of qualifications between states and territories.

Ensure public service pay increases are not out of step with those of the private sector.

End government funding of elections.

Ensure that political staffers who wish to be pre-selected for elected roles have at least 5 years of work experience in private enterprise.

2. Be the party of home ownership:

Put in place bold policy initiatives to encourage and facilitate home ownership for all Australians.

Remove all government tax imposts on the purchase of the family home for first home buyers.

Work with banks and legislate the creation of special savings accounts that will be exempt from tax if saving for the deposit for a first home.

Require councils to expedite planning approvals for high-rise apartments and broad acre land subdivisions. Tie council Financial Assistance Grants to performance.

Financially support the creation of new public housing but put in place a mechanism to assist public housing tenants to ultimately purchase the property.

3. Be the party of free and liberal education:

Take control of the National Curriculum ensuring that it instils the basics of reading, writing and arithmetic, teaches history and geography and educates young people about our form of government.

Remove social and political fads subjects from the curriculum and hand back responsibility to parents.

Provide financial education and teach money management in schools.

Make political advocacy or activity within schools by teachers and school staff illegal.

Create a national small business education authority with the brief to deliver affordable business courses via private sector training organisations.

4. Be the party of liberty, free speech, racial and religious equality:

Demand reform at the ABC via legislative change to ensure balance, openness and transparency.

Remove all FOI exemptions, require the publication of the

remuneration of staff in line with standards applied to ASX-listed firms.

Legislate that social media companies cannot exclude community members on the basis of political views, only on the basis of the advocacy of violence or criminal activity.

Ensure that our universities fully support free speech and research.

Legislate to stop activist blackmail campaigns against companies and individuals on the basis of their political, religious beliefs or business activities, i.e., if a business activity is legal then a campaign that sets out to deliberately damage that organisation should not be permitted.

Amend section 18C of the Racial Discrimination Act.

Reject the division of Australia on ethnic and religious grounds and promote an integrated, egalitarian community.

Conclusion

These are just a few suggestions but, if implemented effectively, have the potential to send a profound message about the positioning of the Liberal Party with the young and restore faith with the older members of the community and small business.

And, to return to the issue at the start of this essay, it's my firm conviction that a revitalised Liberal Party agenda is the best way of leapfrogging the bleak growth projections in the Fifth Intergenerational Report and the best choice for this country.

Let's back the "Forgotten People" because, 80 years on from the Menzies address, they are again being taken for granted and ignored.

Let us create an agenda that excites people and truly unlocks the entrepreneurial and creative potential of all Australians.

Let's permit them, and encourage them, "To strive, to seek, to find and not to yield".

And guess what?

They will do the rest.

Campbell Newman AO served as Premier of Queensland from 2012 to 2015 and previously held the role of Lord Mayor of Brisbane from 2004 to 2011. During his Premiership, Campbell Newman was involved in the conception and delivery of major infrastructure projects. He is now the Chairman of Arcana Capital, syndicating commercial property investment opportunities for sophisticated investors, a Director and adviser to a number of start-up technology companies and a regular commentator on *Sky News Australia*. Before politics, Campbell Newman worked for six years as an executive for Grainco Australia in the grain storage, handling and logistics industry and also for four years as a management consultant. He also spent 13 years in the Australian Army and served as an officer in the Royal Australian Engineers.

24

WHY VOTE LIBERAL?

Jacinta Price

Australian conservatives have not been skilled at getting their message across or at bringing public attention to their outstanding achievements on behalf of Indigenous people. Those on the Left are very good at mythologising and having their myths accepted and propagated by the mainstream media. It is time we started developing policies based on truth rather than harmful stereotypes. Only the Coalition is capable of doing that in the age of political correctness and cancel culture.

My Warlpiri grandparents lived through desperate and dangerous times. They were born in the bush out of contact with the rest of the world. They survived frontier violence, including the infamous Coniston Massacres., that took the lives of perhaps 200 people in the country in which they were born and grew up. My grandfather was arrested, chained and walked, with several others, hundreds of kilometres then trucked another 100 to Alice Springs where he was induced to labour for the army for five shillings a week.

In the early years after the war, they coped with inadequate rations, spasmodic medical and educational services living in a humpy they built themselves. In the 21 years between 1947 and 1968, my grandmother endured 12 pregnancies. She lost five of her children, still born or in infancy and had a baby taken from her alive but was told that she had died. We now know that she was rescued; her twin brother was dead by the end of the year of their birth. Yuendumu then had the highest recorded infant mortality rate in Australia and one of the highest in the world. It also had one of the world's highest homicide rates.

But life was still safer and more secure than it had ever been before. The frontier violence had ended, internecine violence decreased, food and water supplies were always reliable and they had clothes and blankets and money to buy more of what they needed.

So, what did conservative governments do during this time to improve the lives of my Warlpiri grandparents and their surviving children? The now anathematised policy of Assimilation was applied yapa-nyayirni (those of the full descent like my mother and grandparents) in the 1950's as it had been to yapukaji (those of mixed heritage) since the thirties. Assimilation was most clearly defined in 1963:

The policy of assimilation means that all Aborigines and part-Aborigines will attain the same manner of living as other Australians and live as members of a single Australian community enjoying the same rights and privileges, accepting the same responsibilities, observing the same customs and influenced by the same beliefs, hopes and loyalties as other Australians ...

... the formal government position on assimilation ... was not that Aboriginal culture should be suppressed but that over generations cultural readjustments would be made.

Paul Hasluck, Minister for Territories from 1951, had shown deep concern for the welfare of yapa (Aboriginal people generally) for decades. He acknowledged the 'grim history' of frontier violence that my grandparents had lived through. He wanted protection and segregation replaced with policies founded on legal equality and citizenship rights, with some special measures to raise those needing them to living standards equal to those of all other Australians. My grandparents were obviously among those who required 'special measures'.

During those years, many significant advances towards racial equality were made –

1952: Mining royalties paid for the first time to benefit yapa.

1954: Most yapukaji granted full citizenship rights having been able to apply for them since 1936.

1959: Yapa on missions, settlements and stations eligible for child endowment and pensions.

1962: Right to vote in Commonwealth elections extended to all yapa.

1964: Ward status, prohibited areas, restrictions on movement and association, prohibition on buying and drinking alcohol all removed. Full rights extended to yapa-nyayirni.

1967: Referendum allowing the counting of Aboriginal people in the national census and the Commonwealth to take responsibility for Aboriginal Affairs from the states.

1968: Granting of award wages to yapa workers.

1969: Training allowances for those on remote settlements.

1970: First hand back of reserve land to Aboriginal residents by Victorian Liberal government.

1971: First Aboriginal member of any parliament, Senator Neville Bonner, sitting with the Liberals.

1974 to 1977: First Aboriginal MLA in the NT, Hyacinth Tungatulum sitting with the CLP. First Aboriginal member of Qld parliament, Eric Deeral, sitting with Nationals.

1976: NT Land Rights Act passed by the Fraser Government.

2010: First Aboriginal Federal MP, Ken Wyatt, sitting with the Liberals.

2012: Election of the Giles government in the NT, the first to be led by an Indigenous Australian.

Up until that stage, many Christian and Humanitarian groups, as well as Communists, agitated energetically for citizenship rights for yapa. In the NT, the Half Caste Association and, later the Australian Half Caste Progressive Association, lobbied hard and successfully, on behalf of their own people. These activists wanted to be treated differently from their yapa-nyayirni relatives and openly stated that this was the case.

Full citizenship rights were not extended to my mother's family and other yapa-nyayirni until activists classified as 'wards' organised themselves in the Northern Territory Council for Aboriginal Rights (NTCAR) in 1962. The Social Welfare Ordinance was passed in 1964 at last extending citizen's rights to yapa-nyayirni.

In the NT, the Northern Australian Workers Union had shown little interest in supporting the struggle for the rights of yapa workers. In fact, unionists generally had vehemently opposed equal rights for yapa, and other 'coloured' workers. "Members of the 'coloured race'" and Asians were not allowed to join the union until 1947 though "'half-castes' or 'coloureds' with one 'white' parent were. The union leadership openly admitted that it supported full pay for yapa workers in the pastoral industry in 1927 because they believed that it would lead to the elimination of yapa workers from that industry altogether.

As late as 1964, when the first yapa union organiser was appointed, yapa workers were still thought of as potentially threatening 'a general depression of living standards for all' with 'non-union aborigines ... becoming potential scabs' during industrial disputes.

During the campaign for equal wages for yapa pastoral workers in the late 60s, the union movement "was responding to national pressures and showed little enthusiasm for the fight". The NAWU did not authorise the famous Wave Hill strike of 1966, but was compelled by public opinion to support it.

Yapa workers themselves were not given the chance to put their own views directly during the equal wage hearings. The union refused to call yapa witnesses but insisted on speaking for them. They put up a 'sporadic hit-run presentation' and those on the bench had to do their thinking for them. The Left's claim to be the champion of minority ethnic groups is a very recent phenomenon.

There were problems with Assimilation that could be called unintended negative consequences. Too often yapa were expected to give up their culture and identity in order to succeed. The removal of the ban on alcohol has had a devastating impact on many communities and led to the untimely death of thousands. The granting of equal pay and entitlement to welfare benefits has led to high levels of unemployment and welfare dependency. The granting of Land Rights has led to loss of initiative and rent seeking and control by Land Councils rather than traditional owners themselves. The complexities of the situation made mistakes inevitable. Conservatives do a better job of reform; they handle complexity much better and look for genuine answers rather than impose predetermined shallow, ideological solutions. They are interested in truth rather than slogans.

Those on the Left have distorted history, dismissing the positive achievements of conservative governments and refusing to admit their own errors. They have convinced too many Australians that they own us politically and only they can solve our problems. They insist on telling us what our problems are. Their identity politics have led to those with no experience whatsoever of traditional culture and language, of the worsening crises in remote communities, speaking for those who do live with those experiences, and they never get it right. They can't. They insist that yapa can't take the initiative and change their lifestyles in order to 'Close the Gap' condemning those in the bush to a life of poverty, violence and ignorance.

They mercilessly attack yapa who express views that don't fit into their false narrative. I have seen the 'whatever it takes' attitude in action at every election. They throw massive resources into campaigns against yapa Conservatives. They send in the CFMEU and Get Up. I have witnessed bribery, intimidation, rumour-mongering and even death threats used blatantly. All of the available weapons are used against those yapa who have a mind of their own and oppose the disastrous stereotyping of us by the Left. They are happy to replace yapa women leaders with ineffective white men.

If gaps are to be closed, then behaviours must change. Every human community in the whole of our history has needed to adapt culture, values and behaviours to solve novel problems as the world changes around them. Aboriginal Australians are as capable as anybody else of doing that, if those with their own agendas get out of the way and stop insisting that they don't have to change; the rest of the world has to. That's never going to happen. Aboriginal Australians can adapt in ways that can be called genuinely Aboriginal. It is not about becoming 'more white'. It is about solving new problems their own way.

We must heed the words of the remarkable Neville Bonner who once warned of those attempting to imitate the Black Power movement in the US, "Beware there are those among us who will pit coloured against white and white against coloured, Australian against Australian – they mean to destroy, to inflict conflict on this nation." The Black Lives Matter movement now seeks to do the same.

It is up to the Coalition now more than ever to hold strong to our conservative values and not buckle under the insidious influence of 'woke' ideology. 'Woke' ideology favours not truth nor logic but is an attack on individual freedom, free speech, dignity and facts. Australia's most marginalised have and will continue to suffer if the Left maintain their stranglehold and sustained ideological crusades. True equality is recognising and respecting another human being's agency not convincing them they are victims, incapable of solving their own problems.

When I am asked why I call myself a Conservative, my answer is simple. I am aware of what Conservatives have achieved in the past. When I talk to others, who call themselves Conservative, I am welcomed and treated with respect. If they disagree with what I have to say, they are happy to engage me in respectful debate. They don't vilify me obscenely, try to shout me down or defame me. They don't threaten me with violence or pay rumour mongers to attack my character. Conservatives value truth and decency. It's a no-brainer, really.

Jacinta Nampijinpa Price is a Warlpiri/Celtic woman from Alice Springs. She has worked as a Cross-Cultural Consultant for nearly 20 years to create understanding between Indigenous and non-Indigenous Australia. She is deeply involved within her community as well as communities throughout the Northern Territory. In 2015 she was elected to Alice Springs Town Council. Jacinta and her mother, former NT Government Minister Bess Price, have, for many years, advocated against domestic violence and the need for positive cultural change. Throughout the platforms of television, visual art, music, women's AFL and local government, Jacinta has worked with a number of initiatives to empower young Indigenous children, girls and women.

25

TO THINK, TO SPEAK, TO ASSESS AND TO ACT

Senator Jim Molan AO DSC

Since Secretary Pezzullo's email and similar realistic statements by the Prime Minister, the Defence Minister, and many others, calls for action on our strategic environment have proliferated. But not from all. "Drums of war" might be reverberating around strategic commentary, but still there are those who line up with the comedy character Basil Fawlty's quote: "Don't mention the war!". We should be thinking about conflict and war, we should be speaking about it amongst ourselves, we should be assessing what the nation should do and we should be acting effectively.

Katrina Grace Kelly (*The Australian*, 22 May) thinks that because war is appalling, it is wrong to talk about it. But war is so appalling we must talk about it. Ignoring human experience of conflict and deterrence, but with a token nod towards "not putting our heads in the sand", Kelly denies the brutal role of power in the world. She seems to think that by keeping quiet, our world will see the error of its ways and we can all move to peace and happiness. Last time we tried that, in the 1930s, it did not end well.

"Speak softly and carry a big stick" is very good advice, but only if you already have the big stick. Many well-intentioned Australians seem to think that any stick is big enough, that Australia does not even need a stick, or that even having a stick is provocative. That thinking is wrong but is particularly common on the left, such as in the writings of Max Suich (*AFR*, 16-19 May) and Dennis Argall (*Pearls and Irritations*, 20 May).

Australia is frighteningly vulnerable because, as a nation, we have so little self-reliance and no resilience, especially in shipping, ports, liquid fuels, industry, supply chains, pharma, and stocks. In defence, we lack hitting power, we cannot fight for long enough and our forces are not big enough. Recent Defence studies have clearly stated this. Even at the end of the 10-year investment in the ADF, I doubt we could fight effectively against a peer adversary for more than a few days and I invite anyone to demonstrate I am wrong. Australia has vast security potential, but we seem to have decided, with few exceptions, to not realize it.

War is part of the spectrum of conflict. War is possible because so much of the region is heavily armed. War is becoming more likely because armed forces are moving in close proximity to each other, big issues are at stake and China is aggressive in word and deed. War is not made more likely due to thinking and speaking about it, as long as that creates a realization that Australia should be doing more for self-reliance and resilience, and armed forces' lethality, sustainability and size. In many other parts of the world, this would be called national security, because it takes a nation to defend a nation, not just a defence force.

As a member of the Morrison government, the biggest challenge I face in advocating the above position is that the Abbott, Turnbull and especially the Morrison governments have improved our national security position so much, not just defence but national security in its broadest sense. That must be repeatedly acknowledged. By 2013, after the Labor years, our national security and the effectiveness of the ADF was disastrous. Now the ADF is the best it has been for fifty years with money allocated to weapons, defence industry, intelligence, security and legislation. With the government deservedly talking up its role in achieving that, most Australians think the extra $270bn allocated over ten years buys defence perfection. Only by speaking about war can we put this expenditure, its priority and its timeframe into perspective.

The current threat environment Australia faces is clearly more complex than that faced in living memory. The Morrison Government understands this and is doing more than any previous Government to prepare for the uncertain future. Alternatively, the Australian Labor Party (ALP) is unprepared and unorganised when it comes to our National Security. To highlight this, the ALP's official websites Policy page, entitled 'What we stand for', makes no reference to National Security. The closest they come is talking about Defence Industry development. The Greens are irrelevant and most other public comment is purely tactical – about submarines, tanks and jets. They are not the key issues. The key issue is strategy.

I am immensely proud that the Morrison government has done more for defence and security than any other government since the end of the Vietnam War. The last years of the Howard government were meaningful for defence but Labor blew that away before it could be consolidated. The basis of our national security is our economy and the stability of our society, with our success evident in jobs, health and the last budget. The government and Australians have been remarkably successful in beating COVID and bringing the economy back, and nothing should have a higher priority. Nothing is more important for national security.

The recent budget kept up the delivery of what this government has promised across many challenges in addition to health and jobs. We have now built defence spending to over 2.0% of GDP, with 2% being a floor not a target. Rhetorically, we seem to be recognising that we face the most uncertain strategic environment since 1945. As well,

ASIO and other security agencies have been funded to historic levels, a block of legislation has been passed over the last six years which has brought us well into the 21st Century and we have started the road back in liquid fuel, general manufacturing and particularly in defence industry. Many of our recent achievements are based on the 2020 Strategic Update announced in July 2020, with the PM giving the best Australian speech on defence and security at the strategic level I have ever heard when he launched that strategy and committed $270bn to defence over ten years.

Despite how well this government is doing, the question that still needs to be addressed is: Are we doing the right things in national security and are we doing enough? You cannot even consider that question without thinking and speaking.

As a soldier for 40 years, I lamented the lack of resources generally allocated to defence, but I knew that it is government's business to take risks. We take risks on any number of social issues, on tax, on energy, on politics. The people expect this of us. On most issues, the consequences of getting the risk wrong, of failure, is less than it is in national security. But even in national security, all governments take risk. But how can you take calculated risks without thinking, speaking and particularly assessing all risks?

The risk that we took leading into World War Two was based on our blind faith in the Singapore Strategy. We understood that the naval base at Singapore would be fortified and the Royal Navy would send forces to our region in the case of war with Japan. Everyone knew from the 1920s that Japan was likely to be our enemy, but we arrogantly underestimated them. Australia, like most allies, was woefully unprepared for war in 1939. Even more damaging, based on our belief in the Singapore Strategy, we felt that we could send the best of our army to North Africa, our navy to the Mediterranean, and our air force to Europe.

But if there was any risk calculation conducted in the 1920s and 30s, it must have been based on wilful ignorance. It had been made clear to Australia at Imperial Conferences that if the Germans were active in the North Sea, then at best limited naval forces would be sent to Singapore. We knew it, but it was not something which led government to plan for a high degree of Australian self-reliance and resilience. We grasped at a strategy we knew to be faulty because to think we might have to look after ourselves was beyond our comprehension. We must never make that same mistake again. We can defend ourselves and we must.

Who paid the appalling price at the time of this wilful ignorance? Our inadequately equipped and trained servicemen and women sent north in desperation to be killed, injured and imprisoned. Let us never forget Vivian Bullwinkel and Bangka Island. And of course, the nation thought that we would be invaded and subjugated as the Japanese forces approached Australia. It was not brilliant strategy and planning that removed what was considered an existential threat to Australia. It was the heroism of our defenders and the courage and luck involved in the battles of the Coral Sea and Midway.

Heroism and luck. How moral is it for politicians to overly rely on these for national security? As Churchill rightly pointed out, at the pinnacle of leadership, politics and strategy are one and the same. We continually revert to a belief that the US will save us, and that the presence of the US marines in the Northern Territory will guarantee US attention. But the US warfighting capability is 30-50% less than it was at the end of the Cold War and the recent Biden defence budget proposals did not carry support for the Indo-Pacific that many expected. That should terrify Australians who, without thinking, default to US strength whenever the issue of Australian security arises. And the US Marine presence in the Northern Territory should be understood as temporary, because as soon as tension in our region increases, the US Marine elements are more than likely to re-embark on their ships and sail away. That is what they exist for and that is what they do.

Rhetorically, we are recognising that China is the biggest threat to our security since World War Two. Given the magnitude of the possible conflict we face, much of our security will be up to us. Of course, we should be in alliances. Alliances are our first line of defence, but alliances are only as strong as each alliance member. The US has a severe problem in facing China. The US Indo-Pacific warfighting commanders have been telling Congress they cannot guarantee to deter China and are vulnerable in a number of ways. A recent four-star Indo-Pacific commander predicts war over Taiwan within 6 years. The Quad is the way to go but it is nascent. Japan is powerful as is India, both in different ways. But the Quad is not an Indo-Pacific NATO and has a long way to go to become a warfighting alliance capable of deterring China. We must assume we are responsible for our own defence whilst embracing allies.

The first step in an assessment that might lead to action is to make a judgement on what type of war Australia might face. Our population has trouble thinking about and assessing war because it has no recent memory of serious wars. To revert to the more popular football analogy, in the recent decades we have played two away games with unimpressive military results (Iraq and Afghanistan) and now we must prepare for the big home game, the decider.

So, we cannot say if what we are doing is right for national security without some detail about the nature of the threat we face. Reference to "drums of war" and vague reference to a "China threat" do not tell us anything useful about how many ships or tanks or planes we should have or how we should fight. Until we think and speak openly about the threat in sufficient detail, it is impossible to assess how prepared the nation should be, or what sacrifice the people should make for that preparedness. The Coalition is the government of national security, but it is the people's money and the people's security, and they must be brought with us. There is no security risk in speaking openly about these issues as our likely adversaries will already know more about Australia's national security than 99.99% of Australians. In particular, our likely adversary will know if we are bluffing.

In the absence of other guidance and as a basis for thinking and speaking, I offer my assessment of the kind of conflicts or wars that I think Australia should prepare for, and which should drive our comprehensive risk analysis, our planning and assessment and then our action. The application of many informed minds could, of course, improve my humble version, but they are:

- A continuation of the grey-zone conflict Australia is experiencing now and which the government is handling well. Grey-zone is best defined as "that limbo land between peace and war" and consists of trade and diplomacy aggression, theft of IP, cyber-attacks, influence operations and intimidation such as the "little blue men" of the maritime militia set against the Philippines.
- An enhancement of grey-zone conflict, for example, massive cyber-attacks, unattributable biological attacks, enhanced trade and diplomatic pressure, pressure against allies or all-encompassing action against our maritime trade and our air routes amounting to a blockade. Our ports are our single point of failure in the security of this nation and our capacity to carry our imports or exports in our own ships, or to secure our ports, is almost non-existent. Our sea ports are one of the many weak points of pressure that can be used against us.
- War between the US and China could see Australia as collateral damage though Australia is unlikely to be the main target initially in such a conflict; but Australia may be attacked directly from within that war by cyber, by missiles aimed at coalition forces or strategic targets and with our sea and air movements heavily to totally restricted, more direct

attacks on Australia may eventuate depending on who wins the initial round of battles in such a regional war between the US and China. China's aim will be to win decisively early and to force the US out of the region. What price Australia then?

- Regional war in the Middle East, or elsewhere, alone or in conjunction with opportunistic conflict in our region. Should Iran close the Gulf in a war with Israel and/or Saudi and the Gulf Arab states, Australia will be deprived of 90% of our liquid fuel, with US stocks still 40 days away from being able to power vehicles even if sea lanes are open. As well, the US, given its limited military capability, may be made weaker in our region if it has previously deployed forces to the Gulf, the Baltic or the Black Sea.

These types of conflict and war scenarios, or something like them, created by the Office of National Intelligence, should be our planning and testing scenarios for the ADF and the nation. From such scenarios, the tasks for Australian government action fall neatly out of these scenarios, and actions and acquisitions can be justified. I list my version of the tasks against which we should decide how to act, as follows:

- Form, complete or reinforce alliances, as alliances are our first line of defence. Remember that an alliance is only as good as the soft and hard power capability and intent of each member. The Coalition government is doing well in this area. Sadly, in the post-war period, most US allies used their alliance with the US as an excuse not to spend money on their own defence and so alliances became ineffective.
- Minimise grey-zone conflict impacts, such as cyber, influence, and trade aggression, which we are effectively managing now, but we must also be prepared to manage enhanced grey-zone conflict described above, which are likely to be far worse.
- Be capable of contributing minor military forces to alliances

for small out of region deployments, as Australia has done since 1945, as an option for government.

- Be capable of deploying significant combat forces with the US and other allies, into the region to deter conflict or the escalation of a conflict. This gives the government of the day options. Deterrence only works if those who want to deter are willing to use their forces, and the forces are capable against an aggressor. Therefore, such a deterrent force must be willing and able to fight, and if Australia joins such a deterrence focussed force, losses will be inevitable and success is not guaranteed. This would be a monumental decision for the Australian government, as it was in 1940, given we are a 'one shot' military at present, and the risk involved is monumental.

- Plan to defend the homeland against collateral attacks from within, in a US/China war, such as massive cyber-attacks, blockades and direct missile attack. Australia can do very little to deter a war between China and the US, but it can take steps to deter such collateral attacks on Australia by being prepared for them through national resilience and specific defence and so lessening their impact.

- Be capable of expanding the national security capability dramatically to defend the nation against direct attack and possible eventual invasion, if a war between China and the US does not go in favour of the liberal democracies and the US is forced out of the region. An extreme scenario perhaps but one that must be at least prepared for.

If these assessments do exist in the classified areas of government and are used as the basis for action to meet the above tasks, it is very difficult to see the results that we should all be able to see. If they don't exist, they should. They are terrifyingly massive, which is probably why there is a reluctance to address them, but they are the logical outcome of our current strategic environment and the PM's Strategic Update from 2020.

Such comprehensive preparations take time. It is my fervent wish that war situations never arise, but the least Australia can do now, to deter war, is to start prudent planning and preparation so that we can make mature judgements about the risk we take, particularly if, as is any government's right, we decide not to take further action. If deterrence fails, we must be able to fight and win. The critical step, then, is to assess. The 1930s alternative, that is, ignoring the problem and adapting a strategy of hope, is immeasurably worse and irresponsible; and planning now costs little.

What the Morrison government has done for national security is, by comparison with post-war efforts in Australia, spectacular. But the allocation of funds, the running of programs and even the possession of military capabilities is never an end in itself. What is of the utmost importance is what those forces can do, not what they have. Is our current investment likely to be sufficient to remake a defence force designed for post-World War Two tasks? My judgement is that it is not. Is ten years too long for us to hope that we can make the changes necessary? It is far too long. Can we make the ADF and the nation capable of deterring war or if that fails, winning the kind of war we may now face? Of course, we can and any other view is defeatist. The most important question is not how much we are putting into defence, it is, can the nation and the ADF deter the next conflict and war and if deterrence fails, as it may, can we win? Yes, as long as we think, speak, assess and act – now.

Senator Jim Molan AO DSC is a Liberal Senator for New South Wales and served in the Australian Army for 40 years. Retiring at the rank of Major General in 2008, his service included a broad range of command and staff appointments in operations, training, staff, and military diplomacy. His career saw him deployed to Papua New Guinea, Indonesia, East Timor, Malaysia, Germany, the United States and Iraq. He has been an infantryman, a helicopter pilot, commander of army units from a thirty-man platoon to a division

of 15,000 soldiers, commander of the evacuation force from the Solomon Islands in 2000 and with service in East Timor in 1999. In April 2004, he was deployed for a year to Iraq as the Coalition's chief of operations, during a period of continuous and intense combat. For distinguished command and leadership in action in Iraq, Major General Molan was awarded the Distinguished Service Cross by the Australian Government and the Legion of Merit by the United States Government. Following the 2013 federal election, he was appointed for a year to the full-time position of the Prime Minister's Special Envoy for Operation Sovereign Borders. Senator Molan has a Bachelor of Arts degree from the University of New South Wales and a Bachelor of Economics degree from the University of Queensland.

26

CONSERVATIVES MUST DEFEND CLASSICAL LIBERALISM

Senator the Hon. Amanda Stoker

There are times of stability and times of upheaval. When it comes to conservative politics, we have been experiencing the latter for at least the last five years.

Shifting voter trends, growing public discontent and the emergence of new political challenges have sparked major changes in centre-right political parties across the western world.

These changes can be seen in some of Australia's closest friends and allies, the UK and the USA, where the political orthodoxies were overturned with the successful Brexit vote and the election of Donald Trump. Since Brexit, the UK Conservatives have made major gains in Labour's heartland, while the policy consensus in the GOP substantially shifted under President Trump.

While Australia is yet to experience political shocks of this scale, we are not immune from their effects or the circumstances that caused them. As we deal with these challenges, Conservatives must resist attempts to jettison policies and values that have made us one of the freest and most prosperous nations in human history.

Changes on the centre-right

The changes in the electoral map are not without their benefits. At the 2019 UK election, the flow of votes from Labour to the Conservatives in England's north led to the collapse of the so-called red wall, with the Conservatives winning seats like Leigh and Don Valley – both of which had been held by Labour since 1918.

This not only prevented the election of a Prime Minister who self-identifies as a socialist, it allowed Boris Johnson's government to break the Brexit stalemate and act to fulfil the referendum mandate to leave the European Union.

Unfortunately, there have been some on the centre-right who have attempted to adapt to this political upheaval with policies and proposals that would make us less prosperous and less free. Theresa May, Johnson's predecessor, took this very approach during her short time in number 10.

May's policies for the 2017 UK election included curbs on executive pay, restrictions on foreign takeovers of UK firms, and worker representation on company boards. According to one academic analysis, the Conservatives' 2017 election manifesto was the most left-wing since 1964.

This embrace of economic nationalism has been even more evident in the US, where the positive economic impact of Trump's tax cuts were undermined by the imposition of tariffs on a host of countries ranging from geo-political rivals like China to close allies like Canada.

According to the non-partisan Tax Foundation, Trump's tariffs were equal in their impact to $80 billion worth of new taxes on Americans, equivalent to one of the largest tax increases in decades. By their calculations, the effect of those tariffs would be to reduce long-run GDP by 0.23 per cent, wages by 0.15 per cent, and employment by 179,800 full time jobs.

Oxford Economics, likewise, estimated that US and retaliatory tariffs would lead to tariff-driven price increases costing households between $490 and $1,000 per year (depending how the tit-for-tat trade war played out), wiping out much of the $800 tax cut middle-income households got, on average, in 2018 from the Trump administration.

Of even greater concern than Trump's approach to trade policy are the shifting views among the US's broader conservative movement.

Several prominent politicians – including likely presidential candidates – have abandoned fiscal conservatism and their previous support for free markets in favour of rhetorical attacks on capitalism. They've done this despite clear evidence capitalism has been the most effective mechanism for lifting people out of poverty in human history.

Joining these politicians are a disparate group of intellectuals, journalists, and political activists calling for an end to the conservative coalition that has existed since the post-war era – a coalition that has combined elements from classical liberalism, traditional and religious conservatives, and foreign policy hawks.

Views and perspectives among this disparate group differ, but their goals were spelled out at a 2019 conference on National Conservatism – a term around which many have coalesced. Broadly speaking, they envision a much larger role for government. In the economic sphere they want higher tariffs and greater support for America's industrial sector (with one speaker calling for a National Institute of Manufacturing). They also want to more aggressively use state power to legislate morality and fight the culture war.

In the words of Sohrab Ahmari, a writer who has helped spearhead the push for a new conservatism, their goal is "To fight the culture war with the aim of defeating the enemy and enjoying the spoils in the form of a public square re-ordered to the common good and ultimately the Highest Good."

To achieve these goals, these national conservatives are calling for important classical liberal ideas – ideas about the importance of individual freedom and limits on state power – to be cast out of the broad church of American conservatism.

As Israeli political philosopher, Yoram Hazony, said in his conference speech, "We declare our independence from neoliberalism, from libertarianism, from what they call classical liberalism. From the set of ideas that sees the atomic individual, the free and equal individual, as the only thing that matters in politics."

Importance of liberalism

Ironically, in attempting to rid American conservatism of classical liberalism, these national conservatives are attacking the very ideas on which America was founded – the ideas that provide the philosophical underpinnings of the Declaration of Independence and the governmental structure set out in the US Constitution.

Ahmari conveyed his own attitude towards the ideas of America's founding when he expressed a preference for Spanish colonisation of the Americas over the founding of what became the USA, stating that "Part of our work is recovering the Hispano-Catholic founding of America, which ... enjoyed a much wider geographic sphere and cultural span than the second, Anglo Founding."

For Ahmari, classical liberal ideas are an impediment to waging all-out war against his opponents in the culture war. But if victory in the culture war comes at the expense of the freedoms that underpin our quality of life, then it is no victory at all.

Classical liberalism is the political tradition that delivered the abolition of slavery, led to universal suffrage, and unleashed the greatest engine for economic progress in human history, free market capitalism.

The ideas of classical liberalism are not only important to American history. Fundamental liberal principles like the freedom of all individuals to live their lives in accordance with their values, provided they respect the equal freedom of others, are also at the core of what has made Australia one of the freest and most prosperous nations in human history.

Sacrificing these ideas would amount to sacrificing the aspect of our society that is most worth preserving.

Thankfully, liberal ideas are still deeply engrained in our culture – even though they are taken for granted and undermined by collectivist ideas like identity politics. They are what underpins the dynamism and innovation in our society.

But liberal ideas operate best when they are paired with conservative values like prudence, opposition to radical change, and respect for the institutions that have been proven to work over time – institutions of government, like our Westminster parliamentary system and the common law legal system and societal institutions like the family.

Together, these classical liberal and conservative ideals ensure that our society remains both vibrant and stable, nestled between the chaos that can occur without order and the tyranny that exists without freedom.

The danger of a remote and detached political class

Nevertheless, there is much that Australians can learn from the circumstances that have led to the rise of national conservatism in the US, and ignited populist movements across the western world.

These movements highlight the danger of a nation's political class becoming remote and detached from the public it serves.

No country's political class is immune from this risk, but it has undoubtedly occurred to a far greater extent in the United States than it has here in Australia.

The US Congress's perpetually low approval ratings speaks to the lack of trust and esteem in which America's political class are held, as well as the lack of understanding and human connection that politicians ought to have with their constituents.

At the time of writing, only 26 per cent of Americans approve of how Congress is handling its job. Admittedly, this is higher than in the last months of Trump and Obama's presidencies, when it was 15 per cent and 11 per cent respectively, but it is well down on the 2002 high of 63 per cent.

The election of Donald Trump was in some ways a symptom of this problem. The public had become tired of governments from both sides of politics failing to deliver on their promises – whether it be grandiose promises of "Hope and change", or clearer commitments, like reining in illegal immigration. The result was that in 2016, almost 63 million Americans turned to a reality TV star and real-estate mogul, who promised to "drain the swamp".

Why have the American political class become remote and detached?

Population size provides part of the answer, as it is much harder for politicians to remain connected to the people they serve when each member of congress represents approximately 711,000 people.

It also the result of the US political system, which is designed to make legislative change exceptionally difficult. This has its benefits; it makes it harder for bad laws to be passed. But it also leads to politicians being unable to deliver on their promises, leaving legitimate issues of concern unaddressed.

This problem has only increased as the hierarchical media landscape of the 20th Century has fractured. The internet has turned everyone into a potential publisher, even fringe extremists, and with no requirement for quality or accuracy, it is now far more difficult to achieve public consensus.

The problem of a detached political class also exists in much of the European Union, where decision-making power has progressively been taken out of the hands of national governments and placed in the hands of Brussels-based bureaucrats.

Like in the US, the institutions of the EU have been deliberately designed to limit the influence of the public. But rather than dividing power and pitting institutions against each other in open political conflict – as the US constitution does – the EU has limited the public's influence by concealing the decision-making process within a byzantine bureaucracy and providing democratic accountability as a me fig leaf.

The result, again, is that many of the public's concerns go unresolved, leading to frustration and social discontent.

One of the healthier responses to this discontent occurred mere months before the election of Trump, when the British public seized the once-in-a-generation opportunity to "take back control" by leaving the EU and returning powers to their national parliament.

In other EU nations, the public have shown their discontent with the political class by voting for once-fringe parties, ranging from Italy's Five Star Movement to the Sweden Democrats – a party with roots in Swedish fascism and white nationalism.

Challenges for Australian Conservatives

Australia is not immune to these forces. There are signs that voting patterns are shifting, with Labor increasingly favouring its cosmopolitan inner-city voters over its traditional working-class base.

But social discontent has been limited by both our political system, and the actions of a succession of governments.

Although there are aspects of our political system that are designed to make reform more difficult – such as our bi-cameral legislature – they do not make it so difficult that nothing can be done. By and large Australian governments have been able to delivered on their key election promises and our compulsory and preferential voting system has helped prevent our political class from becoming too remote and detached from the public – aided by our relatively small population.

Widespread social discontent has also been kept at bay by successive governments being willing to respond to the public's concern on issues like immigration, with both rhetoric and action. This factor is crucially important, given the destabilising influence unfettered illegal immigration has had on political systems around the western world.

Despite this success, we must not be complacent. Many of the intellectual trends that created the discontent that led some on the centre-right of American politics to lose faith with classical liberalism are already present in Australia. These include identity politics, cancel culture, intersectionality, critical race theory, and the many other aspects that make up the Woke ideology.

One particular danger is the abandonment of important concepts like personal responsibility and small government. These ideas are not only necessary for the cost and sustainability for government, they also help sustain trust in our democracy.

When politicians offer to solve problems that are properly the domain of individuals and families, they slowly erode freedom of choice and deprive individuals of the satisfaction that comes from personal accomplishment. And, as governments fail to deliver on their grandiose promises, they gradually undermine faith and confidence in our democratic institutions, strengthening the appeal of fringe populists and extremists.

How should Australian conservatives respond?

So how then should conservatives respond to these challenges? How are we to ensure that our conservatism does not merely become progressivism driving the speed limit?

The answer is that we must robustly defend and champion the liberal principles that have enabled us to thrive. First among these are the core values of freedom of speech and freedom of conscience.

We must make the case for these values, not merely because our beliefs should be heard, but because these freedoms are fundamental to what it means to be human. They are at the heart of what is necessary for a person to find their purpose in life, for their personal and spiritual development, for their education and their sense of meaning. They are also at the heart of our prosperity, for they make possible the curiosity and creativity that is at the heart of innovation. They feed our ability to solve problems, which only occurs when we can question, contend with difference and change our minds.

We must make the case for these values from first principles, pointing out that it is only through having the freedom to think and believe, the freedom to discuss what we think and believe, and the freedom to hear other thoughts and beliefs that we are able to learn and develop as individuals. Without these freedoms we cannot develop the critical thinking skills necessary for us to thrive, nor know for sure whether our thoughts and beliefs are correct.

We must make it clear that people can only be persuaded through discussion and debate; that attempting to silence your opponents, whether through the law or a social media mob, only creates resentment and hostility, which in turn leads to a divided and intolerant society. It pushes dangerous ideas underground, where they can fester and grow unchallenged until, often bursting out in more extreme and violent form. Far better that they be confronted in debate, when the only risk is that we might be offended.

We must counter the dangerous notion that words are violence. This concept, which is readily taught in our schools and universities, will continue empowering the repression of our fundamental freedoms until it is discredited.

Rather than embracing the economic populism of the US's national conservatives, we must make the case for the free market – not just because it drives economic progress but because it is the only economic system based on free and voluntary exchange; because unlike policies that require government to pick winners and losers, it utilises humanity's inherent self-interest to incentivise wealth creation through service to others. In doing so, it is both effective, efficient and moral.

We must re-assert the importance of a lean and efficient government; a government that is responsive to the concerns of the public, but doesn't attempt to transform human nature; a government that provides basic rules and regulations that are necessary, not one that strangles businesses in endless red tape.

We should actively reject any move towards a politics that divides our community according to their immutable characteristics, whether it is by race, sex, or sexuality, even when this is done with good intent.

And, crucially, we must resist any move to undermine these basic liberal principles through the state.

These tasks cannot be left to the minority of conservatives and classical liberals who are in public life. Everyone must play a role, whether that be by educating your children or refusing to pile on when someone is being cancelled, even if you don't like them or their views.

None of these arguments is new, but as President Reagan said, "Freedom is never more than one generation away from extinction. We didn't pass it to our children in the bloodstream. It must be fought for, protected and handed on for them to do the same."

Senator the Honourable Amanda Stoker is a Liberal National Party Senator for Queensland. She is the Assistant Minister to the Attorney-General, Assistant Minister for Industrial Relations, as well as the Assistant Minister for Women. Senator Stoker studied law at Sydney University and commenced her legal career at Minter Ellison. She was associate to then Justice Ian Callinan AC QC on the High Court of Australia, and Justice Philip McMurdo, who was then on the Supreme Court of Queensland's commercial list. After some time prosecuting for the Commonwealth in Brisbane and Townsville, she joined the private bar. As a member of Level Twenty Seven Chambers, Senator Stoker practiced in commercial law, administrative law and corporate crime. She has served as Vice-President of the Women Lawyers Association of Queensland.

27

WE ARE THE MASTERS
OF OUR FATE

Professor James Allan

I write this as most of the Western democratic world is slowly emerging, at last, from the tight grip of the lockdownistas, who are people from the upper echelons of the public health class, the press, and the political class. Barring a Sweden here and a Florida or South Dakota there, the near uniform response of politicians has been to copy the methods of an authoritarian one-party Chinese dictatorship, lock people in their homes, and effectively impose the greatest inroads on our freedoms and civil liberties of the last three centuries.

And, by the way, that's not just me saying so. Recently retired United Kingdom Supreme Court (their highest) Justice Lord Sumption, has been saying exactly that now, almost as long as I have. And that is to pass over, in polite silence the lopsided effect of these lockdowns – lopsided in that they have hurt the poor far more than the rich, the gap having widened noticeably; lopsided in that the young have paid far more of the lockdown costs than the old; lopsided in that big business and bureaucrats have done well while small businesses and entrepreneurs have been devastated and many an owner bankrupted; lopsided because the politicians imposing these despotic, draconian 'shelter in place' rules have themselves paid virtually none of the costs – they have not even had the good graces to take a token pay cut; and lopsided because if you factor out deaths in old age facilities, the Infection Fatality Rate of Covid is estimated by leading Stanford Professor John Ioannidis to be 0.2 percent, about that of the flu.

In other words, it has not been a particularly good 18 months for selling the credentials of Western democratic government, of a journalistic class that jettisoned its day job as the sceptical probers of despotically heavy-handed politicians, and of a supposedly (but not much visible in fact) freedom-loving populace. And, in my view, the Covid response of Australia may yet prove to be worse than that of the northern hemisphere democracies as we have opted to go down the route of making Australia a sort of affable, minimum security Supermax prison where citizens cannot leave their own country without begging for (and usually not receiving) bureaucratic dispensation. You see, I said to start that most of the Western world is at last emerging from these massive over-reactions to a virus nowhere near as lethal as the Black Death or even as the 1918 Spanish Flu (apparently you can name viruses after Western countries but not after countries with non-white majority populations, at least according to the lunacies of today's woke, identity politics overseers who enforce these new 'racism is everywhere' orthodoxies in the media and in government. Go figure!). But Australia is not emerging. We have inadvertently tied ourselves to a de facto suppression and eradication strategy that every day looks stupider and stupider – though to be fair to myself, I predicted all this in the pages of the Spectator Australia back in April 2020.

In very simple terms, then, it is incredibly easy to be depressed about the state of democracy in Australia at the moment. Still, the editors have asked for a bit of optimism from contributors, on utilitarian grounds if no other. And so, my contribution in this chapter will be on the theme of how Australia's democracy could be improved. That is the big picture upon which what follows will focus. I will start, then, by outlining what I see as three problem areas in our democracy that are fixable.

Now, of course, what is probably our biggest problem – made painfully clear during the pandemic – is the current state of federalism in Australia. We have the democratic world's most emasculated States, indeed the only ones that do not have income tax powers so the link between spending and accountability for that spending has been broken – our States being mendicants (meaning that States that impose overly long lockdowns, for instance, do not themselves pay much if any of the financial costs); we have a division of respective powers that for a century now our top court has gradually realigned ever more in favour of the centre, in others words our top court employs the world's most pro-centre interpretive approach; we have the world's worst vertical fiscal imbalance; we have few Australians who seem to see that the main point of a federal system is difference, experimentation and injecting internal competition into the country, which is why proper federal systems like those in Germany, Switzerland, Canada and the US are per capita wealthier than unitary systems like those in France and (in de facto terms) here and that real federations actually have fewer, not more, bureaucrats per capita; and we have almost no plausible candidates for judicial high office who display the slightest affinity for proper federalism and interpretation of our Constitution in line with the federalist intentions of those who had the legitimate authority to make it.

In his brief tenure as Prime Minister Abbott wisely set up a body to look into what might be done to fix our federal system but that went when he was defenestrated by Prime Minister Turnbull and it is hard to see any future Liberal Prime Minister reinvigorating that idea, alas. So, I will limit myself to outlining three problem areas in our democratic arrangements where the chances of reform and improvement are remotely realistic. Here, to purloin the words of the 19th Century poet William Henley in his famous poem Invictus, we are "the masters of our fate".

Problem One

Our voting systems make it harder to hold political parties accountable. In the Senate, we use an Irish style STV proportional voting system. Now, I am no fan of any proportional voting system. They are usually sold as delivering a rough and ready proportionality between the percentage of those voting for Party X and the percentage of seats Party X gains in the legislature. Fine. But what all such proportional voting systems also do is that they kill majoritarian results. No party can plausibly ever win a majority. So, unlike majoritarian voting systems (such as First-Past-the-Post and the preferential system we use for the House of Representatives) all the compromising and bargaining happens after the election, beyond the control of the voters. Just look at Germany or Israel or any user of a proportional voting system. In majoritarian systems you end up with two big parties – call them the 'Ins' and the 'Outs'. These are broad church coalitions of the Left and the Right. Before each election, each party has to internally resolve its position on a host of issues, resolutions that will involve disagreement and compromise internally. But whatever the positions ultimately taken, they are more or less openly put to the voters and, to some extent, are constraining in the future. Proportional voting systems look good in a very superficial way, but their effect is significantly to disenfranchise the voters in favour of insider party elites who come together after elections to bargain and compromise and form coalition governments.

Now, as STV is used only in our Upper House, it is somewhat easier to countenance. Still, Australia is one of only three democracies in the world with a powerful Upper House – the other two being Italy and the US. Ours comes from the fact that our Founders copied big chunks of the US Constitution, including its uber powerful Senate. Yet in the US, which uses a two-party-producing First-Past-the-Post voting system, if voters in Georgia are unhappy with what a Senator from California votes for, the Georgians can punish someone. There are really only two parties or teams in the US Senate, because of the voting system used, and so Georgians can punish in their State the team (Democrats or Republicans) to which that Californian Senator belongs. Here in Australia, mostly all of us are disenfranchised when a Tasmanian independent or, tiny party Senator from South Australia, opts to block the passage of some Bill or other. That's a problem, one made worse when we moved from ten to twelve Senators per State; nor is there any big ticket fix likely to get through Parliament. A small improvement might be to get rid of 'above the line' voting and make all voters tick their preferred six Senate candidates. That would, at least, reduce the influence and horse-trading of the party machines.

As for the Lower House, the House of Representatives, down there we use a preferential voting system in Australia. When I first came to Australia, in 2005, I disliked the compulsory voting rule here but liked the preferential voting system used for the House of Representatives. Since then, I have changed my mind on both those choices. I now think compulsory voting has more benefits than costs. But ATV-type preferential voting is a problem, a big problem as it transpires, one that I think has encouraged the freedom-ignoring character of the present Coalition government. You see, the superficial attraction of preferential voting, not just putting an 'X' by the one candidate you want as in Canada, Britain and the US, but ranking each one from top to bottom – is that voters get to express what they dislike as well as like. That is very appealing as for many it is whom they do NOT want elected that matters and matters more than whom they DO.

But over time, some of us come to realise that preferential voting – a voting system used only here and in one other country's national elections, so it is rarer than compulsory voting, has a very, very big downside. It is this. Preferential voting serves to entrench the two big or major parties in place. And they know it. They know they can count on their base to vote for them almost come what may. Why? Because at some point on your ballot, you are forced to prefer either the 'in' team or the 'out' team. It cannot be avoided. And so, if you are a right-of-centre voter (it works the same for the other side of politics) and you happen to think your side or team has abandoned its principles and deserves to be punished, you have very few options.

Sure, you can donkey vote or you can prefer the other team (the other main party) at some point on your ballot. I did just that in the 2016 federal election. I put the Greens last, the Liberals second last, Labor third last, and randomly filled in the up-ballot choices. That means that I effectively voted for Labor, a choice I made (and advocated to other conservatives) as a result of Turnbull's coup again Abbott. But notice what is involved psychologically. A voter with a set of views that normally puts him or her on one side of the political divide has to be prepared to vote, at some point on his or her ballot, for the other team ahead of his own.

Given the responses I got from my Spectator Australia columns recommending just that, believe me when I say very few people are prepared to do that.

The obvious non-radical solution would be to move to a NSW-style optional preferential voting system. Yes, I would prefer to go straight to a First-Past-the-Post system but let's be honest, the status quo so obviously benefits the two main parties that that is a pie-in-the-sky desire. Optional preferential voting just might be achievable.

Problem Two

Here is another problem. When someone from the Anglosphere like me looks at his native Canada, or at Britain, or the US, he sees that elected legislators from the governing party are sometimes prepared to vote against their own party's legislation. Over four dozen British Tory MPs recently voted against one of Boris Johnson's 'we'll extend lockdown' legal extensions – against their own party! It happens in

Canada too, though less regularly than in Britain. And in the US, with its non-Westminster system, it happens all the time.

Yet here in Australia, backbenchers are eunuchs, emasculated eunuchs. We can ignore Labor here, even though it is the only Labor party in the world that throws out any of its MPs who vote against the party. The Liberal Party does not have that sort of internal rule. Yet in practice it comes very close. Why? My guess is that party power-brokers have far too much power in regards pre-selections. Vote against your own side because you believe, say, that it is ignoring important freedom-related concerns and you jeopardise your place in Parliament. Or, at least, all but the biggest names in the party do and such big names will probably be in Cabinet (or Shadow Cabinet) where they cannot breach collective responsibility.

So, we need significant reforms to enervate – heck, not enervate but destroy – the sway and influence of Liberal faction power-brokers. Small steps down this path have been taken in NSW. A lot more of them are needed.

Problem Three

Last one I will mention here. Leaving the selection of the Liberal Party leader – of the Prime Minister when the Coalition is in government – solely to the partyroom has to be changed. Canada changed from that system to one where party members have the sole say. Britain changed to one where party members get to choose between two candidates put forward after a vote of the partyroom – so the partyroom retains the biggest say but it can no longer impose its one preferred candidate. That British innovation may just be possible here.

Despite being at heart a traditionalist, I (and I think all of you) have to recognise that a party elite can grow to be out of sync with its core voters.

We saw above that preferential voting makes such disalignment considerably easier. So does the 'caucus alone picks the leader' rule. For any right-of-centre voter awake these past eight years in Australia, the problems with leaving the choice of leader solely to the partyroom or, put differently, with disenfranchising completely the party membership, are patently plain. Think about Britain. In the Brexit vote, about three-quarters of Tory voters voted 'Leave' while a mirror image three-quarter of Tory MPs voted 'Remain'. Left to their own devices the parliamentarians would never have installed a 'Leave' PM, even after the 2016 Brexit Referendum. In fact, as it was, they managed to get Remain-voting Theresa May in as the first post-Brexit PM by gaming the 'here are two names' requirement. Had the polls not been bleak they would not have put Boris Johnson's name forward, knowing he would win in a landslide if they did. So, the British reform is not perfect but it is perhaps achievable.

In Australia, it is now patently plain that party members need some sort of say, even a limited British Tory-type say, into who leads their party. The partyroom has, for many of us, become too disconnected from the core values of its base.

A British-style reform may just be achievable in the medium term. One reformist Prime Minister could bring it about; or a long campaign that asked wannabe MPs to promise to support it.

Bring in those three changes or reforms and democracy in this country would be improved, in my view. All of them are possible. At any rate, that is my optimistic contribution to this book.

Professor James Allan is the Garrick Professor of Law at the University of Queensland and a regular columnist for *The Spectator Australia*. Before arriving in Australia in February of 2005, he spent 11 years teaching law in New Zealand at the University of Otago and before that lectured law in Hong Kong. Professor Allan is a native-born Canadian who practised law in a

large Toronto law firm and at the Bar in London before shifting to teaching law. He has had sabbaticals at the Cornell Law School, at the Dalhousie Law School in Canada as the Bertha Wilson Visiting Professor in Human Rights, and at the University of San Diego School of Law. Professor Allan has published widely in the areas of legal philosophy and constitutional law, including in all the top English language legal philosophy journals in the US, the UK, Canada and Australia, much the same being true of constitutional law journals as well.

28

LIBERAL VALUES ARE UNIVERSAL VALUES

Elizabeth Lee MLA

"Remember, you're the needle and your sister is the thread. Wherever the needle goes, the thread will follow."

My father's words were just words at the time, but I look back now and realise they formed my first lesson in leadership about responsibility, service and leading by example.

I am seven-years-old. I am holding tightly onto my five-year-old sister's hand and I know I cannot lose sight of Mum and Dad. We are in a busy place; we've said farewell to our aunts and uncles, grandparents and cousins and I know we are going somewhere far away. It's exotic and foreign and I know we are getting on an aeroplane. And I know, because my parents have told us, that we will not be back for a long time.

I migrated to Australia from South Korea in 1986 with my parents, John and Cecilia and my younger sister, Rosa (Australian names selected through the church). My parents wanted us to grow up in a country that had a broader view of the world. At the time, Korea was a fairly homogenous society. The university system would have been out of reach of our family and my parents were determined to provide us with an opportunity to spread our wings. My parents brought us to Australia for a better life.

Ours is probably a very typical migrant story.

My parents left behind their family, friends, language and culture to move to a country where they don't look like anybody else; where they don't speak the same language; where they don't know the culture, and aside from one uncle (my father's brother), we did not know a single soul.

We settled into a small unit at the back of a house in Western Sydney. The landlord lived at the main house and we lived in the extended part at the back with its own kitchen and bathroom. My sister and I shared a bunkbed and some of my earliest memories in Australia are of Mum trying to cook an "Aussie" breakfast (when milk that was out of reach for us in Korea was in plentiful supply and sliced white bread was cooked on a frying pan because we couldn't afford a toaster); of weekends exploring the NSW coastline trying to fit into the stereotypical Aussie beach life (despite living in Merrylands and Blacktown - nowhere near the beach); and of our first "rainbow" car (nicknamed as such because it was a Frankenstein-type car with all the different panels made up from spare parts).

My youngest sister, Sara, was born in 1988, two years after we settled in Australia, completing our family. My parents worked as labourers, as cleaners, and in takeaway shops and factories.

After only a few months of English language, lessons before they had to work to put food on the table, my parents would struggle to access basic services and go about our day-to-day activities.

I remember following my Dad to the shops, bank and post office from the age of seven to translate for him.

I remember the kindness of our neighbours, who would help translate our school newsletters and invite us to very traditional Aussie events like pool parties and Christmas summer BBQs – we had never celebrated Christmas in summer before!

In his workplace, my Dad experienced, on a daily basis, jokes and abuse because he was the only "chink" on site who couldn't understand Aussie jokes.

He had a go at small business, not once but twice. Dad went bust, not once but twice. I remember debt collectors coming around to our shabby little house on Blacktown Road and Dad staying up all night worrying about how he would pay the bills.

Through all this, I do not remember the heartbreak of my parents almost losing everything; nor do I remember the anguish of my parents trying and failing, trying and failing again at creating a better life in this new country we were now calling home. I do not remember the frustration, the anger and the torment of the racism that was hurled at my Dad.

What I do remember is my parents being so grateful for the opportunities Australia provided to us to create a better life, a better future.

What I *do* remember is my parents insisting that if someone says something racist or ignorant, it is the view of that person and that person alone. Australia is a great country; Australians are a great people; we are Australian; and we believe in Australian values.

These values are individual freedom and individual responsibility; a society that trusts individuals to make decisions that are best for them and their families; equality of opportunity, of working hard and making a positive contribution to our community.

These are Australian values; these are Liberal values; and these are the values that drive me as an elected member and as Leader of the Canberra Liberals.

I believe that everyone should be free to live their life the way they see fit, without judgment, provided they take responsibility for their own actions and they do not harm others. I believe that government resources should be prioritised for those who may not have the same opportunities as us.

These are Australian values, these are Liberal values.

The reason I am privileged enough to be where I am today, leading the Liberal Party in the ACT, is because of the sacrifices my parents made. I didn't know it at the time and I didn't know it until much later, but this lived experience embedded these values deep inside me. I have always said to my younger sisters that if we don't make the most of our lives here in Australia, the sacrifices that my parents made will come to naught.

I am very proud to be the first Korean-Australian to be elected to an Australian parliament and the first Asian-Australian to lead a major political party. This is not something I set out to do but it's a reality and it is a huge responsibility to be a visible Asian face in Australian leadership.

The saying 'you can't be what you can't see' really speaks to me. I know because as a young girl from Korea growing up in Western Sydney, a life in Australian politics was not an option for me. It was a foreign world, a world in which I did not belong; and if I can play my part, a small role, in inspiring other migrant Australians, especially young women, that they *do* have a place in Australian politics, that they do have a place in Australian public life, then it is a pretty extraordinary privilege that I have.

While the left-side of politics likes talking about diversity and inclusion, it is the Canberra Liberals who preselected and then elected the first Asian-Australian leader of a major party. It is also the Canberra Liberals who elected the first female leadership team in my Deputy Giulia Jones and myself in the ACT. Because that's what

Liberals do. We get on with it. We get things done.

It has been a long time in Opposition for the Canberra Liberals. We have not been in government since 2001. This year, we mark 20 years in Opposition in a Parliament that is only 32 years young.

I am not deluded about the significance of the challenge that is before me.

I have been asked, more than a handful of times, why do you bother? What is the point and why take on the "worst job in politics"?

The enormity of decades in Opposition is not lost on me. I am also acutely aware of the long-term impact of continually 'losing', time and time again. It has a significant impact on morale within the team and it erodes the confidence, faith and belief from Liberal supporters who have devoted their time, funds and energy to working towards a change of government.

Despite this challenge, despite this frustration, despite this bleakness, I believe in the strength of our democracy.

Canberrans are educated, articulate and ambitious and I believe we have what it takes to show Canberra that a Liberal government is best for the future of our great city; I believe we have what it takes to show Canberra that it deserves a government that does more than talk the talk; a government that is led by someone who brings a diversity of life experiences and views; a government that governs for all, not for the select and elite in the inner circle; a government that takes responsibility for its own actions and respects the community.

I believe that the great Robert Menzies was right when he said that "ambition, effort, thinking and readiness to serve are not only the design and objectives of self-government but are the essential conditions of its success."

This ambition, this effort, this thinking and this readiness to serve, are starkly missing from a 20-year-old Labor government; and the uncomfortably cosy alliance it has formed with the Greens, is not in the best interests of our great city.

Twenty years of power in a 32-year-old parliament is an extraordinary privilege that has been afforded the Labor party in the ACT. We, of course, must take stock of our own shortcomings in not being able to topple a government that has, in so many ways, lost its values, its sense of duty and its heart.

Each day we are in Opposition and each day we see mismanagement and incompetence from this Labor government, I am reminded of the importance of my role, sometimes even when those for whom I fight don't see it or appreciate it.

The first speech I made in the Assembly this term I recalled what my father said to me when I had the great privilege of being elected as leader of our party: "You are a leader. What you say and what you do will matter. Always listen, then see, then feel. You must do this – listen, see, feel, before you speak."

At the heart of my father's words was just that – heart. Leadership, but particularly political leadership, is always about the people, acknowledging that voting is an emotional decision based on who and what inspires us and respecting the will and needs of those who may not be in a position to articulate for themselves. Our decisions must be based on courage to do the right things, not the easy things, because our duty to serve others is greater than the disposition to serve oneself.

In her inaugural speech, Dame Enid Lyons, the first female elected to the federal Parliament and the first ever female Cabinet Minister, said she hoped to "never forget that everything that takes place in this chamber goes out somewhere to strike a human heart, to influence the life of some fellow being" and this, to me, is about making a difference to those we serve.

Whilst the privilege and strength of our democracy manifests as the contest of ideas and the spirit of debate, at the heart of what we do and, more importantly, *why* we do what we do, is the heart.

Today, I am a confident leader of a major party in Australia. It wasn't so long ago that I was a seven-year-old girl from Kwangju, South Korea, who could not even fathom dreaming of making a contribution to Australian politics or to Australian public life.

The values that my parents embedded in me all those years ago, the values that I shaped throughout my childhood, schooling and professional life, the values that I bring to my role as Leader of the Canberra Liberals, are what we, as a party were built on and what we, as a nation, were built on.

These are Australian values. These are Liberal vales.

Elizabeth Lee MLA is the Leader of the Canberra Liberals and the Liberal Member for Kurrajong in the ACT Legislative Assembly. Prior to entering the ACT Legislative Assembly in 2016, Elizabeth was a successful lawyer in the private sector and later a lecturer at the Australian National University and University of Canberra. Having migrated to Australia from Korea at the age of seven, Elizabeth moved to Canberra when she turned 18 to study Law and Asian Studies at The Australian National University. Elizabeth is passionate about creating a more connected capital and empowering every Canberran to reach their potential.

29

PRUDENT, PROUD AND PURPOSEFUL

The Hon. David Elliott MP

One of the most fascinating things about Australian politics is the fact that the conservative parties, those being the Liberal and National Parties, are actually the least disciplined. Lay observers would be forgiven for being startled at this fact. The thought of our massive middle-class being anything but averse to change would be a surprise to anyone who doesn't have an intimate knowledge of the running of our great institution.

I often like to present myself as one of the more conservative members of the NSW State Coalition and relish it when my political opponents use it as some sort of vitriolic accusation. But the reality is the one thing that rusted me on to Australian Liberalism, from a very young age and despite my working-class upbringing, was the way in which our version of liberalism embraced change. Indeed, it encouraged and challenged itself to pursue reform as and when the need presented itself. The important preamble here being "as and when".

That being said, we have never been a party of change for the sake of it. Or, indeed, in the case of Kevin Rudd, vanity change.

Our reforms have always been prudent, proud and purposeful. Whether it be State Government asset recycling or John Howard's decade of reforming tax, firearm ownership and reenforcing our role as a regional power, we have much to celebrate as a political movement. Of course, like all institutions, we have our faults. The future of our success relies on existing leaders to ensure our brand is protected and, more importantly, we nourish and nurture future leaders who approach our party with the ambition to continue the legacy of Menzies, Howard, Kennett and Baird, just to name a few. For me, my next contribution to politics will be the latter. We need to make the process easier and less cost prohibitive to ensure that we get the diversity we want without having to constrict ourselves to quotas. It makes no sense to exclude one individual just so we can include another.

The next quarter century will see our party having to face some very diverse policy challenges in the economy, environment, national security, law enforcement and vocation preparation.

The economy

It's a political truism that the Liberal Party has, since its inception, been seen as the gold standard when it comes to economic management. To some that may sound arrogant but, in politics, knowing your strengths is as important as knowing your weaknesses. Our record speaks for itself. The 1999 GST, Baird's electricity sale (ably steered through by Gladys Berejiklian) and of course the retirement of huge Labor debts by both Peter Costello and Jeff Kennett have given Liberals a sense of confidence that continues to this day. The policies established by Frydenberg and Perrottet, over the course of the pandemic, have their genesis in this self-assurance. But they also draw on the fact that we are a party of the times, one that is not locked into dogma and unable to deviate from central philosophies in the way the NSW Labor Movement was prohibited from considering electricity privatization even when its leadership knew it was vital to the state's economic welfare.

For the next generation of Liberals, however, home ownership and superannuation will be the most challenging of all economic policies. Within a generation, Australian workers have gone from holding the same job for life to having three vocations before they reach middle age. In itself, this uncertainty, although hardly a risk, will see the need for more flexibility in the management of superannuation funds whilst at the same time ensuring the flexible workforce doesn't force the finance industry to weaken borrowing regulations, particularly given the thought of 10 percent home mortgage rates are as distant a memory as the Hawke Government is to most Australians.

Likewise, Governments cannot overlook the importance of personal bank savings, as opposed to superannuation. If recent natural disasters, and the pandemic, have not reinforced the need for a "rainy day" account for the nation's Mums and Dads then we have ignored a very important lesson. How tragic it was that the Commonwealth had to open up the superannuation accounts of a large number of lower income workers just so they could survive three months without a wage.

As the NSW Minister for Emergency Services, I've seen enough devastation and destruction to think that, perhaps, it's time for workers between 25 and 50 years of age to be given a tax incentive to directly save a small proportion of their income for an account that can be accessed in case of an emergency, independent of their retirement fund, with any deferred tax liability paid out of the savings when they reach retirement age and can access their nest egg.

Conservation

One of the great weaknesses of conservatism is our inability to sell our conservation credentials, many of which date back nearly half a century. Liberalism in Australia has given away the bragging rights of reform, and the need for reform, to our opponents who have linked conservation with so may other woke causes such as drug law reform and even the proposed Republic, all the while ignoring the fact that the late Duke of Edinburgh had more environmental credentials that any current serving Green Parliamentarian.

For Liberals, the transmission to any alternative energy sources, whether they be nuclear or solar, must be affordable and reliable. It must also consider the social and economic cost of retraining workers and uprooting communities. These decisions are not made easily or, in haste, but they can result in a better outcome for all stakeholders. In my own electorate of The Hills, hardly a hotbed of revolutionaries, the take up of solar panels and the use of recycled and rainwater, is amongst the highest, per capita, in the nation. These decisions have not been made solely because my constituents, rightly, believe we should be good custodians of the earth but primarily, at this point, these practices make good financial sense for them and their families.

National security

Since September 2011, no nation on Earth has been immune from the uncertainty and terror of extremist ideology. It's my view that one of the reasons the world has been so resilient in the face of COVID-19 is because we have been rehearsed in the need to adjust behavior and habits at short notice to respond to unseen threats. The future success of Liberalism in Australia is highly dependent on our ability to reassure the electorate that their government is able to face each and every challenge with the minimal impact on their lives and livelihood. To many this has been our centre of gravity during the pandemic and must be considered by the next generation of leaders as an important lesson because, tragically, there will always be international threats. The Liberal Party's commitment to investment into military, and paramilitary training, and hardware, remain a solid expectation from our base and a moral obligation to our citizenry and friends.

For us to prepare for the future, our party cannot respond to the critics of our great and powerful allies. Our relationships within the Five Eyes network have served us well and we must continue that journey to ensure intelligence sharing, joint exercises and operations as well as mutual protection become synonymous with the very name of our nation. This is not surrendering sovereignty, although I note the same critics of Five Eyes are the very same advocates of further influence by the United Nations; when, in reality, our disputes are now borderless and our enemies are invisible. Given Five Eyes can never be our sole guardian, and that our bilateral relationship with India and Japan has never been stronger, a healthy new journey with our two powerful Asian friends remains essential to secure the future of democracy in our region.

The law

Since the birth of modern Australian liberalism in the 1940s, there has always been a great reluctance within our party to make radical changes to our legal system. This reluctance is based on the blatant mathematical reality that, in our "Broad Church", we have both committed social conservatives serving alongside passionate moderates. No amount of recruiting from certain demographics will ever change that nor will the reluctance of our party base easily allow it.

Whilst modern and future Liberals should not fear change in our family, commercial or industrial laws, we should continue to make sure advocates spell out the case for reform in a transparent and articulated manner. Changes to industrial and abortion laws by John Howard and Gladys Berejiklian respectively are both case studies on how the failure to bring the community on the policy journey has severe and, in some cases, election losing consequences.

With the "gig" economy, same sex marriage, crypto currency

and ecommerce all further rewriting traditional legal norms, the need for potentially radical law reform will be upon us within a decade. Next generation Liberals will need to accept this reality and balance all amendments to our practices against community expectations, without risking our democratic principles. Given our legal institutions underpin the very fabric of our nation and offer certainty and protection to all other elements of society, it is difficult to ascertain a greater challenge for our future leaders than to ensure they do not repeat the mistakes of past conservative governments. The first challenge is to make the case for change. Australians are very skeptical of laws and delight in pointing out inconsistencies and vagaries meaning those who advocate change are favoured targets.

Employment and training

The likelihood of anyone entering the workforce today and, save some military and law enforcement personnel, retiring at the legislated age in the same role is extremely remote. Our employers and Government must prepare for that. Whilst vocational education has traditionally been directed towards the needs of school leavers future Governments will need to prepare for the growing number of mature age students seeking the services of both universities and vocational education institutions.

This great challenge must be met by an acceptance that a reduction in worker incomes acknowledges the cost to business as business invests in training that will confidently return the worker to familiar wages. In this journey, the option to access superannuation to cover training costs and expenses is more palatable, as individuals invest in themselves and secure their future employment. Concurrently, the option for part-time work in a new vocation or longer shifts to allow for extended study, will need to be considered by future Governments in any industrial relations reform. This commitment to support the desires and ambitions of an individual is the cornerstone of Australian Liberalism and would certainly sanction a more flexible and nimbler workforce allowing for large movements in and out of vocations as demands for skills change.

It is essential that, to ensure an adoptable and quality approach to training, industry associations and professional bodies remain as the cornerstone of all future reforms within the vocation and education sector.

Summary

A challenge for the Liberal Party is that two of the most celebrated reforms I have seen in the 35 years since I joined were both more than two decades ago. Whilst we should always avoid chasing vanity reforms, we must accept that membership of an established political party brings with it both the obligation and opportunity to make our government more user friendly. That journey never stops.

For those contemplating a career as an advisor or Parliamentarian, the first question has to be based on what your beliefs are, what they are not, and how far will you go to advocate them. The difficulties facing modern lawmakers, particularly those of us from the conservative side, is the left-wing nature of social media. To do politics well, you must accept that it is not a spectator sport, rather a full-bodied contact sport. There is nothing more valiant than the pursuit and protection of your own beliefs.

The Honourable David Elliott MP is the NSW Minister for Police and Emergency Services and was elected as the NSW State member for Baulkham Hills in 2011. He holds a Bachelor of Arts in History and Asian Studies as well as a Graduate Certificate in Public Policy and Master of Arts (Communication). In 1993, he

joined the NSW Police Media Unit and, in 1995, joined the Regular Army. He was the National Campaign Director of the successful 'No Republic' campaign. Under his administration, David saw a successful 'No' vote in every State of the Commonwealth. In 2000, he was posted to the peacekeeping efforts in Bougainville, Papua New Guinea. From 2004 to 2008, he served as the NSW Deputy Chief Executive of the Australian Hotels Association. In 2008, he was made the Chief Executive Officer of the Civil Contractors Federation (NSW).

30

FOREVER YOUNG: ANZUS TURNS 70

The Hon. Dr Brendan Nelson AO

Brendan Nelson reflects on 70 years of the ANZUS alliance at a joint Menzies Research Centre and American Chamber of Commerce event in Canberra, 23 June 2021. The following is an edited transcript of the speech.

What I'm about to say to you is much about the history of ANZUS, as it is about the future. History is of vital importance for us to understand our future. And when little else in the world seems to make much sense, in my opinion and experience, history is the guiding discipline. It reminds us to where, in our best selves, we know we need to go. And a sense of history also reminds us that there are very difficult decisions that have to be made and the consequences of not making them. It can also point us to new horizons. It can inspire and it also demolishes prejudice.

The most important year in this country's history, by any standard, is 1788. The British first fleet arrived and devastated millennia of rich Aboriginal history, custodianship and culture; but that event and everything that would follow produced the origins of the Australia that we are and the people that we have now become.

The next most important year, to me, was 1942. Fortress Singapore fell and, imagine as an Australian, hearing this the following day when our then wartime Prime Minister, John Curtin, in a national address said, "The fall of Singapore should be regarded as Australia's Dunkirk. And the protection of this country is no longer that of a contribution to a world at war but resistance to an enemy threatening to invade our shores. And that state was not only the Americas, but the entire English-speaking peoples."

Days later, bombs fell on Darwin. We had the United States and Royal Australian Navies, together in the Battle of the Coral Sea, in early May, inflicting a strategic defeat over the Japanese, which led to the ANZUS alliance, formalised in 1951.

The Americans inflicted a major defeat over the Japanese at Midway, which forced them to abandon a seaborne landing at Moresby and instead get to Moresby from the north of New Guinea, across the hinterland. A gripping struggle at Kokoda, Isurava, Milne Bay, Gona, Buna, Sanananda, the American sacrifice at Guadalcanal, miniature submarines in Sydney Harbour, in late May, all made it a desperate, desperate year.

And then, at the end of the war, we, Australia, emerged, inconsolably mourning 40,000 dead. The Americans had 300,000 casualties in the Pacific from December, 1941, to the end of the war. 103,000 dead, half their bodies never found. There's not a day should go by, in this country, where we do not give thanks for American sacrifice in the Pacific and what it meant for the freedoms that we enjoy. Too often, my generation has taken much of this for granted.

The Second World War had three major geo-strategic consequences for Australia. The first is that we knew that we could no longer rely on Britain for our security. We would instead look across the Pacific to the United States. Secondly, it created the conditions for Australia to engage, in time, an emergent Asia, an Asia with which we could engage on equal and respected terms. The third major consequence was it laid the foundations for what would be a struggle that would endure for two generations between communism and democracy.

1942 was also a significantly important year for us, for Liberals. It was the year in which Sir Robert Menzies delivered his Forgotten People radio broadcasts and then subsequently wrote the book, The Forgotten People and Other Studies in Democracy, in honour of his son, Ken, who was serving in the second AIF. In what is a philosophical and values touchstone for us, he spoke of the salary earners, the shopkeepers, the skilled artisans, the farmers, the professional men and women. "Unorganised and unselfconscious", as he said. "Not rich enough to wield power in their own right and too individualistic for pressure politics ... And yet, they are the backbone of the nation and in their children they see their greatest contribution to it."

Sir Robert would later say, in 1944, in looking at a liberal vision for Australia, that true liberals "had great and imperative obligations to the weak, the sick and the unfortunate; and to every good citizen, this country would owe not only a chance in life, but a self-respecting life...".

And for the United States, for me, etched in marble, there in Washington DC, at the Jefferson Memorial, the promissory note that Jefferson wrote in co-authoring the American Declaration of Independence, which speaks not only to America but to countries and citizens around the world who believe in political, economic and religious freedom, "We hold these truths to be self-evident that all men are created equal, but they are endowed by their creator with certain inalienable rights, among them life, liberty, and the pursuit of happiness. And that governments are instituted amongst men to uphold these rights."

Those values, common values of our liberal democracies inform character. Character derives from a Greek word which means the impression left in wax by a stone seal ring. The Greeks called it the stamp of personality; but values are not, for a nation, a notice board upon which we are placing evidence of the latest fad sweeping the country. Nor are they a social media posting which is a description of how we think we're going to be over the next six or 12 months. They are enduring. And we should not, under any circumstances, abandon what Arthur Schlesinger described in the 20th century as historic purpose.

In 1949, Sir Robert Menzies led the Liberal Party to victory and, for the second time, would become the Prime Minister of Australia, the first Liberal Prime Minister and longest serving in Australia's history. The year 1949 also saw President Truman make the decision to commit the United States forces to the defence of South Korea against the Chinese. Our then Foreign Minister, Sir Percy Spender, was ebullient, as the Australian government committed to the Korean War, saying that the United States would repay Australia over a hundred times more than whatever contribution we made.

And so, the ANZUS alliance was formalised in San Francisco on September 1, 1951. It had been born not only of what John Monash had done at Hamel and the breaking of the Hindenburg line, and the leadership of the American troops; nor by what happened in the Coral Sea and the events that followed, but also the milieu in which it was negotiated, conceived and then signed. And never forget also that the Russians were acquiring nuclear weapons.

That ANZUS alliance has four key pillars. It has a political pillar, an economic one, a diplomatic pillar, and then, of course, defence. It has given us Australians capability, intelligence, interoperability, intensity of joint training with the United States, operational coordination and, indeed, a hand-in-glove ability for us to operate both militarily and on intelligence, surveillance, reconnaissance, access to missiles and missile technology. It's given us trade and investment benefits, the exchange of people, research, culture, and a whole range of benefits which too often, we take for granted, or we don't actually think about in our day to day, week to week, and month to month lives.

China is, as we know, Australia's largest trading partner, but the most significant and important economic partner this country has is the United States. It has, on aggregate, represented between 6 and 7.5% of this nation's GDP in the decade to 2019. In 2018, it was 7% of Australia's GDP, $74 billion in two-way trade and investment; then, if you add to the investment made by American and predominantly American owned companies in Australia, employing 325,000 people, it is some 7% of GDP.

When Australia came into the pandemic, we owed the world $1.1 trillion. That is now about $250 billion more than it was when we came into it. The gap between our savings and our investment requirements are about 4% of GDP. The only way we can underwrite further investment productivity, employment, growth and prosperity is if we have access to those very wide and deep equity markets in the United States. And the alliance is the framework for that and a whole range of other things that are important to us.

We are, as we all now know, living through the most consequential geo-strategic realignment in our lifetime. As the Prime Minister, Scott Morrison, said a year ago on the 1st of July, when he was releasing the defence strategic update, "We live in a world that is very similar to and has similarities with the world of the 1930s and the early 1940s ... We are about to emerge into a poorer, more dangerous and less organised world." Our policy as a country, as we now know, overall, is to shape, deter and respond. In terms of shaping, we saw Marise Payne, our Foreign Minister, last year, commit the centre-right government to multilateralism, to drive bilateral arrangements with countries that share similar values with us, but also to drive multilateral arrangements both in our region and globally.

We've seen the Quad at work reinvigorated in 2017. We saw Exercise Malabar and some other naval exercises and we've seen, with the change of the administration in the United States, a re-commitment to these multilateral arrangements, which have been the bedrock of security, particularly in our region, since the end of the Second World War.

I note for the first time, the G7 specifically mentioned Taiwan in its communiqué and then, almost a decade after I was in Brussels, arguing for NATO to take a global approach to Euro Atlantic security, when Madeleine Albright was promoting such a strategic concept that we now have NATO and its Secretary General, Jens Stoltenberg, describing Russia as a threat and China as a challenge.

From my perspective, I suspect that the French, and particularly the Germans, are not ready to outsource their policy on China to the United States, but nonetheless it is quite significant now, that NATO, as the Secretary General said, "Covers all threats from all directions." There were times when I would be meeting the President of the European Council, the Secretary General of NATO or the President of the European Commission, a decade ago, I would always finish the dialogue with a discussion of the Indo-Pacific. And I would say to them, "There's trouble coming and it's going to come out of our part of the world." I remember a very, very senior European official saying to me, "Oh Brendan, no, it'll be years before we can focus on Asia in any serious way." I said, "Oh really?" I said, "If that's the attitude Europe's going to take, you'll find Asia is going to find you a lot quicker than you think, and in ways that you won't like." And when he asked me what I meant, I said, "Well, if the South China Sea is closed for a week, you're going to know about it. You had $700 billion euros worth of trade going through there last year, which was then 2010, and if it's closed, the United

States will be engaged immediately. That will have consequences."

It is very pleasing for Australia, and certainly for me, to see that now, the European Union, and certainly NATO, is recognising the consequential changes that are occurring in our region.

What's shaping us predominantly is the US-China relationship. Just reflect on this. In 1982, the Chinese economy was 9% the size of that of the United States. Within the next few years, depending on how you measure it, the Chinese economy will be as big as that of the United States, perhaps even bigger.

It's also about the fragility or stability of that global base, the rules-based global order, which is so important to us, which we all, to varying degrees, have taken for granted, which has been challenged in recent years. We must address the fragility of certain nation states, the pace of military modernisation and terrorism (which hasn't gone away) and asymmetric, unexpected threats, that are coming from different parts of the world, that we are not expecting.

For Australia also, I think, in a defence sense, we need to be deepening our engagement with the United States on anti-submarine warfare; and we also need to be working a lot more closely on missiles and missile technology.

I was asked recently by one of the defence chiefs, what advice should be given to the Defence Minister, Peter Dutton? I said, "Well, I've made a commitment not to give my colleagues free advice once I've finished these jobs." But I did say to the then President, George W. Bush, "Mr President, I know you've got a book listing good guys and bad guys in your top drawer. Australia, I know, will be on the good guy list, and if we're not at the top of it, I'd like to know why?"

I trust these thoughts will fashion the future consideration of us all.

The Honourable Dr Brendan Nelson AO is a former Leader of the Liberal Party of Australia. Dr Nelson first entered the Australian Parliament in 1996, serving as the Federal Member for Bradfield. During the Howard Government, he served as the Minister for Education, Science and Training and, when troops were deployed to the Middle East, he was the Minister for Defence. Prior to entering Parliament, Dr Nelson was the National President of the Australian Medical Association, becoming the youngest person ever to hold this position. He studied at Flinders University, South Australia, where he graduated with a Bachelor of Medicine and Surgery, then worked as a medical practitioner in Hobart. In 2009, on his retirement from politics, he became Australian Ambassador to the European Union, Belgium and Luxembourg as well as Australia's Special Representative to NATO. In 2012 he resigned as ambassador and took on the role of Director of the Australian War Memorial where he served for 7 years. Dr Nelson is now a Board Director of the United States Studies Centre. He is President of Boeing Australia, New Zealand and South Pacific, the senior company leader in the Oceania region and is the Chairman of the Board for Boeing Australia Holdings. Dr Nelson is also Chairman of the American Chamber of Commerce in Australia.

31

AUSTRALIA AND OUR FUTURE

Gina Rinehart

It's hard to travel Australia and not recognise how wonderful our country truly is. From the spectacular Kimberleys, across great cattle stations, to beautiful Port Douglas and the coastal islands, down to Hobart and much more, we have a country I wish we would do more to value.

Those who've fought for our country, certainly have valued highly, risking their very lives and making huge sacrifices.

For generation after generation, we have wanted to hand down a better country for our children. Sadly, for this generation, I believe this is now at risk, which the younger ones amongst us, in particular, should not want. We need to better appreciate history.

Alluring political words of "free this" and "free that", more taxpayers' money for this or that, helped to turn once prosperous Ceylon, prosperous with its tea plantations and other agriculture, into a country which couldn't support itself with food; instead, its people faced hunger, loss of free speech, consequent damaging riots, property damage, unhappiness, police and military, and a country name change as it struggled with the results of its socialist path.

The story with Argentina is similar. Few knew that 100 years ago

Argentina, with its cattle and grains, which it exported to help feed the world, was one of the richest nations on earth. The cattle barons' beautiful homes, now suffering disrepair in Buenos Aires, remain as testament to those prosperous times.

But then, the increase in taxes and other socialist policies, saw Argentina become not only unable to feed itself, but the socialist policies of Peron and others, saw incredible inflation, people unable to support their families, rioting; and the country has never regained its affluent position in the world, even 100 years later.

Sadly, the economy ruining effects of socialism, don't just last between elections. They last much, much longer. We should be on guard against this and, in particular, the entitlement culture, big government, high taxes and government tape – these are problems that need to be faced, if we want Australia to continue to be the wonderful country that it has been.

Agriculture, mining, small businesses, investment and defence are the keys to our nation and our future.

We need our government to stop making decisions influenced by the media of the moment and instead act to make the bold decisions our country needs.

They need to listen to people like NSW Governor and Member of AmCham (American Chamber of Commerce in Australia), Lindsay Partridge AM, of Brickworks:

> "(Australian governments) are into the rule book to try and find out how they can stop you doing what you want to do, or try and delay you, whereas in America, representatives of the governor will come and see you and ask you how they can help.

> "We need to be prepared to relax the regulations so companies can function. It's just too onerous at the moment, and very difficult for companies to invest in Australia.

"Americans are prepared to take risks and prepared to fail ... whereas in Australia we're very cautious and over concerned with risks and risk management."

Mr Partridge also contrasted unfavourably Australian governments' attitudes to business with those in the US, suggesting Australian businesses deserved "a gold medal just for surviving."

Sadly, excessive government tape makes it hard for businesses, especially small businesses, to survive. Springing to mind are the previous multi generation owners of Fossil Downs, a station in the Kimberleys, who told me it wasn't the difficulties of poisonous snakes, drought, excessive heat over months, flood, fires, isolation, lack of services in the outback, but government tape that forced them to sell the home and station they dearly loved, explaining that John, the husband of the owner and manager, had to get up around 4am each morning, like most do on stations in the far north, but, he wasn't able to get to bed until around 1am, still doing government paperwork.

They couldn't afford to open an office in Perth and have staff to handle it for them. Definitely gold medal! Their conversation on government tape didn't end there!

In agriculture, our government tells us that we will be a $100 billion industry by 2030, but, it keeps piling on government tape to make this impossible, part of this being tape from State or Territory.

Hundreds of millions of dollars of investment lie dormant under government tape in the Kimberleys; young cattle die cruel deaths because of crazy laws limiting wild dog baiting and crocodile killing in the NT, while crocodiles, wild dogs and other ferals mount to record levels; and given clearing laws which restrict clearing, around Australia mean that farmers, pastoralists and their family's pets and staff are unsafe. Ditto their investment.

As the Institute of Public Affairs found, government tape has grown 80-fold in the last 50 years, while agriculture has only doubled in those same 50 years.

We all know Asia is the largest growing market for Australia, and often hear that Asian demand for agricultural products is projected to show sustained growth towards the year 2050, providing opportunities for Australian exporters of high-quality, clean, agricultural products.

But what isn't clearly said, is that we must not lose this opportunity due to our government holding us back through endless red, green and other tape that isn't levied on our international competitors and which drives up the cost of our production and our products.

The government needs to listen to farmers like the straight-talking Tony Seabrook, President of the Pastoralists and Graziers Association of WA. Indeed, all reading this should send to their government members and cabinet, details of government tape that needs to be cut, or made more investment and business friendly. Here are some examples which I have sent to various members of Queensland's Parliament.

AGRICULTURE

Native vegetation red tape

<u>Problem</u>: Laws around 'regrowth vegetation' are preventing economic development.

<u>Solution</u>: The Vegetation Management and Other Legislation Amendment Bill 2018 extended the definition of 'high value regrowth vegetation' to land that has not been cleared for 15 years. The previous definition applied to land that had not been cleared since 31 December 1989. The clearing of high value regrowth vegetation requires approval and is subject to several conditions including

the setting aside of an exchange offset area by the landowner. The Queensland government should re-insert the previous definition of "high value regrowth vegetation".

Regulation of agricultural and veterinary chemicals

Problem: Certain chemicals used by farmers and landowners must be registered in Australia and regulated under Australian law even where those chemicals have been approved by an overseas regulator of good repute.

Solution: Automatically allow the entry of agricultural and veterinary chemicals onto the Australia market where they have been approved by an overseas regulator of good repute, such as US or EU regulators.

Forced removal of infrastructure

Problem: Mining companies are forced to remove infrastructure on farmland even where the farmer or landowner benefits from that infrastructure, such as dams, fencing, and fence posts.

Solution: Either repeal Section 318ZB (2) and (4) of Queensland EP Act, or insert a provision into the Act which allows landowners to agree to receive their land in a certain condition.

Bushfire protection

Problem: Regulation on farmers and private landowners which undermines their ability to manage and mitigate bushfire risk.

Solution: Amend the definition of "essential management" under the Sustainable Planning Regulation 2009 which allows for vegetation clearing on freehold land so that "essential management" means "where it is reasonably necessary to remove or reduce the risk that the vegetation poses of serious personal injury or damage to infrastructure"; and Schedule 21 of Planning Regulation 2017 should be amended to allow clearing of up to 100m from infrastructure for firebreaks, instead of the current 30m.

Native vegetation red tape

Problem: Forgone opportunities to develop high value and privately held agricultural land.

Solution: Reinsert Division 6, Subdivision 1A and sections 22A(2)(k) and 22A(2)(l) into the Vegetation Management Act 1999 as in force prior to 2018. This allowed for the clearing of vegetation on "high value agriculture" (HVA) and "irrigated high value agricultural" (IVHA) land.

Bureaucratic enforcement and penalties for farmers

Problem: Heavy-handed and intrusive enforcement of native vegetation laws by bureaucrats.

Solution: Repeal "Division 1: Enforcement and Investigations" of the Vegetation Management Act 1999 and in its place reintroduce "Division 4B" as in force from 2013 to 2016 so that farmers can undertake vegetation clearing under self-assessable codes of conduct.

Green activists targeting farmers

Problem: Green groups and left-wing lawyers using legal action against farmers and stopping agricultural development.

Solution: Stop government funding of the Environmental Defenders

Office which received $233,000 in 2018 in grants from QLD government.

Management of pests and wildlife

Problem: Regulations limit the ability of private landowners to manage pests and wildlife which can be a threat to livestock, crops, and human health.

Solution: Remove the requirement for a farmer or landowner to obtain a license to manage or eradicate pests and abundant wildlife, such as rats and kangaroos, under the Nature Conservation (Wildlife Management) Regulation 2006. And remove "least concern wildlife" from the definition as a "protected animal" by removing Section 71 (a) (vii) of the Nature Conservation Act 1992. ("Least concern wildlife" is wildlife that is abundant and not threatened or endangered.)

Problem: Primary producers who have applied for a Category H (handgun) licence have been consistently rejected by the Queensland Police Services' Weapons Licencing Branch in recent years without explanation, which is compromising the ability of farmers to manage pest wildlife on their property.

Solution: Add an exemption into Part 5 of the Weapons Act 1990 relaxing the standards for primary producers to obtain a Category H licence.

Mining makes the greatest single contribution to our country, a contribution badly needed, especially now that we are in such record government debt, yet this industry is also saddled with government tape.

It is up to our industry in Australia to stand up and speak out more clearly, real straight talk, not pussyfoot around with words like Australia is well regulated, then complain behind closed doors.

Again, please show government members, what are the government tape burdens restricting your investment and business.

Again, using Queensland as an example:

MINING

Green activist lawfare

Problem: Environmental groups engage in vexatious 'lawfare' where they use the legal system to delay project assessment with the aim of discouraging development. This causes delays and imposes onerous costs on project proponents. Specifically, under Section 260 of the Mineral Resources Act 1989, any entity may lodge an objection to an application for the grant of a mining lease. This has led to the number of objections steadily rising, causing longer delays and expense.

Solution: Amend Section 260 of the Mineral Resources Act 1989 to allow only entities with a direct property rights interest in the development to lodge objections to mining lease applications.

Problem: An individual or their representative can lodge a legal objective regarding the same project through two separate avenues – Section 260 of the Mineral Resources Act 1989, and Section 160 of the Environment Protection Act 1994. Separate to this, the same individual could potentially also lodge a legal challenge under relevant local government planning laws, depending on what given local government planning laws allow.

This allows for frivolous legal challenges to be made multiple times, even where a court has recognised those challenges to be frivolous.

Solution: A provision should be inserted into both Section 260 of the Minerals Resources Act 1989 and Section 160 of the Environment Protection Act 1994 which prohibits the same individual making a legal objection under one of the Acts where an objection has been made under the other Act.

Government funding of green activists

<u>Problem</u>: Anti-mining groups lodge legal challenges to disrupt and delay investment in mining projects. The Environmental Defenders Office (EDO) is one such group which has been actively involved in instigating challenges to coal mining developments in Queensland. According to the Queensland EDO's 2017-18 annual report, the organisation received over $270,000 in funding from the Queensland government. The government should not provide funding for anti-mining environmental activists.

<u>Solution</u>: Immediately cease all government funding of the EDO and other environmental groups engaged in anti-development lawfare.

Red tape on infrastructure

<u>Problem</u>: Project proponents often have temporary tenure over land, rather than acquiring the title to that land. In these cases, areas within that tenure may be used for short-term activities, followed by rehabilitation before the land reverts to the activities of the landowner. The preferred method of relinquishing tenure may be through progressive certification, where an area of the tenure is certified as rehabilitated and relinquished to the landowner.

Section 318ZB(2) and (4) of the Environmental Protection Act 1994 prevents progressive certification by imposing a responsibility on proponents to maintain the rehabilitation in the same condition as at certification; in effect, this means that proponents cannot allow the area to revert to the landholder with infrastructure which was built by the proponent during their tenure, forcing proponents to remove infrastructure that could be repurposed by landowners.

<u>Solution</u>: Amend the Environmental Protection Act 1994 to allow for a legislative exemption from Section 318ZB(2) and (4) where, as part of the transfer process, the landholder provides a statement that

they are satisfied with a given level of rehabilitation or any transfer of existing infrastructure.

Red tape on water licences

Problem: There is no statutory timeframe for decisions for an Associated Water Licence under Subdivision 2 of the Water Act 2000. This allows bureaucrats to prolong the approvals timeframe.

Solution: Amend Section 1250F of the Water Act 2000 by inserting the requirement that the Chief Executive must decide to grant, grant in part, or refuse to grant an application within 7 days. Reasons must be given in writing for refusal.

Red tape on mine rehabilitation

Problem: The Environmental Protection and Other Legislation Amendment Act 2020 created additional red tape for the mining sector. For example, the Act establishes a "Rehabilitation Commissioner" who is to monitor and report on mining rehabilitation practices in Queensland. There are no requirements that the Commissioner have relevant expertise in the area, and there is a non-trivial risk that the Commissioner could be an environmental activist.

Solution: Abolish the role of Rehabilitation Commissioner by amending the Environmental Protection Act 1994 and instead simply detail the terms of rehabilitation in the initial approval process.

Environmental Impact Statement red tape

Problem: The Guidelines which accompany chapter 3 of the Environment Protection Act 1994, outline under what circumstances the government can require the provision of an Environmental Impact

Statement to be prepared by a project proponent.

Many of the circumstances are subjective, vague and broad, which provide too much discretion and authority with bureaucrats, with the effect of delaying the approval of major projects in Queensland.

Specifically, the Standard Criteria for an EIS under schedule 4 of the EP Act include provisions such as "intergenerational equity", "the public interest", and "any other matter prescribed under a regulation".

Solution: Remove all subjective considerations which could trigger the need for an EIS.

This means removing "Appendix A – Standard criteria" from the Guidelines and remove Section 3.1: Cumulative impacts.

Fees and charges imposed on project proponents

Problem: In addition to the payment of taxes and royalties, project proponents are also subject to cost recovery obligations and fees and charges associated with the submission and processing of applications for permits to government.

Industry should not be required to pay for the cost of government regulation, over and above payment already made via taxes and royalties.

Solution: All industry cost recovery and fees and charges should be abolished, for example by repealing Schedule 5 of Mineral Resources Regulations 2013.

Cut bureaucratic red tape for COVID economic and jobs recovery

Problem: Approval time frames and slow bureaucratic assessment of applications and provision of permits will undermine QLD economic and jobs recovery from COVID lockdown.

<u>Solution</u>: There is a provision under the State Development and Public Works Organisation Act 1971 which allows the relevant Minister to cut through bureaucratic red tape through the classification of a given project as a "prescribed project". The designation of a project as a "prescribed project" allows the Coordinator-General (which is a function inside the Department of State Development) to intervene and fast-track approvals. The QLD government should classify all major resources projects as "prescribed projects".

How many approvals, permits and licences do you think we at Roy had to complete before construction, then with more required for construction?

I asked this question of one former Australian Prime Minister who guessed "about 40". But it wasn't 40, or 50, or 100 or 1,000. It wasn't even 2,000 or 3,000.

There were more than 4,000 pieces of government tape we had to deal with before we could even start to build. More than 4,000!

And then more for construction. What small or even medium sized company can pay for all that?

How many people would dedicate high-risk money, many years of effort and undertake a project, knowing that it would require over 4,000 pieces of regulation to be complied with before any prospect of being able to start construction, and then have to go through even more tape, approvals, permits, and licences before producing income; then go through years of more compliance tape burdens. I don't know any country in the world which has to go through so much government tape as we do in Australia.

For a mega project like Roy Hill, that will pay billions in various forms of taxation whilst providing decades of opportunities for many, and other benefits, is it really in the best interests of Australians to burden, delay and risk such projects with thousands of approvals, permits and licences?

Too many in Government and media don't recognise that mining, agricultural and small business profits are needed so we can reinvest, investment being essential if we want to maintain our standard of living, or, if we want our living standards to improve.

Sadly, few have even a clue that their tape and tax do nothing to encourage investment in mining, agriculture, small business or indeed, any industry.

They might mention the word investment but fail, year after year to take the hard decisions that they should, to significantly cut Government tape and tax to make Australia, our very high-cost country, more appealing for investment.

We in business need to help the government with specific examples of regulation that need to be cut. As we all know, our export industries need to be cost competitive internationally. How long can we afford this onerous government burden, this massive slab of government fat?

I'll put my hand up and say the very first tax that should go is payroll tax. This tax along with stamp tax, was meant to be removed when the States got more revenue via the GST. That was back in 2000! Why doesn't our federal government remind the States of this and even reduce their share of GST if the taxes aren't dropped as was meant to have occurred?

And if I may add a message for business, please don't lobby government for more handouts, be that for green or whatever is the flavour of the moment. More handouts mean higher taxes.

Red, green and other government tape is not something that we can't change. Governments can act to reduce it. Other countries have done this with great success, such as our neighbour Singapore, India under the very dedicated leadership of Prime Minister Modi and the United States under the previous strong leadership. If these countries can do it, Australia can too!

I would suggest, a first step is to significantly limit the low-hanging fruit, the duplication of tape between state and federal governments. Projects and businesses should not be burdened with three layers of government tape. My suggestion is where tape extends to mainland Australia, the federal government cuts its tape.

Again, those in small business, please let government members know which of their tape and taxes are restricting your business and limiting your investment.

I've suggested a broad-brush approach to our north, that would certainly help small business, tourism, and primary and other industries:

Create a Special Economic Zone (SEZ) in North Queensland

Problem: North Queensland has been disproportionately impacted by the lockdown measures and various government support programs making it difficult to get unskilled or low skilled workers for restaurants, hotels, motels, bars, cafes, shops, tourist entertainment etc., resulting in lost tourist income and this is likely to continue for some unknown time to come.

Solution: The Queensland government should make North Queensland (defined as the area above the Tropic of Capricorn) a Special Economic Zone.

This would not only help primary industries and tourism, but many small businesses too.

So, for those who want to see living standards rise, please keep reminding government that mining, agriculture and the biggest private employer in Australia, small business, are necessary to help fund our hospitals and kindies, to help our elderly, maintain our infrastructure, provide funds for crises, and very importantly, support and fund our police and defence forces.

A government's first and primary task is to protect and defend its nation.

Although there is record spending in the defence budget, too much of this money and focus is tied up in spending on the department and not on the front-line troops, technology and the equipment we need. It is grossly insufficient to enable us to become a "poisonous barramundi" if under attack, Singapore stated it strived to become a "poisonous shrimp" to deter other countries from trespassing.

Please let us never forget our military put their lives on the line to protect us, usually risking these lives several times a day when on difficult overseas missions. It's no small task signing up to the military – so we should respect and be very grateful for our troops, not demoralise them through not tested reports such as the recent 5-year Brereton inquiry, diverting our troops from their training.

Given all the serious challenges we face as a country, it was shocking for many good Australians to see the Defence Department order our military to divert to holding rainbow teas and to strip 3,000 of our most highly trained military personnel of their medals.

It is up to each of us who values our troops and the defence of our nation to constantly make our Prime Minister and Federal Government aware that we expect them to honour their first responsibility to our nation and to include sufficient budget resources to do so.

We also should be terrific at supporting our returned servicemen and women who, too often, aren't able to transition smoothly into civilian life. It is nothing short of tragic to see so many returned military personnel suicide, especially following the years of an unnecessary public inquiry.

If you have served your country in very difficult and dangerous missions, sacrificed part of your own life being away from your family, even when they may have needed you, spent much of your adult life training hard to join such effort, to then have your government, the one who ordered you overseas, to treat you like this is beyond disgraceful.

Whenever we see our military, let's always thank them for their service and help them in more ways that we can. Our government has let them down very badly. Indeed, more so, given the then Afghanistan government never complained of our troops on their soil. Yes, the media has stirred up the potential for some people in Afghanistan to try to get compensation for civilian tragedies. Very sadly, most wars include civilian tragedies, but this may open the door for compensation calls to Australia, even though our troops were not the only ones with ammunition.

Our country owes a debt and thanks to those who are bravely fighting another war, in the media to try to save our country and our young from the slippery socialist path. Yes – helping Australians to try to leave a better future for the next generation.

Thank you to media leaders like Andrew Bolt, Paul Whittaker and Rowan Dean, and extra big thanks to the longest media battler of all, Alan Jones! What a patriotic Australian, what a star.

Gina Rinehart is a leading figure in the mining and agricultural industries in Australia. She is also a leading figure in Australia's Olympics efforts, being patron of four teams – swimming, rowing, volleyball and synchronised swimming – making her the largest single non-government contributor to the Olympic effort in Australia's history. Mrs Rinehart is the Executive Chairman of Hancock Prospecting Group, Roy Hill and the iconic pastoral

company, S. Kidman & Co. She is also the founder of Australians for Northern Development and Economic Vision (ANDEV), National Mining and Related Industries Day and National Agriculture and Related Industries Day. Mrs Rinehart is a Governor of the American Chamber of Commerce in Australia. She has been awarded an Honorary Doctorate from Bond University together with other prestigious business awards. She was CEO Magazine's Chairman of the Year in 2014 and 2017 and has received their lifetime achievement award.

32

SHRINK YOUR CLASSROOMS, SHRINK YOUR COUNTRY

Dallas McInerney

Three men walk into a bar, a Greek polymath, let's call him Aristotle, an Englishman who resides in Washington (via Balliol College), let's call him Christopher Hitchens and the Governor of Texas, let's call him George W. Bush. Hitchens doesn't hesitate on the opportunity and goes deep into a single malt, it's a club soda for George and Ari refrains. The conversation amongst these three naturally turns to heavy matters of conscience, culture and how best to nurture the intellectual development of youth and civilisation generally (what else would they talk about?).

Ari tees off and offers some entry level advice, "give me the child for the first seven years and I'll give you the man". This doesn't really register with Hitchens but it has caught Bush's ear who has his own thoughts on education. Bush is concerned about the plight of minority students on whose behalf terrible assumptions are often made by those charged with their schooling. Bush tells Ari of his belief that reading is the new civil right for black kids and too often, minority American children experience an achievement gap; "too many believe these kids were not meant to learn", Bush relays to a nodding Ari.

Hitchens is now engaged and brings forth what he considers is needed for all good discussions – a comment from Hitchens! "A barbarian never takes the city until someone holds the gates open to them", he intones.

Let's torture this fantastical story further. Name the bar the 'Last Chance Saloon' and situate it in any city in the Anglosphere or, right here in Australia.

Having pioneered and led from the front during the Industrial revolution, Western Civilisation and its constituent nation states are at risk of being at the back of the pack as we move through the technology and knowledge revolutions. School students from developing worlds often outperform Australian, New Zealand, American, Canadian and Irish students.

Australian school students are experiencing a decline in learning outcomes in both relative and absolute terms across major global educational indices, with notable concerns in the key domains of literacy and numeracy. This coincides at a time of record resources and support being extended to Australian schools while being led by a highly credentialed and committed teacher workforce.

So, what is going on? Having invested so heavily in the inputs of school education (funding, resources), what accounts for the oftentimes, disappointing outputs (PISA and TIMMS scores etc.) of Australian schools? Critically, how do we arrest the decline and how much time do we have as world moves to overtake us?

Aristotle's claim (later appropriated by the Jesuits) speaks to the lasting power of a child's formative experience and the influence of early instruction in shaping the future contours of both mind and character. So much flows from childhood educational experience, including the life path charted for and by the student during those early years. In modern educational policy, the focus on the 0-5 years of early development and foundational learning, gives expression to the Aristotelian creed, though no educational faculty would acknowledge the intellectual providence of their research.

Aristotle was correct of course; the early years count for so much and are rightly considered a harbinger of life's possible rewards and riches. Any philosophy that is concerned with individual attainment, opportunity, reward for effort and the community dividends of rich intellectual traditions must first concern itself with the start of the journey – schools.

This must be an ongoing project for conservatives; in recent times, it was considered an off Broadway pursuit by the Right as more celebrated policy endeavours found favour and delivered prominence.

Hitchens' was a figurative observation, as they often were. In this instance, he was regaling a Manhattan crowd who had gathered to hear him promote his best-selling book, "God is not Great". He was speaking of the dangers of a sleeping America not attuned to the growing domestic risk of a new entrant, Islamofascism. A recent instinct for accommodation and the acceptance of the unacceptable had left the Unites States, according to Hitchens, with a massive internal security risk and cultural vulnerability.

Hitchens' barbarian observations were figurative, as they often were, but also deliberate. An avowed supporter of Trotsky until his death, Hitchens was channeling the Trotskyite tactic of 'entryism'. This involves securing an influential foothold in an organisation or movement by benign or even legitimate means, ahead of unleashing damaging or a countering suite of influences. Think the long March through the Institutions.

Where Hitchens was alarmed by America's crisis of self-confidence, conservatives need to be alarmed, or at least alert, to the influences and pedagogy that have been allowed to enter the Australian school education system, including on their watch. What has gained entry or a hold in some places, is a vision of education that promotes and celebrates a soft skills vision of curricula, one that can privilege insanely nebulous pursuits such as self-reflection, collaboration or empathy, as ends in themselves. They are sold to parents and students as being indispensable skills for the 21st Century, as if they magically dawned on humanity as salvational tools at 12.01am, January 1st, 2001!

None of these as standalone attributes are really contestable, but when they take the place of knowledge, content and foundational information or worse, paraded as being actual sound educational tenets to the exclusion of everything else, Houston, we have a problem (more on Texas later)!

Have we forsaken or neglected the fundamental civic and community mission of schools to prepare generations for informed citizenship and ultimately, leadership, powered by investing in one's dignity through scholarship? Do conservatives even have an agreed and distilled position of the purposes of school education in 2021? If they do, it is not debated or talked about nearly enough. The pursuit of other interests and bright lights have meant they vacated the field and the results are now before us.

What increasingly finds favour in school education circles is an approach that discounts the importance of knowledge attainment and subject specific content in favour of grievance-tinged presentations of 'themes' or 'perspectives' sold with tag lines that are uncritically digested by parents, such as 'contemporary, student-centred inquiry'.

The aim should be for our schools to be citadels of learning and development, powered by reason and contestability; however, there are too many examples that have children spending class time that lacks a rigour or long-term reward, such as being encouraged to explore their feelings, find their 'voice' and having the right quota of culturally relevant experiences.

Where is the content that recognises the liberating and enriching power of capitalism? The NSW School course of "Society and Culture" appears as the obvious unit of study that might, for example, recognise the liberating and enriching power of capitalism, its role in unprecedented wealth creation, its partnership with democracy against autocracy and the emancipation of women?

It doesn't.

It does, however, have students design and undertake self-directed projects in the areas of gender, identity and power. The great modern success story of capitalism and its uplifting power over the human condition is a big miss for today's kids, though you might find some lamentation about white privilege in corporate boardrooms with a Ross Gittens article on comparative wage justice thrown in somewhere.

It is not only misguided aspects of content but also the diminishing breadth which presages longer term problems for Australia's future knowledge base and shared understanding of each other.

We risk shrinking the great educational and knowledge panorama that should be available to all school children without interruption or interference.

Consider the attack on the western canon and the truly bizarre contrivance of grievance hunters to find fault with any traditional text; nothing is sacred, especially the Sacred! Shakespeare is now problematic for school children we are told. The Bard could be racist or homophobic, for these activists; no curricula or instructional text can or should be neutral and accounting for context is either an inherently prejudiced notion or just gets in the way of a jolly good act of intellectual vandalism. It is actually a miserabilist mindset that promotes this lunacy.

You will need to look long and hard for sufficient measure of automaticity, Christianity and citizenship in today's prevailing approach to education and learning.

Children need to learn how they will both internally and externally adjudicate their encounters with difference and conflicting perspectives; such friction can fire the intellect. Alas, it will not be developed in students who are educated on a diet of dismissal and consensus where all things deemed 'controversial' are initially presented in a judgmental or unbalanced manner; no room for interrogation or examination, just blithe consumption.

Ironically, or predictably, those texts which are cultural bulwarks against racism and discrimination are also targeted for excision from curricula; a growing number of states in the USA are following each other in removing Harper Lee's timeless masterpiece *To Kill a Mockingbird*.

On the basis that the text includes the 'N' word (Scout is chastised by her father, Atticus, for using the word), it is now considered by a growing number of American school boards as unacceptable and triggering. It is foolhardy to think this trend will not soon gain prominence in Australia.

On matters of the South, George W. Bush, as Governor of Texas, was the first major conservative figure since Margaret Thatcher to deliberately attach their political career to education policy; and, thereafter, made it a centrepiece of his Presidential campaign. As Governor of a border state, with a high Hispanic population, Bush was appalled at the achievement gap that showed up in minority student cohorts in Texan schools and set about fixing the malaise with a focus on instructional, knowledge-based learning, founded on strong early literacy skills. No more was he prepared to accept these kids suffering, what he described as the 'soft bigotry of low expectations'.

Decades later, there is a lesson from the Bush approach to minorities and Australia's approach to Indigenous education. No school, or Australian, can be, in any way, satisfied with the abject failure in Indigenous education that has persisted for too many decades. It is a failure that reflects on us all.

Albeit guided by good intentions, the approach to Indigenous education that gained entry and found favour in Australian schools has left them too far behind in their learning journey.

It is a point that has led Australia's keenest intellectual and leading Indigenous figure, Noel Pearson, to emphatically declare and implore others to agree that there is nothing *sui generis* when it comes to teaching Aboriginal children; and, alternative culturally specific approaches are not the way to go. They are a rebuke of identity informed pedagogy.

Like Bush, Pearson does favour accounting and considering the context of these children, but to eschew proven strategies such as direct instruction in the name of cultural considerations is just wrong. The timidity on the part of Conservatives to more fully enter this debate at an earlier point, arguably accounts for some of this failure.

A reorientation of interest and attention to school policy and pedagogy by conservatives is overdue; moreover, there needs to be a political recognition for those who make such an investment that the problems are manifest and the stakes, high. Action is needed, in large and quick measure, lest our children be intellectually coddled to the point of a scholastic enfeeblement.

Early attention should be given to a curatorial crusade across all Australian school learning material; not for the purposes of replacing 'progressivist' or leftist content with right-wing dogma or conservative treatises – that, too, would be a betrayal of student needs. Rather, we need to curate the content and replace the ephemeral with the abiding, the superficial for the universal and the self- loathing with the confident.

If we commit to such an undertaking, then even three disparate figures such as Ari, Christopher and George could be moved to raise a toast in approval of our schools.

One question remains, are we willing to stand guard at the gates?

Dallas McInerney is the Chief Executive Officer of Catholic Schools NSW, the Approved System Authority for the State's 595 Catholic schools. Prior to his appointment, Dallas spent 15 years in financial services across a variety of functions with companies such as the Insurance Australia Group, MLC and NAB. He is a Director of the NSW Education Standards Authority (previously known as the Board of Studies) and a Director of Catholic Commission for Employment Relations. In 2018/19, Dallas served on the State Executive of the NSW Liberal Party.

33

THE POLITICS OF THE MIDDLE

Caroline Di Russo

I have always been fascinated by politics. I grew up in the bush, a barefoot farm kid from a migrant family and I vividly remember politics being typical dining table conversation. My Nonna would cook for at least 10 of us every day and there was never a shortage of lively debate, staunch opinions and constant frustration with +20% interest rates and that "ratbag" Graham Richardson. I left the farm to go to boarding school, then went to university, worked in the legal profession, and eventually started my own business. It was only after going into business that I properly began to appreciate how much government policy directly affects those on the ground and how little the political class understands, engages and reflects the people they're meant to serve.

The closer I keep an eye on political goings on, the more mindful I have become of the increasingly tiresome and tribal nature of our political discourse. It's like watching the chihuahuas on the ends of the political spectrum yell at each other through a plate glass window as the rest of us look on partially bemused and partially disappointed at the state of it all – as well as acutely aware of the fact we're paying for this circus. In the midst of the squabble, the voice of middle Australia invariably gets lost.

So, who is middle Australia?

Well, it's one of those things you know when you see it. Trying to define it precisely is like trying to fashion *petit fours* with a shovel. Ultimately, its subjective depending on your precise values and priorities and from where you are looking.

For me, middle Australia comprises those people who are busy keeping their show on the road with the least amount of fuss: they're working, raising kids, paying the mortgage, and saving for an annual holiday. And while we know middle Australia isn't all that politically engaged, they are well-versed in fairness and know when someone is trying to sell them a bridge.

They are decent, aspirational and imperfect at the same time.

In reality, the sentiment on the ground is always more nuanced than our national discourse would have us believe. People don't live in little boxes and they don't necessarily support every ideological position in their notional political territory. The idea that you can't be centre-left without being willing to die on the hill of woke is as untrue and politically infantile as saying you can't be centre-right unless you oppose same sex marriage.

Middle Australia is why the major federal political parties need a 40% primary vote to take government. It also illustrates why, as the Labor Party has moved further and further to the left, their primary vote has plummeted from 43.38% in 2007 when Kevin Rudd sold himself as a centrist, to 33.3% in 2019 when Bill Shorten told us the financial cost of his climate change policy didn't matter because the consequences of doing nothing were greater, and despite the middle being lost in the fray, they take their revenge at the ballot box. It's where the reclamation occurs. The last three 'climate change' elections tell us this is so.

The fact is, the cost and consequences of all policy matters and, particularly, any policy which is likely to affect something as fundamental as the cost of living. While Australians do care about the environment and reducing pollution, that can rub against their immediate concern of being able to pay their household bills. The immediacy of the latter concern doesn't mean Australians don't care; it just means they know their limits and prioritise as best they can.

That is more than we can say for much of the political class, the activist set and the commentariat. They think poverty means driving a C-Class and everyone can just shell out for a roof full of solar panels.

Earlier this year, Anthony Albanese announced that the ALP was "competitive". Actually, it's hard to think of a time when Labor has been less reflective of community attitudes and as weak in delivering its message. The reality is, the entire country would be better served by a strong Opposition; and an Opposition, just like a Government, will be stronger if they can read the middle of the room.

Unfortunately for Labor, they either aren't interested in the middle or they think they understand it when, in fact, they don't. The latest slogan they've trotted out is 'we're on your side'. Whose side is that and why do we have to choose sides? Using class warfare as a political weapon has never been particularly fruitful territory in Australia. Compare this approach to Bob Hawke's 'Bringing Australia Together' and 'Let's Stick Together'.

Now, Bob Hawke was not without his flaws, but boy could that man gauge the mood of the nation. His approach to framing the political narrative was a perfect cocktail of perceived fairness and aspiration, with a sprinkle of larrikin imperfection. Whether you liked him or not, it's undeniable that he spoke directly to the middle. Hence, his enduring political success and legacy.

And while we are fraternising with the Labor party of the 80s and 90s, let's get back to that "ratbag", Graham Richardson.

When I first started watching Richo commentate on Sky News, I kept getting this awkward uneasy feeling. It took me a little while to realise the cause of my consternation, but it eventually dawned on me: I now sympathised with almost everything he said. Because, instead of indulging the elitist and divisive palaver of identity politics, the hallmark of the modern Labor Party, he spoke about fairness and common sense solutions to problems. It wasn't performative ideology; he was rollicking in the old 'fair go' territory of the Labor party.

So, how is this relevant to the Liberal Party and centre-right politics? Because the Liberal Party needs to avoid vacating the middle, as the Labor Party has largely done, by hitching its cart to each and every fleeting and fashionable political cause.

Remember, the Liberal party is also at its electoral and policy best when it speaks to middle Australia in its own way: the small business owners, the regional Australians, the tradies with an investment property in their nest egg and the aspirational class. We also know them as the 'forgotten people', 'Howard's battlers' and the 'quiet Australians'. It's not a party hidebound by any one political ideology but one anchored in a diverse tapestry of community values – the 'broad church' so to speak.

Historically, the party's electoral success hinges on policies which keep the country safe and prosperous and which encourage Australians to work hard, be aspirational, support themselves where they can and be compassionate and caring to those who cannot. The Liberals have made it easier to do business and have encouraged industry and productivity; and we know that a healthy economy gives rise to a stronger middle class, which in turn, gives people greater freedom of choice and opportunity to continue growing.

As the Labor Party moves further from the middle, it focuses on politicking instead of developing policy which is electorally palatable. Their main shtick is trying to frame the Liberals as the party of big business and the big end of town. This is simply not true. The party of big business is whichever party lets big business get its way. Those businesses are crony corporates and they are not driven by principle; they are driven purely by self-interest. They are not free market capitalists and, in fact, they welcome regulation because they have the staff to manage it and the market share to pass on the cost.

Crony corporates pretend to care about free markets the same way socialists pretend to care about people.

Small business doesn't have that luxury, hence why they support the streamlining of regulation and the reduction of red tape. This is why they have always found their natural home with the Liberals and why the party does its best work when it sticks to its proverbial knitting. It's how the party has won elections, albeit at State level; but compare that success to the disaster which was the 2021 Western Australian State election. We saw blue-ribbon Liberal seats fall to Labor for the first time and the irresistible temptation was to blame COVID-19 and move on; simply say that all opposition parties around the country suffered election defeats and the Liberals never really stood a chance.

The real issue is the sheer number of voters who jumped ship, first in 2017 and again in 2021. People once knew what the party stood for but are no longer sure if it still stands for it.

There were too many announcements in too many areas, and none with enough detail. It was the ultimate political soufflé. And, despite a term of repeated government failures, the punters didn't see the Liberals as a viable alternative and decided to skip dessert.

The most contentious policy was the 'green energy policy' which included a renewable energy infrastructure investment, closing the Collie power station and reducing government emissions to net zero by 2030. It was described in the media as a Greens-style policy which was heavy on ambition but light on substance; and, despite framing it as a job creation policy, the Liberals struggled to demonstrate why that was the case and this did not go unnoticed.

Unsurprisingly, it only impressed people who weren't going to vote for us anyway, while simultaneously repelling traditional Liberal voters and anyone on the fence.

Another issue was the perception that candidates from religious backgrounds didn't appeal to the mainstream voters. The extent to which this affected the vote is hard to gauge but it is a timely reminder of the importance of choosing candidates who reflect the community as well as the values of the party. It's also a timely reminder of the power of perceptions and the need to effectively manage the party brand.

So, how do the Liberals best use what it knows, to get to where it needs to go?

Well, in the lead up to the next federal election and beyond, the party needs to focus on its bread and butter: reduction of red tape and government waste, tax reform, competitive federalism, productive infrastructure, job creation and the encouragement of economic growth. The party itself needs to continue to engage with small business and the middle, keep their concerns front of mind in policy development, and give them a reason to trust the Liberals with another term.

In relation to candidates, the party needs to be thoughtful and bespoke in its preselection processes: be mindful of local demographics, and preselect well-rounded candidates who reflect their electorate and appeal broadly. An election isn't won appealing to a niche market.

To achieve this, the Liberals should decentralise power in the preselection process, have a good long hard look at what it considers to be meritorious, and select on that basis. Why is this important? Because how the party behaves and promotes internally, ultimately reflects its external brand. Whether we like it or not, people can spot a spiv a mile away – and the party should avoid making the difficult job of getting elected any harder than it needs to be.

Finally, for any government to continue to be electable, particularly one looking for a fourth term, it needs to remain relevant and have something substantive to offer; but also, be mindful of the road travelled, look back at what did and didn't work, and make changes for the benefit of the country beyond the political short term.

This government wants to be remembered for how it made the lives of Australians better, not for the hard conversations it avoided or the scandals it poured cold water on. It must be practical and authentic in its message and execute it with conviction. Its job is to do more than simply manage the decline of the country. It must be courageous. It must embrace the middle and it must drive substantive reform.

This barefoot farm kid is keeping a watchful eye.

Caroline Di Russo is a lawyer by profession with over 10 years' experience specialising in commercial disputes, corporate insolvency and reconstruction. She is a columnist for the _Spectator Australia_, _Penthouse Australia_ and contributes to the Menzies Research Centre. She is also a regular contributor on _Sky News Australia_ and is Chair of the WA Liberals' law and intergovernmental subcommittee.

34

HOW LONG WILL THE AUSTRALIAN CONSTITUTION ENDURE?

Peter King

First made in 1901, and since condemned as outmoded, ramshackle, unintelligible and impossible to teach in schools, a mystery to those who should be its masters, costly to change and out of step with modern Australia, the Australian Constitution has been remarkably resilient. Four main criticisms are that the Constitution does not reflect the nation's status as an independent country and a Federal Parliamentary Democracy, that its framework is not suitable for the economic, social and political development of the nation, that as a Federation there is an inappropriate balance between the Commonwealth and the States, and Territories and, that it fails to ensure fundamental democratic rights are guaranteed.

There have been detailed official reviews to consider these concerns. Australian Governments in 1929, 1942, 1959 and 1988 authorised reports based on Constitutional Commissions or Conventions some of which were costly, all thorough and extended over several years. The last was by the Hawke Government, initiated by the Victorian Government, and then taken over by the Commonwealth. In 1998 the Australian Constitutional Convention, established by the Howard Government, reviewed the fundamental issue of the country's monarchical foundation. Attending that Convention, as I did with leading and other figures of the day, I saw first-hand how passionate for and against constitutional change many Australians are. Apart from these official reviews, there are leading writers on the Constitution, Judges and others who have written books, articles and Judgments calling for reform including a Bill of Rights and more recently for new covering clauses to acknowledge Indigenous Australia.

Yet, more than 120 years later, the Australian Constitution has endured. It is one of the world's oldest written constitutions. As former Chair of the World Heritage Committee, categorised under the World Heritage Convention, it is a significant item of intangible cultural heritage. Some of the criticisms made have validity. It compromises some ideals. Yet practical politicians know sometimes the good with the bad is necessary for an outcome. The criticism that it is derivative may also be correct, but when analysed that is the very reason for its strength, and endurance. It was made by the Founding Fathers, or Framers as they are now called, based on two powerful constitutional traditions, that of the United States of America being a written constitution, and that of Great Britain being an unwritten constitution, with a third tradition at its core, which may properly be described as the Australian tradition. Each is a remarkable contribution.

The American Constitution is the first and critical source of the Australian Constitution. It says a lot for the independent spirit of the Framers that they looked across the Pacific and drew strongly upon the American model. The United States of America just over 100 years earlier had rebelled against the Imperial Crown, which the Framers were determined to retain. The American model powerfully influenced those colonists who first sat down in 1891 and, over the next 10 years, wrote the Constitution. Its fundamental structure is based upon the American doctrine of separation of powers, as a guarantee of freedom. The principle is that political freedom is best preserved by keeping separate the functions and roles of the three key arms of Government, the Legislature or Parliament, the Executive Government or bureaucracy, and the Judiciary or the courts. Law makers, administrators and dispute resolvers each in this worldview have their place. The result is at the core of the Australian Constitution, a guarantee of political, social and economic freedom.

Events since 1901 have reinforced the strength of the separation of powers ideal, which has become a strict doctrine in the hands of the Judiciary but with Australian characteristics. Accordingly, a Federal Court may not, by law, be given non-judicial roles such as investigation, and vice versa executive agencies of a government may not be given judicial powers or roles to perform. All such laws are invalid. This is the Boilermakers' principle named after the 1956 High Court case of that name. This strict approach guarantees independence of the Judiciary from Government, and confidence in the rule of law. It has also led through judicial activism to the development of new constitutionally protected freedoms, derived from the words used in the founding document. An example is the freedom of political communication, derived loosely from the words 'directly chosen'. Based on this freedom the Judiciary have struck down laws both Federal or State whose terms, operation or effect is to impair the freedom of political communication, e.g., laws which restrict campaign material, or even laws operating outside the election period which restrict public criticism of other laws and the law-making process.

In short, the doctrine of separation of powers has become a raw topic of continuing relevance with the Judiciary and is still seen as fundamental to stable constitutional Government in Australia. It is embedded law, in the sense it overrides other laws. Its reach has been extended by decisions of the Judiciary to State as well as

Commonwealth legislative powers. For example, in the recent case of Williams, the High Court struck down a funding agreement between the Commonwealth and Scripture Union Queensland to provide religious education to Darling Heights High School, but where the Parliament had not made a law authorising the program. Under the separation of powers doctrine, the Executive's initiative directed by the Howard Government was struck down because the Legislature had not approved it.

The perceived role of the Judiciary is also strictly conserved. Recently, the conservative Queensland blogger ex-Army Major Bernard Gaynor was prosecuted on multiple occasions in the NSW Civil and Administrative Tribunal, an executive agency of that State, by the Anti-Discrimination Board of NSW upon complaint by a discrimination activist Mr Garry Burns. Burns and the ADB complained that Gaynor had blogged public criticism of discrimination activists like himself. Burns and Gaynor are residents of different States. The Constitution provides in Chapter III section 75 that disputes between residents of different States are matters for the Commonwealth Judiciary. The High Court held that the NSW Parliament's laws giving its Executive power to decide Burns' complaints were invalid. NSW's laws denied Gaynor the protection of due process of law.

Apart from structure and respect for freedom, based on the separation of powers ideal, the text of the Australian Constitution also owes much to its American model. A powerful example is the express freedom of religion provided for by section 116, discussed further below. The Bill of Rights, part of the text of the American Constitution, likewise provides for a guarantee of religious freedom. The Australian Constitution also provides that the Commonwealth may not take a citizen's property except on just terms, that is by paying him or her full compensation. Karl Marx, and President Xi, obviously spurn that freedom; but in the spirit of Hume, the Australian Constitution denies Government the power to take property, or reshape a nation by any political doctrine depriving another of property unless with full recompense. The American democratic tradition of freedom and protection of property rights is an integral part of our Constitution, not to be abandoned lightly. In short, the American tradition is vital to the Australian constitutional framework.

Can the same be said of the British contribution to the Australian Constitution? Yes, but not for the reasons most think. Its more obvious influence is in the express role of the Crown in Chapter II. Every act or omission of the Australian Executive is an act for and by the Crown. Yet, at bottom, Government by the Crown is just a reflection of a convention in all constitutional monarchies like the Commonwealth and the States, an exoskeleton of administrative convenience. More fundamental is the role of the Crown as a centre of power in itself, and its meaning. That function is not a convention, but introduces something basic and fundamental not often associated with other constitutions, but understood by most Australians if referendum results count. Properly characterised, the Australian Constitution is the constitution of a religious polity and denominates Australia a Christian nation.

Sir John Downer, on 3 March, 1898, along with Patrick Glynn, another of the key delegates from South Australia at the Constitutional Convention of that date, described the new nation as 'a Christian Commonwealth' founded upon the inheritance of English law and traditions, to be reflected in the express terms of the Preamble. Higgins, who became a justice on the first High Court, and others, objected. Downer, however, pointed to the official name, the Commonwealth of Australia, on which all had agreed, and the Preamble. The Framers, with an eye to the future, did not merely adopt Matthew Flinders' territorial name, Australia, but embraced it in the context of a commonwealth. The document then emphatically stated that, the people, "humbly relying on the blessing of Almighty God, have agreed to unite in one indissoluble Federal Commonwealth under the Crown ... and under the Constitution." Only the people of Western Australia were not recorded as having made that invocation, but they later did when they pleaded to be joined with their fellow colonists to form the new nation.

It might be said against this analysis that, in section 116, the Framers provided that, "The Commonwealth shall not make any law for establishing any religion." The key emphasis, in contrast to the American Bill of Rights, is upon the gerund, the present tense. That is, no law can be made by the Parliament for establishing any new religion; it says nothing about prevention of assistance to the religion recognised by the new polity as already established under the express terms of the Preamble and the central role of the Crown. Beck and others have claimed that section 116 provides for a wall of separation between Government and all religions. However, that is only partly true. The roles of the Crown, in its administrative and religious aspects, both in fact and at law as part of the Preamble, expressly recognise Christianity as an established religion. Accordingly, the Commonwealth, through the Australian Heritage Commission, has duly provided for the construction of Waddell's towers on St Mary's Cathedral in Sydney, and the crypt of St John's Cathedral in Brisbane. This is not a mere polemic, but a fundamental protection, of contemporary relevance.

That Christian foundation may not be seen as a reason for denying the right to practice other religions, protected by section 116. Recently, a Sudanese man, born an Islamist, converted to Christianity in Australia after arriving as a refugee and was accepted into a longstanding Baptist congregation. As a non-citizen in Australia, he was liable to be deported. But, from the time of his conversion, he was no longer an alien, but a non-alien, non-citizen who fell outside the banishment provisions of the Migration Act 1958. Had he been deported to Sudan, he faced certain death as an apostate. His belonging to an Australian community, linked to a constitutionally recognised religion, was a feature guaranteeing his life. However, the Christian tradition, at the heart of the British contribution, still plays a key role, valued by many.

Turning lastly to the Australian tradition, which is focussed on the core notion of community, the word "Australia" is significant. To quote Alfred Deakin, the word looks backwards and forwards, and whether you are Paul Hogan or Linda Jaivin, when a crowd choruses 'Aussie, Aussie, Aussie', as it did at Wimbledon after Ms Ashleigh Barty's recent success, it rings true. There is an aftertaste, an impression of the larrikin to be sure, even of coarseness, but that obscures a moral compass that comes from inner strength and bright confidence. There is an assuredness, a lucidity, which overreaches legalistic jargon, professional training, and study. It is that easiness in context, a determination not to be distracted by any irrelevancy, that is at the heart of any characterisation of what it means to be an Australian, and part of the Australian community.

As for the remainder of the official title 'the Commonwealth', it has powerful resonance, historically, and by the example of others. Four of the United States, including Virginia and Massachusetts, are self-described commonwealths. Its etymology is sourced to the traditional Anglo-Saxon word for a political community with a sense of tribe founded upon the common good. Some objected to the word, when adopted in 1891, because of its association with res publica or republic and others for its use by Cromwell. But the core Anglo-Saxon meaning derives from the commonweal, a community where supreme power is vested in the people. The central notion is community, in which every citizen has a part, and is therefore respected, to provide for a common quality of life or outcome. That quality of life refers to the individual's perception of his or her position in the context of the culture and value systems in which they live. Obvious indicators of such quality of life include wealth, employment, the environment, physical and mental health, education, recreation and leisure time, social belonging, religious beliefs, community safety, national security and freedom. Only the full name, the Commonwealth of Australia, and what it means, captures that tradition and sense of belonging to that community.

It is appropriate, briefly, to mention history. Australia is extraordinarily ordinary. For at least 65,000 years, mankind has occupied the landmass, Australia. Vast reaches of the countryside have proved productive, some areas highly productive. Whether the dark emu analysis is accepted, undoubtedly correct for the Riverina in NSW and the Western Districts of Victoria, or rejected, the land itself has been, and is capable of feeding, large numbers of humankind. As Egypt was to ancient Rome, Australia has the agricultural capacity to be the storehouse of the planet that can feed, if pressed, with grain and meat, 7 billion. Rich agricultural and grazing lands, hardworking and innovative farmers and back up structures with agents and facilitators who get the products to market, is the key to that unique feature. Its richest resource however lies in its people.

Putting history aside, the Australian tradition's respect for community, expressed in the Constitution, is robust and of continuing relevance. It is a constraint, and a source of freedom. It confirms the Framers did not make a republic but a gradualist constitutional monarchy. It also embeds certain unrelinquishable protections of some basic human rights, particularly freedom of religion, freedom of ownership of property, freedom of association and the freedom of political communication. And it conserves the Federal structure with the core regions, the States. Those regional communities, although large, still matter and not just for sporting events. COVID-19 has demonstrated the continuing relevance of the Federal structure to such an extent that it is now sensible to revive that cooperative initiative of the Framers, the Inter-State Commission found in section 101.

Looking forward, the Constitution is an expressed scheme of government or, as Sir Robert Menzies wrote in 1967 in Central Power in the Australian Commonwealth, it is "not a straight-jacket; it is a frame of government."

Most significantly, for present purposes, it is the three traditions that lie at the core of the Australian Constitution that underpin and make the Constitution strong and explain why it will endure. Each of these traditions has contributed to the core values of the Australian Constitution of freedom, of orderly change and prosperity under one authority sourced to God, and of community, in many different and diverse contemporary settings. The Australian Constitution, favoured by such features, will, for these reasons, endure for many years. It will endure for at least another century.

If it ever fails the wit and initiative of the Australian people, it will only be because it was discarded, not from within but from without, not by Australia but by the failure or collapse of those political traditions from which it has been caste.

The Framers wrote a document that is not parochial, but universal; not a short term fix, but permanent.

Peter King is a Barrister-at-Law at Queen's Square Chambers. In 2001, he was elected to the Australian Parliament as the Federal Liberal Member for Wentworth. Prior to entering Parliament, Peter was a Judicial Member of the Administrative Decisions Tribunal of NSW. In 1987, he served on Woollahra Municipal Council and was elected Mayor in 1990-91. During this time he also served as President of the NSW Liberal Party. Peter King is a graduate of Sydney University and, in 1975, was awarded a Rhodes Scholarship, gaining his Masters Degree at Oxford University. While there, he won his Oxford Blue in rugby. During his time practising, Peter King has appeared in cases for farmers against banks during the drought, helping to keep many farmers on their farms; and has been involved in several commercial and constitutional cases including Spencer v Commonwealth (2010) and Gaynor v Chief of Defence Force (2015).

35

IT IS TIME TO TALK PRODUCTIVITY

Senator Ben Small

The coronavirus pandemic ushered in the most profound restrictions.

As a bicentennial baby living in 2007, three things were a comfortable certainty in life – John Howard was the Prime Minister, share markets only went up and economies continually grew. I found myself part of a new generation of Australians who were beginning to make their way in the world, with a blind ignorance that we were the beneficiaries of some two decades of continual economic growth. This is understandable when you consider that when Australia was beset by the recession that we 'had to have', "Ice Ice Baby" was on top of the charts, the Simpsons had only just begun screening for the first time and Dustin Martin was in nappies.

Of course, 2007 was to mark the year that these comforts were ripped out from asunder bicentennial babies such as myself. By the end of the year, what would become known as the Global Financial Crisis (GFC) was well and truly underway, as bank bailouts began and share markets wobbled in preparation for enormous falls. The Australian people evicted John Howard from both the Lodge and the House of Representatives and, with his departure, the Liberal Party's appetite for serious industrial relations reform died. Indeed, 'dying' wasn't sufficient, with then Opposition Leader Tony Abbott later declaring that WorkChoices was "dead, buried and cremated" as he publicly ruled out any industrial relations reform in the next parliament.

While the entrails of WorkChoices have been picked over extensively by others, I contend that the Liberal Party has learned the wrong lessons from its defeat.

It is seldom, if ever, acknowledged that the legislation was carried by a Minister with no significant experience in workplace relations; rushed through Parliament without appropriate scrutiny – despite receiving 202 significant and almost 5,400 minor submissions; the Senate's public hearings were held within a week; the report tabled two days after the conclusion of the hearings and proposed without having taken the time to prepare the Australian people for the reforms, explaining the problems and building a public case with the vocal community support of the business sector. Indeed, through the eyes of voters, there was no obvious need for the legislation at all.

Rather, the lesson that the Liberal Party took from the 2007 defeat was that industrial relations is a debate that we will never win.

Industrial Relations is not the third rail of Australian politics and, as Liberals, it is imperative that we dispel this myth. After all, Michaelia Cash did manage to get the Australian Building and Construction Commission reinstated, established the Registered Organisation Commission and abolished the Road Safety Remuneration Tribunal (which was the Transport Workers Union's attempt to bolster membership at the cost of owner-drivers losing their livelihood) and we went on to win the next election. If we distil the WorkChoices saga down to a single root cause of failure, it was that the Prime Minister could not look down the barrel of a TV camera and honestly declare that all Australians would be better off. My deep and sincere conviction is that, as a Coalition Government, we are again in danger of being unable to argue that all Australians will be better off under our leadership – but this time, from inaction.

The rising standards of living that reflected Australia remaining free from recession for a world record 113 quarters didn't just happen by accident. Instead, the microeconomic reforms of successive Governments continued to drive growth and prosperity, notwithstanding occasionally significant economic headwinds from events such as the Asian Financial Crisis, Dot-com Bubble and the GFC. Over time, the drivers of that almost 30 years of continuous economic growth became known as the 3Ps; population, participation and productivity. With population growth at generational lows and participation rates already at record highs, it would follow that productivity holds the key to our future prosperity – yet the word was not mentioned once during the 2021 Budget Speech delivered by Treasurer Josh Frydenberg.

Economists are a quarrelsome lot, rarely agreeing on much at all. Indeed, it was once said that when three economists went shooting, the first missed by one metre to the left, the second by one metre to the right and the third exclaimed "we got it". Even in this most intangible of disciplines, one of the rarer areas of economic consensus seems to be the notion that lunch is never free – an aphorism that has remained iron-clad for generations. The structural spending seemingly demanded by Australians on health, aged and disability care alone poses a deep fiscal challenge, without considering rising regional tensions and the staggering cost of pandemic stimulus spending.

Healthy and wealthy societies are those that can afford to provide for the vulnerable. If you needed any evidence of how quickly people turn on others when the security of lives and livelihoods is threatened, you need only have watched octogenarians being trampled in the toilet paper aisles of Australian supermarkets last year. This is ultimately why Liberal Governments have historically focused so strongly on economic management, as it is our economic outperformance that underpins the Australian way of life.

And so, the time for a national conversation on productivity is upon us once more, irrespective of whether it is politically convenient. Australia's sluggish productivity growth in the decade from 2010 lead to the slowest per capita GDP growth in the last sixty years, even before the impact of COVID-19. Living standards have begun to stagnate on the back of this, making the load of almost unprecedented Government debt even heavier to bear. It is impossible to contemplate any reform to drive productivity without tackling the "Byzantine complexities, rigidities and perversities that foster adversarial relations within workplaces and militate against productivity enhancing innovations", as former Productivity tsar Gary Banks so eloquently put it.

The temptation for Liberals is to argue that Australia must dismantle the Fair Work Act in its entirety and begin again. The existence of a quasi-judicial organisation at the centre of a workplace relations universe, the so-called Fair Work Commission (FWC), with its propensity to insert itself wherever possible between employers and employees whilst steeped in excessive process and almost totally beholden to precedent, is total anathema to Liberals who honestly believe that most Australians are fair-minded, reasonable and require little Government in their lives.

Whilst I share that instinct, the reality is that economic data doesn't support the view that Australia's workplace relations system is fundamentally dysfunctional. Ultimately, as the economy recovers from the COVID-induced recession, Australia has proved, for the second time in the last two decades, that our economic framework, inclusive of our workplace relations system, weathers a global economic crisis more successfully than almost any other nation on earth. Of itself, this supports a view that we ought to bring a 'renovator's mindset' to the productivity challenge of workplace relations reform, rather than wielding an ideological sword in demolishing Labor's Fair Work behemoth.

It is not to say, however, that there is not clear evidence of conduct within the Australian workplace relations system that threatens productivity, even within the status quo. The Maritime Union of Australia (MUA) has an appalling track record of selfish, thuggish and militant conduct that harks back to its treasonous strike activity during World War 2 under the auspices of the Seamen's Union of Australia as a predecessor. At the time of writing in 2021, the MUA have just 'negotiated' an enterprise agreement with what Janet Albrechtsen rightly called a Corleone mafia clause.

Not satisfied only with the perversion of a free job market through a requirement that 70 per cent of jobs filled by Hutchison Ports be chosen from a list of "family and friends" provided by the union, the same deal includes a provision guaranteeing that no jobs will be lost to automation and introduces 20 days of paid domestic violence leave. In the same week that news of this dodgy deal broke, the MUA landed a separate agreement that raised wages at Webb Dock for its members by up to 47% over 4 years.

Such a stunning abrogation of managerial prerogative and accountability might be fatal for a business in a truly competitive market; however, the costs of selling out to these industrial thugs will instead be borne by every Australian, as 98% of our trade is conducted through ports. This doesn't just make every Australian business that either imports or exports fundamentally less competitive, but it also increases the cost of living for every single Australian to benefit those 'lucky' few invited to join the MUA's racket on the wharves.

The behaviour of the amalgamated Construction, Forestry, Maritime, Mining and Energy Union has long been lamented by our courts. Federal Court Justice Katzmann put it best when he said: "The Union has an appalling record of contravening industrial laws. It has frequently been excoriated in this Court for its recidivism ... Further the Union's overall record is indicative of an indifference to, if not a disdain for, the law. Simply put, the Union behaves as though it is above the law."

My suggestion that reform not dismantle the workplace relations system that allows such treachery against the national interest is a pragmatic reflection of the fact that Australian voters are largely ambivalent to union corruption, intimidation and thuggery. It is a political reality that such a fight is inevitably drawn down ideological lines, and gives rise to the opportunity for a debased misinformation campaign to be run by well-funded unions.

Instead, the renovation of workplace relations in this country must be predicated on what I'll call the three pillars of a world-class workplace relations framework that is fit-for-purpose in a new age where the imperatives of being responsive to changes in our social, economic and technological environments are a given; simplicity, certainty and flexibility. It is incumbent on the Liberal Party to glove up and fight for this renovation, thereby ensuring that we unleash new productivity gains that will drive real living standards higher.

Traditionally, any workplace relations system has sought to rebalance power between employers and employees. We must shift the debate, as contemporary industrial relations is not a feudal dispute between the wealthy elite and the impoverished peasants of the Dark Ages; nor is it taking place in an economy devoid of job opportunity with massive breadlines. In modern Australia, there simply isn't a gross power imbalance that unfairly favours bosses, meaning that the FWC's judicial and inflexible approach with undue influence from partisan interests is no longer, if it ever was, fit for purpose.

Take, for instance, the tens of thousands of Australians who, in recent years, have shunned traditional employment for working in the gig economy as an independent contractor. They want in because our inflexible system of awards is beyond what most mere mortals can comprehend. Take the more than 100 different pay rates in the Retail Award, or the absurdity of being paid a different rate to deliver a plate of food to a customer than to collect the dishes afterwards under the Hospitality Award – this inflexibility and complexity mean fewer jobs for Australians.

So-called independent contracting is simply a market response to the total unworkability of traditional employment structures for those who want to earn money outside other parts of their life, such as caring responsibilities, a primary job, study, or sport. Staggeringly, the Transport Workers Union Secretary Michael Kaine claims that "those individuals have no capacity to determine what the value of their work is and what they should be paid" and are therefore in desperate need of the protections of traditional employment models.

Yet, if I told you that you could engage in work that didn't require a job interview, didn't require a uniform, and didn't require you to show up for shifts or apply for leave, most people would think that it hardly sounded like a job at all – and that's because it isn't. Work in the on-demand economy is not a job within the construct of a traditional employer-employee relationship, and yet people are flocking to it. People work in the on-demand economy because it works for them, often presenting unlimited opportunity for economic reward, unlike working to the cap of a minimum wage under an award. Our response shouldn't be to force regulation onto this emergent work – instead we could take heed of the signal that our traditional employment system is broken. In the context of our changing economy, flexibility unlocks work for those who want it, drives productivity growth and in turn leads to better outcomes for all.

The question remains, however, as to what the Liberal Party might hope to achieve in initiating a national conversation on significant industrial relations reform. In my view, both the organisation at the centre of our workplace relations system (still largely as Labor designed it in 2009) and the freedom for businesses (especially small and medium enterprises) to directly engage with employees ought to be central to an effort to promote simplicity, flexibility and certainty.

In terms of renovating the FWC, the Productivity Commission

made a number of pertinent recommendations in its 2015 review of Australian workplace relations. It is contended by some that successive Governments have "stacked" the FWC with members who are at one extreme or the other in terms of being pro-employer or pro-worker. This is a gross over-simplification; yet, at the same time, the mere perception of such a problem in an organisation of such significant economic and cultural importance can't go unremedied. Fixed tenure terms with no opportunity for re-appointment, along with a clear separation between the functional and governance roles within the FWC would go a long way to achieving this, whilst also ensuring that the organisation is more consistent and in touch with the dynamic and evolving nature of workplace relations in the new age.

A second, and equally important proposal from the Productivity Commission, is removing the minimum wage determination from the auspices of the FWC and creating an independent, evidence-based and specialist organisation to effect such a profound annual decision with a greater emphasis on forward looking economic, social and technological trends. Those charged with contributing to the determination must seek the best evidence that they can find, rather than consider the best evidence presented to them. This change in modus operandi is fundamentally at odds with the quasi-judicial approach of the FWC, notwithstanding that the FWC's expert panel does consider some empirical evidence in its determinations. A contemporary, data-driven approach unshackled from historical precedent ought to see wages increase more rapidly in those sectors where productivity and profitability increase, whilst sectors without such bounty are not crippled by unaffordable wage increases that lead to negative employment outcomes.

Liberals rightly consider awards and penalty rates an anachronism from a time long lost to the annals of history, yet the real issue is that it remains so difficult for employers and employees, in smaller businesses, to achieve simplicity and flexibility in an alternative arrangement. Individual Flexibility Arrangements, designed to continue the best elements of Australian Workplace Agreements, cover less than 2 per cent of employees. We must recognise that decisions are most effectively made closest to the relevant information, so it stands to reason that an employer and employee working cheek by jowl in a small business are best able to determine what is fair, reasonable and accommodates both business need and individual desire – rather than a tribunal member in an organisation obsessed with process, historical precedent and the vested partisan interests at play.

This is where I believe that we, as Liberals, can make a significant and lasting contribution to productivity in Australia. We believe in individual responsibility and reward for effort, requiring only the equality of opportunity as a precondition. We also believe that fundamentally, most Australian employers and employees are fair-minded and decent.

These ought to be the tenets of reform for workplace relations, initially in small business as a test case, such that we might finally wean the Australian economy off award dependency. Creating a pathway for enterprise-level contracts that do not require formal FWC approval, can be a condition of employment and further permit non-cash benefits in the discharge of the no-disadvantage test would empower business to innovate, driving productivity and real living standards higher.

Carefully managed, I believe that we owe it to all Australians to restart the national conversation on productivity. There are always political costs to any reform; however, the costs of inaction in reforming workplace relations to suit modern Australian cultural, societal and economic realities will see our standard of living decline. Our ambition as a nation must be matched by our ambition as political leaders – as Peter Costello once said, you can't lead reform if you don't believe in it.

Senator Ben Small was elected as a Senator for Western Australia in November 2020 after the retirement of Finance Minister Mathias Cormann. Prior to entering Parliament, Senator Small had a successful career in the maritime oil and gas industry. This culminated in his working as the Marine Manager at Woodside Energy, handling large marine services for major offshore projects. He has been a small business owner, starting a bar restaurant showcasing local produce. All these experiences have led to his passion for industrial relations reform in order to deliver better outcomes for working Australians.

36

BEING RIGHT

The Hon. Barnaby Joyce MP

People become curious about politics after a period of life in uninspired observation. The question is often put: What is the reason that you are on the political side that you are, the Left or the Right?

Let me offer a very abridged and parochial view from someone of the Right who wants to stir you from your political slumber.

The Right are driven primarily by their desire to replace the State with their personal, individual belief structure; their own money, underpinned by their own assets and enterprise; a blueprint designed so that an individual, born to more meagre circumstances, not graced with a better education, not in communion with those who would be their benefactor, can nonetheless, transcend any disadvantage through the economic and social stratification of life, limited only by their innate abilities.

This is achieved, in a proven way, in small business, where you are master of your own destiny, limited, unfortunately, by a far too excessive involvement of the State through its impost of taxes and regulations.

The Right believe in the role of the family and religion, not the State, as having primacy in the development of the child into an adult; a belief in a Divine as the star for guidance, rather than a family's upbringing of a child being subject to the direction of, and interference by, the State.

The State's flaws are mimicked by the market dominance in mega-business which often succeeds at the expense of small business. Big business has an open door to the highest levels of government. They are bed friends as the upper echelons are only wealthy from the administration of others' wealth. They did not create the wealth; they were merely a very good applicant at an interview.

Socialist statements, calling for government help from big company executives are really not so surprising. The political wanderlust of some on the Right to depart from the philosophical reservation comes because of a failure to understand that individual commercial endeavour of the Right, should derive from a lived experience.

The Right are often self-confident and possibly impatient with those whom they see as living from the efforts of others as opposed to those who went without, early in life, to buy security for their later years. In other words, the Right back themselves in and respect others who do the same; they are unapologetic in their view that the cost of those who live from others' taxes must be absolutely ringfenced.

This belief in themselves leads to an impatience because their lives may seem limited but their aspirations are not. Unchecked, this can lead to arrogance. Unchecked, this arrogance is an ugly intrusion into the egalitarian principles that underwrite the freedom of the individual, the opportunities they enjoy and the aspirations they hold.

Their individuality means, often, that they are not the best team players because they have a bad habit of speaking their mind but, as a grace, they have the fortitude to strike out, take risks and accept the consequences.

The benefit from their endeavours comes with a responsibility to society that gave them the security to earn, but it is not an unbridled contract.

The Left are driven by the romantic notion of delivery on social policy and a disconcerting lack of respect for expense and debt, exemplified by an inability to navigate a considered path to repayment. At times, it appears they lack an earnestly held self-confidence and fall back on the State as a form of a quasi-eternal parent who allows them to stay at home forever. The paternal government will pay for the substantive issues of financing the "groceries" and will even borrow to do so.

They ultimately need other's assets to pay for their inability to commercially venture out for themselves. This is resolved by the Left's belief that they enjoy some sort of licence to take from those who have embraced risk and justify this by saying that the creator of wealth is no more economically relevant than the beneficiaries who seek to share in it.

The State is most manifest in social services and social infrastructure promoting the mantra that all government is essential. To this end, they create crises for which it is immoral for others not to succumb to their overtures. The object seems to be to create, in unsuspecting citizens, a rolling crisis of guilt in order to justify their call for the maintenance of government expenditure.

Today it is climate change and COVID-19; tomorrow it will be another existential crisis. In between, always, there will be a new social program that must be provided for, regardless of cost; a tithing on the endeavours of the prudent and the industrious, redistributed by the willing, often left-wing, bureaucracy of the State. After all, the State seems to be administered by the bureaucracy with the bureaucracy advocating for, and on behalf of, the State.

The public is left to wonder what was the purpose of the voting process if unelected bureaucracy rule at the behest of the Left.

Of course, the State has a range of essential tasks such as to protect the vulnerable, educate our children, provide a competent health system, defend the nation, protect individual rights, build the necessary infrastructure but, above all, do this in a way that promotes social cohesion. The State must have a plan to make the nation as powerful and as prosperous as possible in order to increase the opportunity and the security of its people.

Only the Right embrace this philosophical viewpoint.

In politics, these two groups, the Left and the Right, are supposed to be divided by a timber table in the middle of the Parliament. In reality, the table today exists merely as furniture because of the similarities in the resumés of those who reside on either side.

Of course, with the Right and the Left, there will always be similarities; but, we are reaching an ideologically dangerous fork on the political road where "similarities" become "mirror images". When this occurs, the public have little choice. The Right must assert what it stands for, promote its values and persuade an often unconvinced electorate that the Left only have answers when they seek overwhelming access to other people's money. The Right's obligation is to assert the primacy of a world in which endeavour, opportunity and ambition are rewarded, and the State takes a back seat.

The Honourable Barnaby Joyce MP is the Deputy Prime Minister of Australia and Leader of the Federal National Party. He is the Minister for Infrastructure, Transport and Regional Development. He was first elected to the Australian Parliament in 2004 as a Nationals Senator for Queensland. In 2013, Barnaby was elected the Federal Member for New England and was Deputy Leader of the National Party. During 2018, he was appointed by Prime Minister Morrison as Special Envoy for Drought Assistance and Recovery. Prior to entering Parliament, Barnaby worked in regional banking and, for 10 years, operated Barnaby Joyce and Co in the western Queensland town of St George. He studied Accountancy at the University of New England.

37

THE MEDIA MARKET DROWNING IN A SEA OF WOKENESS

David Maddox

In more than two decades as a journalist, the politician I have interviewed most has been Nigel Farage.

Throughout, he has spoken to me in various guises – UKIP leader, Brexit Party leader, star turn on the American conservative circuit.

The most recent interview was ahead of his latest project presenting a primetime show on the fledgling but not trouble-free start-up news channel, *GB News*, here in the UK.

"I see broadcasters all pushing the same kind of agenda, doing pretty much the same as they have done for decades," he said.

"People are bored with it, they have had enough of it, they keep turning it off. They turn it back on like a drug. Then they can't bear it and turn it back off again."

"I think there's a huge opportunity here to reshape broadcasting. I think there is a huge opportunity here to reverse the metropolitisation of our entire political argument where everything is looked at through that lens."

Just as he was in politics with Brexit, Farage is still the great disrupter.

The original cause of leaving the European Union may have been won but the conservative, small c, revolution continues.

And what more fertile territory to seek change than the "stale", as he put it, broadcast media market?

Enoch Powell once described the media as "the sea", it sets the political weather but more than that it defines social norms and a sense of right and wrong.

So, when we look at the extraordinary changes in recent years in what is often called the woke agenda whether it is the Marxist Black Lives Matter, the environmental extremists of the Extinction Rebellion or the assault on human identity through the transgender movement, we have to look at it through the prism of the media treatment of it.

Just in Britain alone, there have been stunning developments.

- A man who complimented a female colleague's dress was disciplined for sexual harassment.

- An author who expressed concerns about biological men being accepted as women and given access to women's prisons, dressing rooms, et cetera, was sacked by her publisher.

- Lecturers threaten to go on strike unless a statue to an Oxford college benefactor, Cecil Rhodes, is removed.

- British Police officers and the England football team took the knee when faced with violent protests over the death of a black man in America.

- The Free Speech Union, set up in Britain to defend people from being "cancelled" for expressing their views, provided defence for 700 people in its first year.

- The Scottish Government has brought in a law which has banned "wrong thoughts" in the privacy of people's homes.

- The UK government attempted to block including language in a new law on maternity leave for senior ministers that identifies a person who is pregnant as a woman.

These are just a small selection illustrative of a wider picture.

It is worth noting that recent polling evidence now suggests that the general public have woken up to the change in society, especially over freedom of speech.

A ComRes poll of 2,000 people commissioned by the actor turned politician, Laurence Fox (himself a victim of cancel culture), in February 2021, showed that 50 per cent agree "freedom of speech is under threat" while only 24 per cent disagreed. This, Fox argued, directly comes from the assault on traditional and conservative values. It is hard to disagree with his conclusion.

None of these things would have happened with very little mainstream challenge, without the tacit consent of the mainstream media, at best a silence in the place of a challenge, at worst, open support. We see it repeated in western democracies around the world, particularly the Anglosphere.

Part of the problem is the collapse of the traditional newspaper market which is where the strongest resistance to wokeism can still be found.

Using the British example, in February 2020, *Press Gazette*, the newspaper industry magazine, reported that, in 20 years since 2000, newspaper circulation had plummeted by two thirds with national titles seeing sales drop from 21.2 million a day to 7.4 million. For example, in January 2000, Britain's leading newspaper, *The Sun*, sold 3.6 million copies. In January 2020, that was down to 1.3 million. It now struggles to break a million.

Instead, we have a media market dominated by broadcasters and the new rising giant set to dominate the future, social media.

The change in the UK media landscape was confirmed in the News Consumption Report in August 2020. This showed that 75 per cent get their news from the television, 65 per cent from the internet, particularly social media and 35 per cent newspapers. The strength of social media was highlighted by the fact that Facebook alone matches newspapers with 34 per cent. Similar numbers are true of other western democracies.

In a new media market dominated by broadcasters and, increasingly, the social media giants, it does not take much to see that the woke liberal agenda has their support.

In Britain, the taxpayer-funded BBC is a monolith that dominates the market and uses its position to define what is impartial, which the smaller players at *ITV* and *Sky News UK* follow. *Sky News* in Britain is as woke as *Sky News* in Australia is conservative.

In 2007, Paul Dacre, editor of the Daily Mail, the most significant British newspaper editor of the 21st century, said: "It's my contention that the BBC monolith is distorting Britain's media market, crushing journalistic pluralism and imposing a monoculture that is inimical to healthy democratic debate."

In recent years, the BBC and other major broadcasters all followed a similar path. They were anti-Brexit in their coverage, they have unquestioningly lionised Greta Thunberg and the climate change agenda. They left no space for those questioning lockdowns and joined in the unquestioning support for the vaccine, demonising those who raised questions.

Brexit provides a good example of the problem. BBC bias was highlighted in a 2018 report by the thinktank Civitas which revealed that, between 2005 and 2015, only 132 of the 4,275 guests asked to speak about the EU on BBC radio's flagship Today programme on radio, supported leaving the EU.

It goes much further.

In December 2020, the Campaign for Common Sense (CCS) published findings which showed that in the November before on the main BBC comedy shows on television and radio, there were 268 slots of which 74 per cent were given to 99 comedians with publicly pronounced left-leaning, anti-Brexit or woke views, while only four slots were given to two comedians with explicitly conservative, pro-Brexit or anti-woke views.

Perhaps, though, the more pernicious threat comes from the social media giants. We only need to see the banning of Donald Trump from their platforms and the active suppression of stories critical of the Biden family to see that there is a political agenda.

The ban on Trump on the false pretext that an out-of-control demonstration was an attempted coup was also followed by other conservative accounts being cancelled. It is worth noting though that Twitter still allows the Supreme Leader of Iran and the General Secretary of the Chinese Communist Party to keep their accounts and Tweet.

As well, like all monopolies, they acted to destroy the one social media platform that allowed a consistent conservative voice, Parler.

Facebook funded Black Lives Matter and electoral efforts to secure a Democrat victory in the 2020 US election. They wear their politics on their sleeve and the once "platforms for free speech" are increasingly intolerant of conservative views while promoting liberal and woke ones.

So, what can be done? Is all lost?

Start-ups like *GB News* offer a challenge. Television stations like *Fox News* and *Sky News Australia* ensure there is a different perspective as well. Australia has also led the way by ensuring Google and other internet giants have to pay for newspaper content, but newspapers have to reimagine their products for the 21st Century.

Perhaps most of all, the monopolies and giants like the BBC or big social media companies need to be broken up and more competition allowed into the market.

There is no doubt that there is an appetite in voters for conservatism, patriotism, tradition and Christianity. The 2019 UK general election, where woke Labour lost its historic working-class seats in the north to the Conservatives was proof of that.

The issue is recreating a media market that reflects those values.

David Maddox is an award winning, campaigning journalist with two decades experience covering British politics. He is currently political editor of the *Sunday Express* and chief leader writer for the *Daily Express* in the UK. He also acts as an adviser to several thinktanks and has written speeches and articles for UK Conservative Party politicians.

38

IT IS TIME TO TALK NUCLEAR POWER

Senator the Hon. Matt Canavan

Unique among large, developed nations, Australia has a legislative ban on nuclear power. The ban was introduced via a Greens' amendment in the Senate on December 10, 1999. There was fewer than 10 minutes of debate on the matter.

The Howard Government at the time was seeking legislative support to build a new research reactor at Lucas Heights. A Greens' Senator, Dee Margetts, moved an amendment to the enabling legislation to prohibit the construction of a "nuclear power plant" anywhere in Australia. With no immediate prospect of a nuclear power station being built, the Government accepted the amendment so it could proceed with the new research reactor at Lucas Heights.

There was almost no national media coverage of the ban. The Lucas Heights reactor was built and Australia continues to lead the world in nuclear medicine. However, we remain an outlier when it comes to nuclear power. Of the top 20 richest nations in the world, only three do not have nuclear power: Australia, Saudi Arabia and Italy. Saudi Arabia is building a nuclear power station and Italy gets much of its imported electricity from France, where three-quarters of the electricity is produced by nuclear.

Our status as a nuclear outcast is the more remarkable given that Australia has the largest reserves of uranium in the world. We export uranium to the world but ban its use here.

There is a myth that post Fukushima, the use of nuclear power will decline. In the decade since Fukushima, Japan initially shut its reactors (although some now have been restarted) and Germany announced that it would move away from nuclear; but other European nations have not joined Germany. The only other European country that has plans to shut nuclear power stations soon is the United Kingdom and they are building new nuclear power stations to replace the old. Poland plans to start building its first nuclear power station in 2026.

The future looks bright for nuclear power when you look at things on a global scale. There are 443 nuclear power stations in service, only a third of these are in Asia but 60 per cent of the 54 new nuclear power stations, under construction, are being built in our Asia-Pacific region.

Over the next 30 years, the International Atomic Energy Agency predicts that global nuclear power capacity could increase by 80 per cent and possibly triple in the Asia-Pacific region.

The lack of plans for nuclear in western countries is partly due to the lack of popular support for nuclear in the west. Michael Shellenberger, an environmentalist himself, details in his recent book, *Apocalypse Never*, how activists, in the 1960s, intentionally distorted the science to turn people away from nuclear power.

The green activists adopted the well-worn tactics with which we are now all too familiar, from sagas like Adani and coal seam gas. In the 1960s, the Big Green movement spent big on lobbyists, legal action and public relations. Their rhetoric knew no bounds of hyperbole, with Ralph Nader claiming once that "A nuclear accident could wipe out Cleveland and the survivors would envy the dead." Then Jane Fonda starred in the anti-nuclear disaster film, *The China Syndrome* and a fortnight after it premiered, the Three Mile Island nuclear accident occurred.

Nuclear's popularity has never recovered. It remains the least popular energy source, even less popular than coal despite all the vitriol heaped on that energy source in recent times. There is now an unconscious bias against nuclear in western societies.

That unpopularity has created a self-fulfilling spiral. Exaggerated concerns over nuclear's safety have led to more and more regulation. More red tape has pushed up the costs of building nuclear power stations in the West. Nuclear's resulting high costs prevent some being built which then means that there are few real world examples of operating plants to dull the concerns over safety.

The increased costs of nuclear in the West are eye-watering. Nuclear power stations used to be constructed within around 5 years. Over the past decade, the time frames for construction have blown out to 17 years.

These issues are stark in the case of the UK's Hinkley Point nuclear power project. The UK Government backed the project in 2008 with an expected cost of A$4 billion and completion by 2017. The costs have now blown out to over A$40 billion and construction is not expected to finish until 2026.

Despite these challenges, there remain compelling reasons why Australia should not turn its back on nuclear technology. We should keep the nuclear option on the table, given technological developments, the need to protect the environment and the collapsing security situation in our region.

The cost increases in conventional nuclear power stations have encouraged some to find solutions. Renewable energy costs have come down in recent decades not because of scientific breakthroughs but because of scale efficiencies through mass production. So some are seeking to take the same approach with nuclear and build nuclear units in factories for transport to a plant site.

These are the so-called Small Modular Reactors (SMRs). They keep the basic details of large nuclear power plants but seek to reduce their size and standardise their design so they can be made in a production line. Multiple companies in the US, the UK, Canada and China are at various stages of installing pilot plants.

Unfortunately for Australia, none of these demonstration projects will be conducted here given our nuclear energy prohibition; but the smaller size of these plants could be well-suited to Australia's smaller and dispersed population. One reason to remove our nuclear blanket ban is to allow companies to start investigating nuclear innovation, like SMRs, so that we are ready if any of them prove to work.

SMRs may also produce waste that is easier to manage as some designs are not refuelled in their operating lives. A small town in South Australia, Kimba, has recently voted 62 per cent in favour of hosting a radioactive waste facility in their town, although this will not be a facility capable of storing waste from energy. This followed an extensive, years long information campaign explaining the risks and benefits of the facility. The public support in Kimba proves that Australians will support nuclear if the risks are properly explained to them along with the benefits of the industry.

Despite the recent cost explosions of nuclear, it remains more cost-effective than renewable energy. Michael Shellenberger calculates that between 1965 and 2018, the world spent $2 trillion on nuclear compared to $2.3 trillion for solar and wind, yet nuclear today produces around double the electricity provided by solar and wind. This makes the continuing opposition to nuclear, from many climate campaigners, nonsensical.

In mid-2021, climate protestors graffitied the front of Parliament House to demand action on climate change. If they were serious about their apocalyptic predictions, they would embrace nuclear given its carbon free footprint and production of reliable power; but most climate campaigners also oppose nuclear which completely undermines their Armageddon-like concerns over industrialisation. More likely, they are most worried about capitalism and the climate is just a backdoor way to attack that system.

Whatever your thoughts about the climate, nuclear energy is much better for the environment than its alternatives. The biggest environmental issue in the world remains air pollution. Air pollution is estimated to kill over 4 million people a year, much of it generated by the burning of wood and other biomass in parts of the world where electricity is not available.

Nuclear power provides reliable electricity and avoids the burning of organic matter. Researchers Pushkar Kharecha and James Hansen estimate that nuclear power's air pollution cutting benefit has prevented the deaths of 1.84 million people since 1971.

Nuclear does less damage to the natural environment, too. Wind energy takes up 250 times more land than nuclear power and solar takes up 150 times more land. Nuclear doesn't just have a low carbon footprint, it has a lower footprint full stop. And, nuclear is just safer. Despite the high profile of major nuclear accidents, nuclear has resulted in far fewer deaths than that from dam failures, oil rig explosions and even, on some measures, the number of people who fall when installing solar panels.

Reliable energy is the only way to ensure that we remain safe as a nation. The day after the fall of Kabul, the *Global Times*, the Chinese Communist Paper's English language mouthpiece, wrote that, "From what happened in Afghanistan, those in Taiwan should perceive that once a war breaks out in the Straits, the island's defense will collapse in hours and US military won't come to help."

While the *Global Times* is prone to bluster, we would be foolish not to prepare for the worst. That means ensuring that we have the sovereign capability to provide reliable energy to industry regardless of the weather forecast. With new technological developments, nuclear energy could be one way of doing that.

We need to keep our options open given the fast-changing security environment we face. There remain many defence specialists who believe that we should be acquiring nuclear submarines but one barrier to that is that we do not have a nuclear power industry. As the former Defence Minister, Christopher, Pyne said when justifying the purchase of diesel submarines, "Australia does not have a nuclear industry. One cannot be created overnight."

That is exactly right. We cannot create a nuclear energy industry overnight. That is why we should remove the prohibition on nuclear power now. Removing the ban won't create a nuclear power industry but it may, at least, kickstart investigations into options. While nuclear energy remains banned, we will make no progress and simply limit the options future Australians have to deal with the energy, environmental and security challenges they will face.

That would be a gross abrogation of our responsibility as leaders. We should make the tough decisions now so that things are easier in the future.

The famous energy analyst, Vaclav Smil, has quipped that nuclear power has proved a "successful failure". It has been successful at producing safe and reliable power throughout the world, but it has failed to sustain the political support to grow and develop, at least in Western countries.

Now is the time to challenge the political myths around nuclear because to succeed, successfully, at overcoming future threats, we need all options on the table. Removing the ban will probably require more than 10 minutes of Parliamentary debate but I believe it is a fight worth having.

Senator the Honourable Matt Canavan is a Liberal National Party Senator for Queensland. He is currently Deputy Leader of the Nationals in the Senate and is the Deputy Chair of the Select Committee on Job Security. Senator Canavan previously served as Minister for Resources and Northern Australia. He was first elected to the Australian Parliament in 2013, being the first Senator for more than 20 years to be based in Rockhampton. Prior to entering Parliament, he was a Director of the Productivity Commission, working on projects ranging from competition laws and housing affordability. He has a First Class Honours Degree in Economics from the University of Queensland.

Lightning Source UK Ltd.
Milton Keynes UK
UKHW021400151021
392260UK00014B/1130